PLANNING·ENVIRONMENT·CITIES

Series Editors: Yvonne Rydin and Andrew Thornley

The context in which planning operates has changed dramatically in recent years. Economic processes have become increasingly globalized and new spatial patterns of economic activity have emerged. There have been major changes across the globe, not just changing administrations in various countries, but also the sweeping away of old ideologies and the tentative emergence of new ones. A new environmental agenda emerged from the Brundtland Report and the Rio Earth Summit prioritizing the goal of sustainable development. The momentum for this has been maintained by continued action at international, national and local levels.

Cities are today faced with new pressures for economic competitiveness, greater accountability and participation, improved quality of life for citizens and global environmental responsibilities. These pressures are often contradictory and create difficult dilemmas for policy-makers, especially in the context of fiscal austerity. New relationships are developing between the levels of state activity and between public and private sectors as different interests respond to the new conditions.

In these changing circumstances, planners, from many backgrounds, in many different organizations, have come to re-evaluate their work. They have had to engage with actors in government, the private sector and non-governmental organizations in discussions over the role of planning in relation to the environment and cities. The intention of the Planning, Environment, Cities series is to explore the changing nature of planning and contribute to the debate about its future.

The series is primarily aimed at students and practitioners of planning and such related professions as estate management, housing and architecture as well as those in politics, public and social administration, geography and urban studies. It comprises both general texts and books designed to make a more particular contribution, in both cases characterized by: an international approach; extensive use of case studies, and emphasis on contemporary relevance and the application of theory to advance planning practice.

Planning·Environment·Cities

Series Editors: Yvonne Rydin and Andrew Thornley

Published

Philip Allmendinger
Planning Theory

Patsy Healey
Collaborative Planning (2nd edn)

Ted Kitchen
Skills for Planning Practice

Peter Newman and Andrew Thornley
Planning World Cities

Michael Oxley
Economics, Planning and Housing

Yvonne Rydin
Urban and Environmental Planning in the UK (2nd edn)

Geoff Vigar, Patsy Healey and Angela Hull with Simin Davoudi
Planning, Governance and Spatial Strategy in Britain

Forthcoming

Ruth Fincher and Kurt Iveson
Planning for Difference, Diversity and Encounter

Other titles planned include

Introduction to Planning
Urban Design
21st-Century Planning

Planning, Environment, Cities
Series Standing Order
ISBN 0–333–71703–1 hardback
ISBN 0–333–69346–9 paperback
(outside North America only)

You can receive future titles in this series as they are published. To place a standing order please contact your bookseller or, in the case of difficulty, write to us at the address below with your name and address, the title of the series and an ISBN quoted above.

Customer Services Department, Macmillan Distribution Ltd
Houndmills, Basingstoke, Hampshire RG21 6XS, England

Skills for Planning Practice

Ted Kitchen

First published 2007 by
PALGRAVE MACMILLAN
Houndmills, Basingstoke, Hampshire RG21 6XS and
175 Fifth Avenue, New York, N.Y. 10010
Companies and representatives throughout the world.

PALGRAVE MACMILLAN is the global academic imprint of the Palgrave Macmillan division of St. Martin's Press, LLC and of Palgrave Macmillan Ltd. Macmillan® is a registered trademark in the United States, United Kingdom and other countries. Palgrave is a registered trademark in the European Union and other countries.

ISBN-13: 978–0–333–69071–0   hardback
ISBN-10: 0–333–69071–0   hardback
ISBN-13: 978–0–333–69072–7   paperback
ISBN-10: 0–333–69072–9   paperback

This book is printed on paper suitable for recycling and made from fully managed and sustained forest sources.

A catalogue record for this book is available from the British Library.

A catalog record for this book is available from the Library of Congress.

10   9   8   7   6   5   4   3   2   1
16   15   14   13   12   11   10   09   08   07

Printed and bound in China

To Ann, Amanda and Christopher

Contents

List of Boxes

Preface

This is a very personal book. Essentially, my credentials to write about skills for planning practice come from the fact that I have been fortunate enough to have had a long planning practice career before coming into the university world for the past decade or so, and it is that practice career on which I draw in this book. My planning practice career ran from 1968 to 1995, excluding three years (1969–72) undertaking a PhD at the University of Glasgow. During this time, I worked in positions of increasing seniority for Luton County Borough Council, the Scottish Development Department, South Tyneside Metropolitan Borough Council and Manchester City Council. I worked for Manchester from 1979 to 1995, with the last six years spent as head of the council's planning service, and it is these latter experiences in particular that I draw on in this book.

Both the book's basic structure and its approach are a product of reflecting on those experiences. So while I recognize that it would be possible to approach this task from a much more theoretical standpoint – Low (1991) argues for example that political theory provides the proper foundation for understanding planning practice – I have taken the view that I can best contribute to debates about skills for planning practice in this way. This has two particular implications for the material that follows. The first is that I have often illustrated what I am talking about by drawing on examples from my own practice experience, usually in a fairly generalized way. Readers who want to access material of this nature in a way that is not so generalized can look at my book about the experience of planning practice in Manchester (Kitchen, 1997), but it seems to me that in this present book the essence of most of the points I am trying to make can be conveyed in fairly brief examples which eschew that level of detail. The second implication of this approach is that I have used the first person singular in this text far more frequently that I would usually advise my students to do in their writing, and probably more frequently than I would say in the abstract is desirable. The reason for this is simply that I want to be clear about when I am drawing on my own experience or expressing a personal opinion shaped by that experience.

My hope in doing this is that I can contribute to ongoing debates about skills for planning practice, because I believe that this is absolutely fundamental if (as for example the British government currently wishes) we are to improve the performance of the planning system and its standing with its stakeholders. At the end of the day, the planning system will be as good as the people who are in it, and whilst planners aren't the only people who shape planning decision-making they are major players in that process. In particular, I would hope that this book might stimulate other planning practitioners to write about their experiences, and to contribute to the debate about skills for planning practice by reflecting on those experiences. It is still relatively rare for planning practitioners to do this, although in my experience it is rather more common for them to complain about the more theoretical contributions that academics make to these debates. It seems to me that this is aiming at the wrong target; skills for planning practice is far too important a subject to be left to planning theorists alone, but practitioners should be asking why they and their colleagues aren't contributing rather than criticizing those who approach the subject from a more theoretical perspective. Both of these approaches have potentially valuable contributions to make, and if this book persuades even a very small number of practitioners to make a contribution reflecting on their own experience (even if that is to argue that they disagree with much of what is in here) then I will be well pleased. In particular, if the book helps to persuade practitioners that the task of developing skills for planning practice needs an effective partnership between them and planning schools, and shouldn't just be left to the academic world alone – as I argue in Chapter 10 – then I will be absolutely delighted.

One of the challenges I have faced in writing this book is the fact that my practice experience (on which I am drawing) is British, when the intention is to be relevant to a wide range of planning practice situations and not just to British ones. One of the reasons this is a challenge is that there isn't much writing about the characteristics of planning practice across the world on which I could draw to set against my own experiences. Another is that it is clearly an oversimplification to assume that in its essence planning practice is broadly the same everywhere, and therefore that it doesn't really matter where practice stories come from; for example, systems and processes, and the cultures of governance within which they sit, do vary considerably across the world. What I have tried to do, therefore, is to draw on my particular practice experiences in ways that offer examples of what I believe to be general phenomena, rather than just to tell stories about British planning practice. To make sense of these examples, however, it is sometimes necessary to provide background material about history, systems, processes, and norms and expectations, because practice always takes place in contexts influenced by these factors. It is also possible that at times I have used British terminology which isn't replicated everywhere else, although I have tried to explain this where I have been aware that it might be a problem. British readers hopefully will find all of this relatively straightforward, although of course they may disagree with the views and interpretations I offer. I invite readers who do not come from

British practice backgrounds to think about how the phenomena I am describing relate to their particular circumstances, and in effect to substitute their own local detail for mine as a way of reflecting on how the broad issues I am describing work out in their own situations. In particular, the self-assessment questions at the end of each of the seven skills chapters should be helpful here, because I have tried to make them as generalized as I reasonably can. My own experiences of talking with planners from outside Britain about practice in their localities have been that it is generally possible to relate quite easily to the sets of circumstances they are describing because I have experienced something like that myself, even if the detail (and quite possibly the outcome) is different because of local characteristics; and so I hope that this also applies to my British practice examples in this book.

TED KITCHEN

Acknowledgements

This book has been a long time in preparation, with various stops and starts as life intervened. There must have been times as a consequence when both the publishers (represented by Steven Kennedy) and the series editors (represented by Yvonne Rydin) had serious doubts about whether this book would ever materialize. First of all, then, I must thank Steven and Yvonne for their continuing belief in and support for this project, and for the helpful comments they have made on drafts at various stages in its stop-start existence. I hope that what has eventually emerged makes them feel that all this effort on their part was worthwhile.

Second, many people have contributed to this project in a variety of ways. As someone who writes in the old-fashioned way of applying a pen to pieces of paper, I need the support of people who can turn my efforts (once they have deciphered my hand writing) into typescript. At various stages, the main burden of this effort has fallen on Faye Baker and Ann Wilson, with Ann taking the lead in recent times, and they have been backed up by the Executive Support Team of the Faculty of Development & Society at Sheffield Hallam University when extra capacity has been needed to move the project along. Ann Wilson in particular has done an important job in the final phases of this project in incorporating changes and in introducing a consistent approach to the numerous text-boxes, and it is mainly as a result of her efforts that a pile of manuscript drafts in recent times has at last begun to look like a book. I am really grateful for their efforts on my behalf, and I hope they feel that the finished product seems worth all they have put into it. I would also like to thank Keith Povey and Mark Hendy for their work at the editorial stages, which has undoubtedly improved the book considerably.

More generally, it is inevitable when drawing upon an extensive planning practice career that I am in fact writing about a large number of people (both planners and many others) with whom I have worked over the years. I am very conscious as a consequence that there are lots of people who might recognize themselves in some of the stories in this book. I can only hope they think what I have written is reasonably accurate, and that in its emphasis on what a positive approach to planning can achieve they can see their own contributions in an appropriate light. Not all of my comments are positive, of course, but if anyone sees themselves in this more critical context then I can at least offer them the consolation that they helped to provide some of the most important lessons in my process of hindsight, even if it usually didn't seem that way at the time. A planning practice career involves working with large numbers of people, however, and while it would be truly amazing if this had all been positive I must say that the balance is very strongly on that side. So, to everyone who has contributed inadvertently to this book from the world of planning practice, a heartfelt thanks is due.

In the academic world, I have been fortunate to spend the last ten years or so with a very supportive group of colleagues at Sheffield Hallam University, and in all kinds of ways these interactions have influenced what is in (and not in) this book. The same could be said of feedback from the students I have taught over this period, and this has specifically influenced the contents of this book in several places. Over longer periods of time I have benefited from many other sets of exchanges as well, and the three that have had the most profound effects on me have been with Patsy Healey, Dick Schneider and David Whitney. I am privileged to be able to call all three friends as well as colleagues, and as a consequence what they think of what I have written in this book matters a lot to me. They have influenced it in more ways than they will ever know.

It goes without saying (but I will say it anyway) that the errors, omissions and other failings of this book are down to me alone.

TED KITCHEN

The author and publishers would like to thank the following for permission to reproduce copyright material. The Association of Greater Manchester Authorities for Box 3.1; The Audit Commission for Box 3.3; The Royal Town Planning Institute for Boxes 4.2, 6.5, 9.2, 9.4 and 9.5; The Canadian Institute of Planners for Box 6.6; The American Planning Association for Box 6.7; Sheffield First Partnership for Box 7.4; and The Local Government Association for Boxes 5.5 and 8.2. Crown copyright material in Boxes 5.4, 5.6 and 9.8 is reproduced with the permission of the controller of Her Majesty's Stationery Office under click license CO1W0000276.

Every effort had been made to contact all the copyright-holders, but if any have been inadvertently omitted the publishers will be pleased to make the necessary arrangement at the earliest opportunity.

Chapter 1

Introduction

Introduction

This chapter begins with a very simple stance on what planning is, for that has governed the way I have set about my task in this book. I then elaborate this approach and talk about the nature and purpose of planning systems which flow from it, before introducing the seven broad clusters of core skills for planning that form the heart of the book. It needs to be recognized, however, that many factors will influence the application of those skills throughout a professional lifetime, and I look in this chapter in particular at two of these: the forces that drive changes in planning systems and processes, and the nature and extent of government support for those systems. In both of these instances, the phenomena I identify from my own experience seem in essence to be the kinds of phenomena that confront most planning systems over a period of time; the British experience may have some particular characteristics, but in essence it has been trying to cope with universal phenomena. The point of these sections is that broad contextual issues, over which the individual planner has no real control, affect in very major ways the performance of the planning system and therefore the working life experiences of every individual planner. Finally, the structure of the remainder of the book is introduced.

Stance

The purpose of urban and regional planning is to make places better for people. This book is about the skills that planners bring to bear on this task.

Some basic approaches

I see planning as being fundamentally something that is carried out for the public good. As such, it needs to be undertaken by organizations accountable to the public whose interests they seek to serve, and at the local level this tends in practice to be an arm of democratically elected local government. This is not necessarily the only model that could be used for these purposes, nor is it one where the structures and working

1

methods used are likely to be the same everywhere. But this is the most common model to be found in Western democracies (although in recent years in Britain, particularly in the field of urban regeneration, there have been several variations on this model), and despite what could undoubtedly be said about the imperfections of local government it seems to me to be an appropriate way in which a public task of this nature should be undertaken. This debate can become more problematic at spatial scales that are broader than that of the individual local authority, because there isn't necessarily a democratic structure at the subregional or regional scales that fits this kind of need, with many planning activities carried out on this basis and many planners employed in undertaking this work.

There is also a thriving private sector in planning, where the primary focus is on the needs and interests of the client who is paying the bill; in Britain in recent years this sector appears to have been growing, not just to meet the needs of private clients but also often to provide an independent viewpoint on planning issues for public sector agencies. There is clearly an issue around the appropriate scale and nature of the private sector in planning in the light of what I have said above about planning as a public activity, especially if the growth of the private planning sector has tended at times to work against the interests of the public planning sector – for example, in attracting staff, or in helping to create situations where the quality of experience in the public sector is diluted by the process of farming out some of the most interesting work to the private sector, as I believe has been the case in Britain in recent years. Indeed, Brooks (2002, p. 17, 18) suggests that there is some evidence from American planning schools that many planning students prefer the idea of working for the private sector because they see it as less frustrating than working for much more overtly political public bodies. My own experience with British planning students in recent years is not entirely dissimilar to this, albeit overlain by a belief among students that the rewards framework in the private sector is better than in the public sector. Nevertheless, and while acknowledging that many planners don't work for public planning agencies at the local level, I think this is the bedrock of planning. Thus, when I talk about planning practice this is mainly what I mean.

The broad nature and purpose of planning systems

Why do we have planning systems at all? And why are they, no matter the differing forms that they take, so widespread throughout the world? The answer is generally that the phenomenon of urban growth in the nineteenth and the twentieth centuries is now widely regarded as being something that we ought to attempt to manage, rather than to leave to the operation of the local market. The reason for this is usually that there are seen to be collective gains to be had from this in terms of factors such as infrastructure provision, the use of land as a scarce resource, the need to ensure that land is available for uses for the benefit of the public as a whole such as open space, and the need for local values and aspirations for the future of their town or city to be given expression. These arguments can collectively be seen as being about public benefit, both directly in the sense of providing certain facilities and services that markets may not supply effectively or efficiently other than on their own terms, and indirectly in the sense that there is a public-interest dimension to many human activities which planning processes can attempt to safeguard. Furthermore, this public-interest dimension is an interactive one; for example, what happens to our town and city centres has a vital effect on what happens to our transportation systems, and vice versa. Planning is therefore about the interactions between the key elements in our urban systems (and rural systems as well, when plans are dealing with rural areas; and also the interactions between urban and rural systems when looking at regional plans for wider areas; and so on), in the belief and hope that looking at these elements in this way will be a synergistic process; it will add value to what would be achieved by looking at each of these separately. To do this, it needs to be holistic; it has to look at the city in the round, both as to its functions and as to its key role players. This is described as follows in the paper produced by the British Department of the Environment in introducing its 'quality' initiative in 1994:

> The life of the city is much more than the sum of its parts. However convenient it may be to talk separately about transport, housing, employment or leisure, it is only when we come to view the whole, to think much more in the round, that we can begin to plan with any hope of success.
>
> Nor can we see the life of our cities as if they were the responsibility only of government, of councils, or planning committees. Instead, we have to see them as products of the whole community, affected by a mass of different influences and supported by a host of different individuals and groups. By considering urban life as a whole and recognising that responsibility rests with us all, we can further improve the quality of urban life. (Department of the Environment, 1994a, p. 24)

So, this picture of planning systems sees them as evolving as a result of three mutually reinforcing pressures:

- a recognition of the need for public benefits to be secured from the development of our cities;

- the synergy that can be obtained by looking at interactions between the key elements in our urban systems; and
- the need to look at our cities holistically.

In turn, these need to be seen in the context of at least four critical sets of observations, which affect very significantly the weight attached to these components in the planning systems of societies:

- The history of the development of our cities (see, for example, Mumford, 1966; Briggs, 1982; Hall, 1996) and of more recent planning approaches to the management of this process (see, for example, Cherry, 1988; Sies and Silver, 1996) is a very variable one. It is clear, as a consequence, that planning has to deal with a wide range of very different situations. The differences between our cities are probably at least as important as their similarities (Marcuse and van Kempen, 2000).
- Local factors clearly play an important role in determining the approach that is adopted to the town planning function, so that what are described above as the collective efficiencies that have been part of the stimulus for planning could not be expected to be found equally everywhere. To take two extreme examples, high-density Hong Kong has always seen efficiency and effectiveness in the use of its scarce resource of land as much more of a driving force in its planning effort than has the land-rich United States of America, where low-density urban development sprawl apparently unconstrained by this perception of land as a scarce resource over much of the country is a common phenomenon (Booth, 1996).
- The achievements town planning actually has to its credit are the subject of considerable debate, be this about the claims that can be made for the benefits that derive as a result of having a planning regime or about the disbenefits that arise as a result of the operations in practice of the planning machine. The first of these is inherently difficult to measure in societies which have had planning regimes for a long time, and so the literature is not particularly strong in this field (but see Hall, 1996; Hall *et al.*, 1973). But the second, which is really about what it is like to be on the receiving end of planning actions, has been the subject of considerable study, and has resulted in some polemical and influential writing over a period of some four decades (see, for example, Jacobs, 1964; Goodman, 1972; Herbert and Smith, 1989; Sewell, 1993). It is clear that one of the common problems that arises is as a result of the institutionalization of planning as part of the bureaucracy of the state, at whatever spatial scale this occurs. The case for planning as outlined above is essentially a case for it to be part of the process of governance; but the very act of incorporation in these terms brings with it difficulties that flow directly from this status, and also from the fact that it makes decisions in which there are often both winners and losers. Some

of this is to do with the process of political control that goes with incorporation within the mechanisms of the state, and this is discussed in more detail in Chapter 7.

• Attempts at defining 'the public interest' in any particular planning situation can be difficult and indeed elusive, although this does not mean that arguments about public interest thereby cease to have any validity (see Taylor, 1994, pp. 87–115). Often, indeed, in a governmental process, the public interest becomes what the public decision-makers eventually decide it is, because this is what their statutory power legitimizes them to do, sometimes after appropriate consultation. This kind of circular argument can powerfully reinforce some of the difficulties experienced in practice with the (sometimes unintended) consequences of planning actions referred to above.

These observations lead to the conclusion that the achievements of planning have not always matched up to its aspirations, but this does not appear to have undermined fundamentally the argument for having planning systems. The fact that planning practice has not always been very effective, while undoubtedly creating operational problems in its own terms in particular localities (Kitchen, 1990), has tended to produce calls for better planning practice rather than calls for the abandonment of the attempt at planning. The present British government's Planning Green Paper (DTLR, 2001) is a classic illustration of this line of argument, even though it could be said that there is a depressing similarity between its diagnosis of the problems experienced by the process of development plan-making and a diagnosis from thirty-six years previously (Planning Advisory Group, 1965); the recommended solution is still to try to do better rather than to give up the attempt. Indeed, planning (and particularly urban planning) appears now to be widely established across large parts of the world as a necessary function of government. The arguments about the need for planning which were at the forefront of debate in the early years of this present century (see Geddes [1915], 1968) have now largely been overtaken by arguments about how better planning can be achieved.

Planning systems, despite their diversity, typically have four common characteristics:

• The preparation of various types of plan that set down rules, policies or guidelines for managing change via the process of development.
• Some method or methods for controlling or regulating those processes of development, often by exclusion; that is, only those developments that pass certain threshold tests fall within these control processes. Examples of this include the ability to proceed with development in Britain where the nature or scale of this is such as to warrant its classification as 'permitted development', or the ability to proceed with

development in large parts of the USA which is consistent with existing zoning ordinances.

- Some requirements in relation to public consultation or involvement in these processes of plan-making and/or controlling development. The extent to which these requirements are set down in legislation, and then again the extent to which they are fallen short of, met or exceeded in practice, vary enormously across the world, and so generalizing about trends is not easy. But in the Western world in general there has almost certainly over the past thirty years or so been the gradual growth of a less quiescent public, less willing to accept that governments at various scales know best and demanding more opportunities to participate in the making of decisions that will affect them. And in varying ways and to various degrees, planning systems have responded to these societal changes. If my own span of practice in British local government from the late 1960s to the mid 1990s is in any way representative, it is very noticeable that the almost complete absence of any sort of effective public involvement has given way to a wide range of attempts at achieving this objective, some undoubtedly more successful than others. This process has been taken even further in the USA, where often very fragmented political structures seem to take planning decisions only when it can be demonstrated that a degree of public consensus exists; and hence working with community interests and mobilizing support for planning action is an essential part of practice (Teitz, 1996).
- A focus on the physical environment, in terms both of bringing about improvements to the built and natural environments through public and private expenditure and of a span of coverage by the main policy instruments (the development plan, and the process of development control) which emphasizes their physical elements. The objectives of planning policies can indeed be economic, or social, or community-based, and the analytical understandings that underpin those policies will need to be as broadly based as possible if the objective of taking a holistic view in the framing of planning policies is to be achieved. But their expression will usually take a broadly physical form; they will be policies about the use of land or buildings which are tested by their ability to promote appropriate forms of development and to resist inappropriate forms. The new focus on urban sustainability which emerged in the early 1990s (Blowers, 1993; Haughton and Hunter, 1994), deriving much of its impetus from the Rio Earth Summit of 1992, might conceivably have reinforced this physical environmental stance, because natural and man-made environments are also the focus of some of the definitions of sustainability which are at the ecological end of the spectrum. The prevailing view has tended to be one that adopts broader definitions, however, which see sustainability as being about the interaction of environmental, economic, political, social and community concerns which have in turn led to a broadening of the operational definition of

planning in Britain towards a focus on spatial planning (ODPM, 2005a). The difference between this approach and the pre-existing approach to physical/land use planning is described by the British Government in Planning Policy Statement 1 as follows:

> Spatial planning goes beyond traditional land use planning to bring together and integrate policies for the development and use of land with other policies and programmes which influence the nature of places and how they can function. That will include policies which can impact on land use, for example by influencing the demands on or needs for development, but which are not capable of being delivered solely or mainly through the granting or refusal of planning permission and which may be implemented by other means. (Ibid., para. 30)

As a consequence, spatial plans should:

1. set a clear vision for the future pattern of development, with clear objectives for achieving that vision and strategies for delivery and implementation;
2. consider the needs and problems of the communities in their areas and how they interact, and relate them to the use and development of land; and
3. seek to integrate the wide range of activities related to development and regeneration. (Ibid., para. 32)

The need for this last point to be achieved successfully in Britain was clearly illustrated by research which showed that old-style development plans were struggling to give any sort of policy lead to urban regeneration processes, but instead tended to follow behind them (Kitchen and Whitney, 2001).

Planning systems of the kind described commonly generate four major types of opportunities for interactions between planners and the customers of the planning service in seeking to influence the decisions that the planning system makes:

- the processes of making development plans;
- the processes of controlling development through the determination of applications for permissions of various types to carry out that development;
- processes of public consultation about a wide range of planning activities, including the implementation of individual improvement projects; and
- adversarial processes, where someone is exercising a right through a judicial or a quasi-judicial process to challenge a decision made by the planning system.

I explore each of these situations in more detail in Chapter 3, but it is important to consider one particular issue which can affect quite profoundly the way planning systems operate in any or all of these circumstances. This is the question of the degree of discretion inherent in the system. Put at its simplest, a planning system which requires precise policies to be expressed in development plans, which requires the process of taking decisions in the context of those plans to stick to their letter as well as to their spirit with only very limited room for the making of exceptions, and which allows considerable room for challenge via the courts of decisions taken by the system on the grounds that they have infringed the requirements of this regime, is a system which allows very little discretion – although at least in theory it generates a considerable amount of certainty about its likely decisions. On the other hand, a system which accepts that its development plans will be expressed in terms of broad policies, which grants considerable room for manoeuvre in taking decisions within this broad framework, and which restricts the opportunities to challenge these actions via the courts, is a system that allows a considerable amount of discretion to its planning practitioners – but may well also create a considerable amount of uncertainty about their likely decisions. Across the world, planning systems can be found which take very different views of this balance between discretion and certainty. Some North American and some European systems are more typical of this first model, for example, with a major emphasis on certainty and a limited amount of discretion, whereas British systems are more typical of this second model, with rather lower levels of certainty and higher levels of discretion – although in practice the extent to which discretion and certainty in such systems are truly the antithesis of each other that this theoretical description would imply is a debatable commodity (Booth, 1996). In reality, these models probably aren't two polar opposites but probably shade into each other across quite a broad spectrum. Effective operation within a planning system requires a good level of knowledge not only about the amount and the nature of the discretion that are available with a planning system but also about how to make the best use of whatever that level of discretion actually is.

Skills for planning practice

My view about skills for planning practice derives primarily from what I have said above about the nature of the planning task. I have chosen for these purposes to break skills for planning practice down into seven broad clusters:

- *Technical skills* – because planners do bring some specific things to the table, that I choose to describe as 'technical', by virtue of the fact that they are planners rather than any other kind of development professional. If this were not so, then there would be major questions to be asked about the need for planners at all.

- *Planning system and process skills* – because planning wherever it is practised takes place within or unavoidably involves engagement with (often highly sophisticated) governmental processes, and planners need to be able to understand how to get things done in this kind of context, not just for their own operational effectiveness, but also to ensure that they can advise their customers about these matters. So this is about understanding the procedural dimensions of planning.
- *Place skills* – because planners need to think about the nature, characteristics and modes of operation of places and how to change these in ways that have positive effects on people's lives. If planning, as I have stated above, is about 'making places better for people', then place skills are particularly about the first part of this definition, with customer skills being particularly about its second half.
- *Customer skills* – because planners need to think very carefully about who they are working for and how the needs of these end beneficiaries (be these commissioning clients or people whose lives will be affected by planning actions, whether or not they are aware of this) can best be met, irrespective of what sector the planner is working in.
- *Personal skills* – because planners need to think about how they conduct and present themselves, especially in face-to-face interactions but also via other forms of communication.
- *Organizational, managerial and political context skills* – because the planning process is inevitably delivered in an organizational context, where issues such as resources, programmes and procedures are important and where the decision-making process has a significant political element, be this in the form of decisions taken by elected representatives (that is, politics with a big 'P') or in the more general sense of 'who gets what, when, how and why' (that is, politics with a small 'p').
- *Synoptic and integrative skills* – because all of this needs to be seen as a whole, driven by a clear sense of purpose, and not as a series of separate parts. The ability to understand and to stick with 'the big picture' is critical to the role planners play in taking an overview and in pulling things together.

I have chosen this particular way of approaching this task as a result of reflecting on my own experiences, and as a result of thinking about the characteristics of the large numbers of planners I have worked with whom I regarded as having made successful contributions. It is clear from the literature that there is no single agreed approach to describing skills for planning practice (a point which I explore in more depth in Chapter 9), and so this particular framework does not draw on any particular school of thought among this diverse material. Dividing skills for planning practice into seven clusters in this manner is useful as a framework for unpicking each of them, but it has one particular drawback that I would like readers to remember as they go through this book. This is that this framework is an analytical construct for looking at each cluster individually, but in practice it is rarely the case that any one of these operates in isolation. Rather, the effective planner deploys this range of skills as a package, and in the light of the requirements of the particular situation. Indeed, while I would hope that all planners possess elements of all seven of these skills packages, manifestly the nature of the mix will vary considerably from one planner to the next. Some people will have a superabundance of some skills and will be rather more limited in relation to others. Some individuals will have a much more balanced range of planning skills than will others and will therefore be seen as all-rounders. Hopefully, planning teams will include people whose skills balance each other, so that the range of what is available within the team is as comprehensive as is needed to tackle the issues they are facing. But almost always, planners will be deploying skills drawn from across this range, and they will be doing this in ways that are mutually reinforcing, rather than utilizing individual skills in isolation. The fact that I take each of these in turn in this book in order to be able to discuss them must not create the misleading impression that planners operate as if each of these seven skills areas were islands scattered across an ocean. Successful planners, in my experience, are successful because they can draw from this complete range and bring to bear all the skills they need to address the situation they face.

Before going on to discuss each of these skill areas separately in the chapters that follow, it is important to remember that planners have to be alive to major changes to the contexts within which they will be operating. The next sections of this chapter therefore discuss some of these issues.

The development of a planning career during a professional working lifetime

Over and above the need to apply planning skills in ways that are appropriate to the particular situations being addressed, there is another major way in which the application of the various packages of skills discussed in the book will vary, and that is over time during the development of an individual's professional career. Different people develop at different rates and to different extents, but a common career pattern involves moving from situations where typically a young planner is a member of a team – applying technical, customer, system and process and place skills in particular – to a situation where increasingly the job involves more managerial and strategic components. As I comment later in this book, it is important in developing in this way not to lose sight of what the process is actually all about, and to become more concerned as a consequence with the efficiency of the machine rather than with what its efforts are actually trying to achieve, not least because such attitudes are likely to impact adversely on the motivation of the people for whom you are responsible. The kinds of skills that are likely to come to the fore in this situation are organizational, managerial and political context skills, and in particular synoptic and integrative skills. This doesn't mean that the other kinds of planning skills will become irrelevant, or that the skills that typify people who are successful senior managers have no relevance to planners in more junior positions, but the nature of the skills mix will change as a planner's role changes throughout a professional career.

This is one kind of change that typifies a developing planning career; the challenges that come with changing roles, particularly when that also involves moving from one locality to another. But there is another kind of change that planners have to be able to adapt to during their professional lives, and that is the challenge of contextual changes. Sometimes these are easier to see when looking back over one's professional career than they were at the time, but when seen over the span of a professional lifetime these sorts of changes can be profound. The best way I can illustrate both the nature and the extent of the contextual changes likely to occur in a professional planning lifetime is to reflect on the major changes of this kind I have experienced during my own planning career.

The forces driving change to the context within which planning operates

Encapsulating the forces that have been driving change during the period in which I worked in the British planning system is no small task. To put this task into context, it is possible to argue that the period of fifty-seven years between the Town and Country Planning Act 1947 and the Planning and Compulsory Purchase Act 2004 spans what may well have been the most concentrated period of change in human history. But to keep the scope of this to manageable proportions, the following paragraphs pick out just four elements in this process of sweeping change, each of which has direct and indirect implications for planning practice. These four are the revolution in communications technology, the changes in the nature of the relationship between government and people, our changing understanding of how economic forces impact upon our towns and cities, and the changing character of British urban society.

We have seen a revolution in communication methods, with the growth in both the use and the potential of information technology which many people argue is still in its infancy (see, for example, Graham and Marvin, 1996). The world's first successful computer was in the process of being developed at the University of Manchester at the same time as the 1947 Act was working its way through its Parliamentary processes. Who at that time could possibly have forecast that all local planning authorities in England by the end of 2005 would be expected to have moved from a situation where in essence all their operations were carried out in longhand to one where they will have enabled public access on-line to their basic statutory planning functions (DTLR, 2001, para. 5.14; Land Use Consultants and Business Efficiency, 2002)? (The basic statutory planning functions are making development plans, dealing with applications for permission to develop – which is known in Britain as development control, but is described differently in different parts of the world – and undertaking other functions of a broadly environmental nature. This package of activities is common to planning services across much of the world.)

We have also seen a huge change in the nature of the relationship between government and people, and this too is a constantly evolving process. The idea that the state 'knew best' in relation to many walks of life and could be relied upon to extend public provision for the public's good was at the heart of many of the measures introduced by the reforming 1945–51 Labour government; so that, for example, Timmins (1996) labels the period 1942–51 as 'the age of optimism'. When I first came into planning in the 1960s most British cities were engaging in large-scale processes of slum clearance and new house-building without any effective processes of public consultation whatsoever, and yet to a very considerable extent most of the citizens directly affected by this process seemed prepared to accept it as being in their best interests. Only forty years later, large numbers of citizens are not prepared simply to sit back and be grateful for whatever the state does, be this at national or local level, but instead expect and demand that their wishes are fully taken into account in making decisions that were once the prerogative of the state. Many people also expect to be fully involved in processes of decision-making as well as to influence their outcomes. The failure of the planning system to engage effectively with people in these senses, as distinct from merely consulting with them, was at the heart of the government's diagnosis of what was wrong with the planning system in its Planning Green Paper (DTLR, 2001, para. 2.3). A full definition of how different 'engagement' is from 'consultation' is not offered in the Planning Green Paper, but a sense of this is given by the following extracts:

> A proper planning system is vital to our quality of life. People can be dramatically affected by the quality of their environment and they

care deeply about new development and how it changes the surroundings in which they live and work. That is why we need a planning system that fully engages people in shaping the future of their communities and local economies. (Ibid., para. 1.3)

And:

To be successful, the planning system needs to have the confidence of many different groups. These include almost half a million direct customers who are applicants for planning permission every year and who want a quick, predictable and efficient service; families and individuals affected by plans and planning applications; and the wider community who care about proposals for the future development of their area. All parts of the community – individuals, organisations and businesses – must be able to make their voice heard. (Ibid., para. 1.5)

This represents a huge change in the perception of the roles of the citizen in planning decision-making, with the citizen over much less than a fifty-year period in effect moving from zero to hero. This also, of course, represents a huge challenge to the planning process, since it would be much easier to conceptualize this as essentially a technocratic process had it not to face up to the challenge of public engagement.

Our understanding of the economic forces shaping our towns and cities has also changed enormously since the postwar years, although it is still possible to argue that this understanding lags behind the ever-evolving nature of the forces themselves. In its essence, however, the 1947 Act system operated on the assumption that a plan would largely be in control of the land use activities that it was seeking to manipulate, and so the key issue in industrial development (for example) was seen as the need to identify sufficient land to accommodate the activities that would come along in order to provide the number of jobs required (see, for example, Keeble, 1964, pp. 187–90). What we have learned from bitter experience, since lots of local planning authorities on this basis allocated land in their development plans which to this day remains unoccupied, is that while this may have been a necessary condition for securing economic development it certainly wasn't a sufficient condition. There are many reasons for this, but increasingly we have come to recognize that one of the most important of these is that contemporary economic processes often work on a global or at any rate a much more than local scale (Hayter, 1997; Marcuse and van Kempen, 2000). So what was once seen for planning purposes as essentially an endogenous variable, which planning processes could therefore attempt to control, is now increasingly seen as an exogenous variable which planning processes have to relate to as best they can.

British urban society also seems to have changed its character very substantially since the late 1940s, and these processes seem to be ongoing. These processes, summarized by Rogers and Power as 'social change and fragmentation', include forces such as urban depopulation, job change, income gaps, ethnic change and race relations, changes in the size and character of the family unit, family and social breakdown, educational change, crime and anti-social behaviour, and social exclusion (Rogers and Power, 2000, pp. 23–52). Each one of these by itself would have represented a considerable challenge to the planning system. Together, they have seen British urban policy turn itself completely on its head. The heroic plans of the 1940s contemplated with equanimity the need for large-scale population 'overspill' from our major cities in order to create acceptable living standards within their boundaries, without (it should be said) much apparent recognition of the fact that the people who would constitute that 'overspill' might have a view about such a forced move and indeed about being described by a piece of jargon that today we might well regard as disparaging. The 1944 Abercrombie Greater London Plan, for example, envisaged just over 1 million people 'to be decentralised, or moved from the central mass' (Abercrombie, 1945, p. 5), and the 1945 Nicholas plan for the City of Manchester saw the need to think about the city's effective population capacity within its then current boundaries as 475,000 as compared with its contemporary population of approximately 705,000, which would have involved a population reduction of around one-third (Nicholas, 1945, p. 167). Just over fifty years later, however, the essential feature of today's urban policy according to the Urban Policy White Paper of 2000 is the need to repopulate our towns and cities through the re-use of 'brownfield' land rather than further 'greenfield' development on the edges of or away from our major urban areas (DETR, 2000).

Similar stories could be told in relation to many countries in many parts of the world; in detail these forces may have impacted on planning in Britain in particular ways, but there is nothing unique or intrinsically British about them. The sheer scale of the forces contained within these four examples alone is surely enough to make us realize that planning practice in the early years of the twenty-first century must be a very different thing from planning practice as it was seen at the time of the passage of the 1947 Act. At the same time, the basic tools that the public sector planner uses (that is, the planner acting within a framework provided by the government at one spatial scale or another and on behalf of the public at large) have not changed very much in their conception. In essence, planners still prepare policy documents (such as development plans) of various kinds, still seek to control other than the smallest scale of development through the vehicle of determining applications for planning permission, and still use a variety of mechanisms for implementing improvement projects of various kinds. These were the key elements of the 1947 Act system, and they remain the key elements of the 2004 Act system, albeit that there has been a lot of tinkering with each of these individual packages in the intervening period. There has also been a huge amount of thinking and writing in this period about the nature of planning itself, so for example we now have a large-scale planning theory 'industry' where for all practical purposes no such thing existed at the time of the 1947 Act; though whether the outpourings of this industry have had a concomitant effect over this period on planning practice is an issue where there remains considerable room for debate (see, for example, Brooks, 2002). Perhaps this identifies two of the problems that planning practice has faced in trying to cope with the tide of change described above; there has been insufficient development of the basic tools for the job, and the intellectual ferment that has characterized activity in the world of planning theory has not for whatever reason fed through into improvements in planning practice to the extent that might have been desirable (see for example the discussion of this relationship in chapter 10 of Hall, 1996).

The practical consequence of all of this for the operation of the planning process is that, during the forty years or so of my professional lifetime, these external changes have profoundly affected some of our most central planning concepts. Again, for the purposes of illustration, I choose four of these (and I develop this argument further in Kitchen, 2002; 2004, pp. 108–15):

- The concept of *certainty* – The idea that the planning system should be able to tell all parties interested in development what is going to happen in any locality, which was originally grounded in legal interests in land (Cherry, 1996, pp. 124–6).
- The concept of *speed* – The idea that the planning system should be able to carry out all of its functions within prescribed timetables, so as not to hold up necessary development and so as to give confidence to participants about how its due processes would operate, which I discuss in more detail in Chapter 7.
- The concept of *public involvement* – The idea that planning decisions should be shaped by public views (always assuming that there is enough agreement to make this possible), which I return to throughout this book and especially in Chapter 5.
- The concept of *sustainable development* – The relatively rather more recent idea that it is the task of the planning system to contribute to the battle against global warming by ensuring that all development is sustainable (see Hall *et al.*, 1993; Jenks *et al.*, 1996; Warburton, 1998; Satterthwaite, 1999; Layard *et al.*, 2001; CAG Consultants and Oxford Brookes University, 2004; Countryside Agency *et al.*, 2005).

Box 1.1 shows what has happened to these key planning concepts in Britain over the period 1966–2004, which is the period which more or less coincides with my own professional lifetime.

Box 1.1   Key planning concepts – the challenge of change

Concept	1966	2004	Commentary
Certainty	Development plans would provide certainty through being as specific as possible.	Development plans would provide certainty through being clear about strategic principles and being specific where this is necessary.	The real issue here may well be, what do we mean by 'certainty'? Do we mean strategic certainty which is about broad directions, or site-specific certainty? It is probably easier for planning systems to provide the former rather than the latter without getting out of date quickly.
Speed	Statutory timetables specified for development plan-making and for development control. The recorded practice, however, was that local planning authorities were struggling to meet these timetables, particularly for development plan-making.	The challenge of speeding the system up has caused that system to be revisited several times, yet many forces such as the continuously growing pressure to engage the public more effectively in planning tend to slow it down. The 2004 Planning and Compulsory Purchase Act represents another try to resolve this problem.	How well resourced the planning system is undoubtedly makes a difference to how well it performs. But public expectations are constantly rising, and efficient and effective systems are not always good at engaging the broad mass of the public both effectively and speedily.

→

→

Public involvement	The concept was scarcely to be found in relation to statutory planning activities, other than via fairly minimal expectations in respect of development plans.	The planning system has been told by the British government in the Planning Green Paper (2001) that it has to go beyond mere consultation and to become much more effective at engaging people, which means taking full account of public views in making decisions.	The expectation is that delivering planning services on-line will make a big difference to the ability of the planning system to deliver more effective public involvement. It needs to be remembered though that more diverse societies may well produce more diverse views; more public engagement does not necessarily equate with greater levels of agreement.
Sustainable development	Although it can be argued that some planning concepts have always contributed to sustainable development, in its modern sense this concept was not visible.	The primary purpose of the planning system is the achievement of sustainable development.	There are major questions to be asked about whether planning really has the tools to tackle this, e.g. persuading members of the public to give up extensive use of the private car.

The point I am trying to make with this extended example is that professional planners can expect during their professional lifetimes to have to cope with contextual change on a very large scale. Box 1.1 shows the extent of change in relation to four key planning concepts over a period that equates to my own professional lifetime, and I hope that readers would share my view that this is indeed change on a profound scale. That said, any view of the future needs to encompass the likelihood that the pace of change is accelerating (Cooper and Layard, 2003). In other words, starting from now most new entrants to the planning profession can expect to have to cope with at least as much contextual change during their professional lifetimes as I have had to. Planners need as a consequence to be alive to changes of this nature, and to be able to adapt their thinking accordingly on a progressive basis. That is part of the reason why I talk elsewhere in this book about the planner as a reflective practitioner and about the importance of professional learning being seen as a continuous process.

Government support for planning

A final factor I want to discuss in thinking about how the context within which planners work changes is that government support for planning can be very variable. I suspect that it is true of most professional planning careers in most parts of the world that they will be heavily affected by this factor. Planning systems exist on a widespread basis, but the extent to which and the ways in which they get used, and indeed how effective they are, will depend among other things on how strongly they are supported by governments at various spatial scales. In Britain, for example, the Thatcher era of the 1980s was a period of time when planning seemed to be seen as part of the problem rather than part of the solution (Thornley, 1991). It was certainly my experience, as senior assistant city planning officer and then as city planning officer of Manchester at that time, that the budget of the planning service over a number of years faced annual cuts as a result of significant reductions in central government financial support for the work of the City Council (Kitchen, 1997, pp. 13–16), and this lack of support for the planning function from central government was reinforced at times by a lack of appropriate support for the planning service at local level from some of the council's political leaders. These things certainly made the planning task much harder than it would have been in a more propitious environment. In addition, some planning powers in part of the city centre were taken away from the city council and given to a newly created development corporation that was responsible to central government rather than locally (ibid., pp. 136–42; Deas *et al.*, 1999, pp. 206–30). That was undoubtedly a hard time for the British local government planning service, and Manchester's experiences were by no means unique. Conversely, the Labour government, particularly over the period 2001–2005, has been extremely supportive of the planning system, 'modernizing' it in a variety of ways (Department of the Environment, Transport and the Regions, 1998a; DTLR, 2001; ODPM, 2002), pumping more money into it in recognition of its financially constrained nature (Arup Economics and the Bailey Consultancy, 2002) in return for performance improvements, and focusing on how it can become more successful through a wide-ranging 'culture change' initiative (ODPM, 2002 and 2003e; McNulty, 2003; McCarthy, 2004; Kitchen, 2004).

This latter initiative is probably peculiarly British, but what sits behind it is a challenge that is facing most administrations across the world – how can our planning organizations be successful in doing what they exist to do, while at the same time being highly regarded by all the parties with key interests in those tasks?

So, what this example shows from my own experience is that government support for planning waxes and wanes over time, and that this can make a considerable difference in particular to how well resourced the planning service is, which in turn affects what it is able to do. The point I am trying to make both in this section and in the previous one about contextual change is that planners have to adapt to changes of this nature over which they have no effective control, as well as to focus on the core skills of the planning job. Thus, in concentrating on the latter, as I do for the remainder of this book, it is important not to forget about the former.

The structure of the book

The chapters that follow then take each of the seven planning skill components in turn under the banner of core skills for planning practice, and discuss what they are and how they occur in practice situations. So Chapters 2–8 cover this ground in the following sequence:

Chapter 2 – Technical skills.
Chapter 3 – Planning system and process skills.
Chapter 4 – Place skills.
Chapter 5 – Customer skills.
Chapter 6 – Personal skills.
Chapter 7 – Organizational, managerial and political context skills.
Chapter 8 – Synoptic and integrative skills.

The logic of this order is that the first four elements are likely to be required of planners even in relatively junior positions, the fifth is about sorting out one's own perspectives, which is common to whatever level at which one works, and the last two are particularly important in senior and/or managerial positions.

I have not hesitated in these chapters to draw on my own experience to provide examples designed to illustrate the operation in practice of the particular skills being discussed, and thus often I am the source for these purposes rather than more formal academic or practice literature. Stylistically, this will often become apparent when the text moves into the first person. There is probably nothing very particular about my practice experience except that it happened to me, but since I have found myself in many of the situations I am describing I have not hesitated to draw on this experience. In particular, I have tried to focus here on positive stories that emphasize the potential power of a planning contribution, because I very much share the view of Leonie Sandercock that

> This 'organising of hope' is one of our fundamental tasks as planners, and one of our weapons in that battle is the use of success stories, and the ability to tell those stories well, meaningfully, in a way that does indeed inspire others to act. (Sandercock, 2003, p. 18)

Whether I have succeeded in my examples by these lights is for others to judge, but my motivation in choosing examples has been to illustrate what is possible and to show how planning and planners can add value.

At the end of each of these seven chapters I have developed a small number of self-assessment topics. The purpose of these is to enable readers to explore some of the material raised in each chapter in their own particular local circumstances by identifying broad issues of which they should be able to find local examples, and then by suggesting some of the kinds of questions that they should be asking about those local instances. Clearly, in detail many of these examples will be different from the examples given in Chapters 2–8, but what this process of exploration should enable readers to do is to begin to understand how some of the generic issues discussed in this book play out in their own particular circumstances.

Chapter 9 then looks at the changing planning skills debate, by adopting four difference perspectives on these issues: the views of some writers, the changing views of a professional body over time (in this case, the British Royal Town Planning Institute), the urban regeneration perspective, and the adoption of a multi-professional approach to urban management. The essential argument presented here is that while there isn't an agreed view of skills for planning practice that emerges from these perspectives, the seven sets of skills presented in this book can be seen in most of these views.

In conclusion, Chapter 10 tries to draw together some of the threads that have been explored in the previous chapters. It revisits in particular the idea that the sets of planning skills discussed in this book do not operate in isolation but are part of the whole package that makes up the effective planner, and it uses the concept of the planner as reflective practitioner (Schon, 1998) as a vehicle for discussing how planners can keep developing their skills. This in turn leads into a discussion of the role of skills development throughout professional life, and of the part the planning education system should play in this.

It seems to me that in essence the basic skills required for successful planning practice are probably not terribly different today from what they have been for most of the past half-century or more, although the balance between them may well have changed. Over this period, however, planning practice seems to have been growing progressively more difficult, and as a consequence the challenge to the skills of professional planners has grown ever more demanding. A good illustration of this is the discussion around customer skills, which I would argue were always needed if planning was indeed seen as being 'for people' but which have come to the fore in more recent times as it has been recognized that this actually means engaging directly with people and not just behaving paternalistically towards them. This has been accompanied (at any rate in Britain) by a sense that planning in many ways failed the tests it was given during the slum clearance period in our major urban areas (which ran from around the mid 1950s to around the mid 1970s) because the quality of the replacement development was too often simply not good enough, and British planning was still struggling to recover from that when it was hit by the Thatcherite whirlwind (Thornley, 1991). This sequence of events tended to create a situation where many British planners working in local government felt beleaguered, and almost programmed to fail; and among other things this might have been one element in the growth of the private sector of planning in recent years referred to above. I am writing this book at a time of greater optimism, however, with a government in office that seems to believe in the importance of planning and that wants to find ways of helping it to succeed, as noted above. This is a huge opportunity for British planning, but it will only grasp that opportunity fully if its skills are sharp and if its practitioners apply them effectively. In turn, the British experience of trying to re-energize planning in these ways will surely offer lessons for elsewhere. If this book can make even a small contribution to this effort, I will be absolutely delighted.

Chapter 2

Technical Skills

Introduction

> If an official wishes to persuade his superiors and political critics that his decisions on a wide range of subjects should be considered authoritative, his most obvious strategy is to maintain that they are technical – to maintain, that is, that public policy has been declared in highly operational fashion and that he speaks as an expert interpreter of it. One who qualifies in the purest sense as an expert – defined here as one who is technically rational – can be judged only according to his competence (assuming that he is honest), not at all according to his personality or character. Give any number of pure experts the same operational objective and they should come out with sets of specific recommendations that differ insignificantly if at all. (Altshuler, 1965, pp. 334, 335)

Faced with these (justified) cautionary words, it may seem somewhat perverse to begin a series of chapters about the skills of planning practice with one that is about technical skills. On the other hand, it was no part of Altshuler's thesis that planning practice was entirely devoid of technical components; his position was that they sat alongside a number of other things that influenced the operating environments of planners, and only became a problem in these terms when things were claimed by planners to be technical as a strategy for obtaining power when it was clear that behind that facade lay other elements of judgement, ideology or perhaps even prejudice which ought properly to be in the political arena. I agree with that analysis. The argument of this book is that technical skills sit alongside six other packages of skills in the make-up of the effective planning practitioner, and that it is the interactions of these skills packages that will actually determine planner effectiveness. Thus, technical skills are part of the whole, but we must be careful not to make them out to be more than they are and not to claim that things are technical (and thus within the specialized knowledge of a relatively small group of experts) when in fact they are not.

On this basis, this chapter concentrates mainly on those major elements in the planning task that in the author's view can properly be regarded as requiring significant inputs of technical skills. These are aspects of the processes of making development plans, of controlling development, and of achieving area or environment improvements. In addition, because many planning tasks benefit from the application of topic-based expertise, an example will be used from the field of retail planning to show how technical components of planning activities in this area relate to other components of decision-making. I illustrate what I want to say about the technical dimensions of planning practice by examples drawn largely from my own career experiences. Much of this also raises issues of planning system and process, and therefore I return in Chapter 3 to some of these major components of planning activity from that perspective. This present chapter closes with some self-assessment topics designed to help readers to explore some of the issues raised in this chapter for themselves.

None of the elements described in this chapter as being technical can be seen as free-standing entities, however. In every instance in the real world of planning practice the application of technical skills takes place alongside the application of several of the other skills discussed in this book, because planning is about trying to deal with problems as they present themselves but as holistically as possible. And problems in societies tend not to present themselves unidimensionally – and perhaps especially not in relation to a definition of technical skills in planning which would make the process of problem-solving uniquely the responsibility of the planner. Nevertheless, it is important that planners do possess the skills that enable the technical dimensions of planning to be seen alongside its other dimensions, because they will be responsible for ensuring that these elements are brought to the discussion table and because others will expect them to do this.

The processes of development plan-making

Box 2.1 shows as a simple linear process 10 steps in the process of development plan-making. There are many different ways of conceptualizing the various steps involved in plan-making, of course, but this is one that many practising planners will recognize from their own experiences. In many ways, it is not dissimilar to several other attempts at generalizing frameworks of this kind (compare it, for example, with figure 2.5 in Bruton and Nicholson, 1987, p. 69). While a very simple diagram like this is helpful for thinking about the basic steps involved in most plan-making activities, there are also some important limitations to bear in mind. Six of these (content, extant planning work, the continuous nature of the process, practicalities suggesting that steps might be taken out of sequence, the problems of public consultation and the problems of spatial scale) are discussed below, with the problems of spatial scale being treated in greater depth because of the issues being raised.

Plan-making occurs almost always in some sort of *context*, which impacts upon it not merely at the start of the process but very often all the way through. A plan-making process is rarely the kind of island that Box 2.1 might be seen as presenting it as being, and if the outcome of the process is to be an operationally useful plan it is important that the process should not be isolated from the real world it will be seeking to influence.

It is not always necessary to go through every step in this chain, because *extant planning work* may render this unnecessary. Most plans do not involve starting with a completely clean sheet. For example, many decisions to prepare plans may arise as a result of concerns raised by the outcome of brainstorming activities about trends and possibilities affecting the area described as step 2, or as a result of political pressures to do something about particular areas or problems. These may in turn mean that part of step 3 is already clear, because the reason why the plan was commissioned (to seek to combat adverse trends or to take advantage of opportunities) will, in turn, determine to a large extent the aims and objectives of the plan.

It is arguable that the process is (or ought to be) *continuous*, with for example monitoring and review being instituted before plan-making has got as far as step 9, in acknowledgement of the fact that the world will not stand still while the plan-making process is under way. While the theoretical arguments for this position are strong, I have argued elsewhere (Kitchen, 1996) that in practice there may well be limits to the capacity of organizations to cope with an intensive activity like plan-making as a more or less continuous process, and that as a consequence they may revert to 'informal' styles of planning between more 'formal' bouts of plan-making activity. The system introduced into England as a result of the Planning and Compulsory Purchase Act 2004, where the plan consists not of a single large document but of a portfolio of documents which can be added to (or subtracted from) on a more or less continuous basis, can be seen as an attempt to catch this kind of idea in statutory form (ODPM, 2004a, 2004e).

Practicalities may dictate that there are very good reasons why steps in the process should be taken out of sequence. For example, it might be decided that step 1 needs to involve some major pieces of fresh survey work to improve significantly existing understandings of the situation and its context. As a consequence, some data bases may well be established which will need to be kept up to date as part of the monitoring and review work which forms step 9, and so in this instance decisions about very significant components of step 9 are to a substantial extent taken right at the beginning of the process.

The precise placing of various types of *public consultation* and involvement in processes of this kind is particularly difficult, because this could take place at any or all of the various stages. The suggestion in Box 2.1 that this should be a component of step 2 in the process and the essence of step 7 is but one way of giving expression to this point. Chapter 5 of

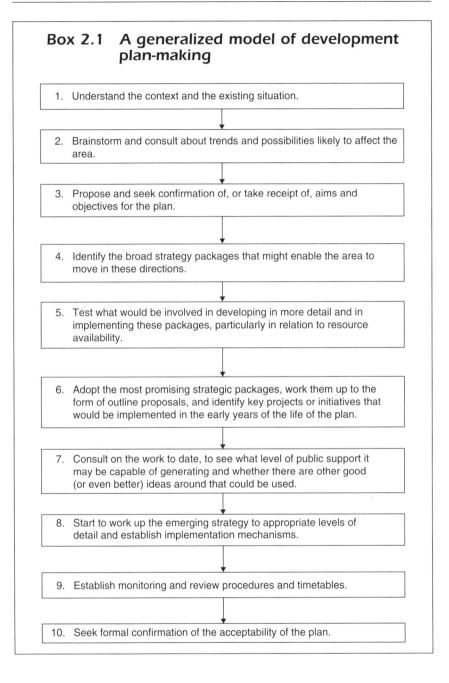

Box 2.1   A generalized model of development plan-making

1. Understand the context and the existing situation.

2. Brainstorm and consult about trends and possibilities likely to affect the area.

3. Propose and seek confirmation of, or take receipt of, aims and objectives for the plan.

4. Identify the broad strategy packages that might enable the area to move in these directions.

5. Test what would be involved in developing in more detail and in implementing these packages, particularly in relation to resource availability.

6. Adopt the most promising strategic packages, work them up to the form of outline proposals, and identify key projects or initiatives that would be implemented in the early years of the life of the plan.

7. Consult on the work to date, to see what level of public support it may be capable of generating and whether there are other good (or even better) ideas around that could be used.

8. Start to work up the emerging strategy to appropriate levels of detail and establish implementation mechanisms.

9. Establish monitoring and review procedures and timetables.

10. Seek formal confirmation of the acceptability of the plan.

this book argues in any event that the most effective consultation takes place as part of a continuing relationship between planners and particular sets of customers, which must mean if this can be achieved that where precisely in the plan-making process specific types of consultation take place is much less important than the quality of the dialogue that is established. In practice, decisions about matters of this kind are likely to be taken according to the prevailing local circumstances and with a particular eye on the amount of time it is intended the plan-making process should consume. The technical view that planners might take about how best to feed the results of public consultation into their plan-making processes should not be confused with the process of thinking about how best to relate to the ever-growing public demand for effective involvement in decision-making, and as I have already argued in Chapter 1 the huge growth in public expectations in these terms is one of the most dramatic changes to practice that I have experienced throughout my career since the Skeffington Committee first turned this visible demand into procedural recommendations (Skeffington, 1969). There is a strong case for arguing that from this perspective public consultation should be seen as part of a continuous process of public debate (Healey, 1997), and the challenge in plan-making is to construct ways of doing this which nevertheless enable the process to move forward expeditiously.

Planning activities can take place at several *spatial scales*, and adjustments may be made to the process accordingly. For example, a detailed redevelopment plan for a particular area of a city may well be required to shape the physical form of the redevelopment process, but the incorporation of such a plan may be seen to be inappropriate as part of a plan for the city as a whole both as to the level of detail it would involve and as to its time-scale. The consequence might well be that the redevelopment plan would be regarded as a separate exercise to that of preparing a plan for the city as a whole, but would be grounded in its objectives and its policies. Indeed, this is actually quite a common problem in planning, where the theoretical view that a single plan can be prepared comes up against practical issues that show different needs in different situations. The result is often a process of 'nesting' plans within plans, and Box 2.2 provides an example of this process from the experience of preparing the Unitary Development Plan for Manchester in the 1990s.

The pattern of 'nesting' plans within plans illustrated in Box 2.2 reflects a very typical planning problem. This is that it is most unlikely that one plan will fit all needs. The characteristics and needs of different localities, and the need to approach issues in varying ways because of the different spatial scales involved (the broad strategic policies appropriate at the scale of a whole city, for example, as compared with the fine detail involved in site specific changes in a relatively small regeneration area), are constant problems irrespective of the planning system that is current, as is the need to understand all the relationships between these elements and specifically the ways they interact. They suggest that there will always need to be different types of plans for different purposes, and that this will always need to be managed in the best practical way within whatever statutory framework exists at any point in time. The Manchester example from the mid 1990s summarized

Box 2.2 Nesting plans within plans: a case-study from Manchester

As part of the process of preparing the Unitary Development Plan for the City of Manchester over the period 1989–95, three parts of the city were regarded as being likely to experience large-scale change relatively quickly, but in a form that could not be precisely anticipated at the time when the UDP's policies and proposals were being drafted. These three areas were:

1. Hulme, to the south of the city centre, where major funding was being sought to create a new agency to oversee the redevelopment of an area characterized by system-built high-rise housing of the late 1960s and early 1970s which was seen to have failed.
2. Eastlands, to the east of the city centre, which was intended to be the location of key facilities as part of Manchester's bid to host the Olympic Games of 2000, the outcome of which was unknown at that time (but which subsequently became the location of the main stadium for the Commonwealth Games of 2002, and the core of a major regeneration area in East Manchester).
3. Monsall, to the north of the city centre, where system-built housing similar to that to be found in Hulme had already been demolished without being replaced, and where as a consequence there was a great deal of redevelopment potential in land availability terms but no certainty whatsoever about how activity of this kind might get funded.

As a consequence, the Manchester UDP defined each of these as 'major urban renewal areas', and provided a broad policy starting-point for separate processes of partnership working which would sort out the necessary detail in each area.

In addition, it was decided to continue with six existing local plans by incorporating them as they stood within the UDP, because these were regarded as still being relevant to the needs of these areas. Each of these had its own particular style and history. The six were:

- The City Centre Local Plan
- The Ringway Local Plan, covering the area of Manchester Airport
- The Green Belt Local Plan
- The Mersey Valley Local Plan
- The Medlock Valley Local Plan
- The Minerals Local Plan, which related to the whole of the Greater Manchester area, and in practice had minimal impact on the City of Manchester because it did not have active mineral working within its boundaries

The patchwork quilt created by one style of planning for the city represented by the UDP as a whole, by the decision to treat three areas as major urban renewal areas to be the subject of later and more detailed planning action, and by the retention of six existing local plans, is undeniably complex, but it was a reflection of the planning challenge as it was seen at the time the Manchester UDP was being prepared.

in Box 2.2 related to a different statutory framework in England to that introduced by the Planning and Compulsory Purchase Act 2004, and it will be interesting to see whether the 'portfolio' approach (a recognition that several different documents together will constitute the development plan) of that Act's provisions will make this task of 'nesting' any easier.

One of the other difficulties with looking at this issue has been the relationship that has existed (at any rate in Britain) between the structure of local government and the areas over which plans have been prepared. In essence, plans are prepared for the areas of local authorities; and as the areas of local authorities change so do the areas over which plans are prepared (although of course it has always been possible to prepare plans for smaller areas where this is needed), irrespective of however (in)appropriate these areas might be in planning terms. So, for example, the abolition of metropolitan county councils in England in 1986 led to the disappearance of metropolitan county structure plans, and their replacement by unitary development plans (a combination of elements of the structure plan and of local plans) for each of the now all-purpose metropolitan district councils. Just as it could be argued that the concept of the structure plan was not very appropriate as a means of providing a strategic planning framework for a whole conurbation, so in its absence could it also be argued that a set of unitary development plans sitting side by side didn't do this job very effectively either. Both cases were a product of a view about the structure of local government rather than of the best kind of approach to planning, but in both cases the planning system had to get on and do the best that it could in the situation in which it found itself. Lots of ink could be spilled debating what are the right areas for plan preparation, and I suspect that this is probably one of those issues where lots of opinions exist but where there is no right answer. Looked at like this, it could be argued that the currently agreed structure of local government is as good a basis as any other for determining the areas covered by development plans, especially since it brings forward democratic accountability for that process in its wake. Nevertheless, I always found it very difficult in Manchester to get participants in the development plan-making process to think about issues on a broader basis than that provided by the city's boundaries, and it was clear that in some cases (for example, when thinking about journeys to work) this was an inappropriate and unduly constraining basis for planning.

Before leaving this topic of spatial scale, there is one other point that needs to be made. It is often thought that the concept of a strategic plan is related to the notion of spatial scale, with the broader the area of coverage the more likely it is that the resultant plan will be strategic in its nature. While it may well be the case that plans for large areas have to be strategic almost by definition in order to avoid being swamped by detail, what is not true in my experience is that it is no longer necessary to think strategically when planning at a more localized scale (see

Box 2.3   Key strategic components of plan-making activities

1. Be clear about the broad directions in which you want to go, and about how to get there.
2. Since this will be unique to each locality, ground it in the history, aspirations, circumstances and people of that locality.
3. Be clear about how 'planning' activities relate to all the other sorts of processes that impact on the relationships between places and people.
4. Look at this in terms of the different sorts of messages to be sent by the plan-making process and by the plan itself to its range of customers.
5. Do not be swayed too much by the latest fashionable ideas unless they are clearly appropriate to the circumstances.
6. The basic principles will probably stand for some time, although they should be kept under constant review, but detailed actions will change.
7. The process will in all probability be opportunity-led rather than problem-led, although it will try to use the former to help solve the latter.
8. The process will probably contain some long-term diagnoses where the direction is much clearer than the detailed action that needs to be taken; so don't prejudice tomorrow by formulating proposals based upon what you cannot know today.
9. The process will need to secure a wide level of general support from the community, as well as achieving as much specific support as possible from those who will have to take action to help achieve desired outcomes.
10. The expression of policy stances will take a variety of forms, of which the development plan will be but one.
11. The most important test of a plan is whether it works in its own terms and in its own area.

These propositions apply to the process of plan-making irrespective of the spatial scale of the plan being prepared.

Source: This box draws on the author's chapter in Tewdwr-Jones, 1996, pp. 125–6.

Kitchen, 1996). All planning activity, at whatever spatial scale, needs to have strategic components to it. I have elsewhere (ibid.) identified 11 propositions as constituting the kernel of the strategic components of plan-making activity that are likely to be relevant to one degree or another at whatever spatial scale that activity takes place, and these are reproduced in Box 2.3. This is similar to the broad argument of Friend and Jessop (1969), to the effect that issues of 'strategic choice' exist at all levels but because they are not always seen as such they are not always well handled. I return to this point again in Chapter 8.

The classic textbooks on town planning used to be very strong on the techniques involved in plan-making (see, for example, Chapin, 1970), but as a field of writing this has been somewhat neglected in recent times.

In its place in Britain has come what is by now quite a long-established tradition of government advice about development plans, although even here the focus has tended to switch from an emphasis on content (Ministry of Housing and Local government, 1970) to a greater emphasis on process (Department of the Environment, 1992a; ODPM, 2004a, 2004b). Indeed, a contemporary impression of material of this nature might well be that the technical component of this kind of advice is dominated by references to government policy advice, to which plans are expected to adhere, and to procedural matters.

An important addition to the plan-making process in England in recent years, however, has been the concept of the sustainability appraisal. This is a consequence of the government's view that the overriding purpose of the planning system is the achievement of sustainable development (ODPM, 2005a). At the time of writing, advice on the requirement that sustainability appraisals of both Regional Spatial Strategies and Local Development Frameworks must be undertaken is still being prepared (ODPM, 2005b), but an intriguing question will concern the extent to which these are seen as technical appraisals as distinct from the extent to which they are seen as a basis for public discussion. This kind of debate in relation to evaluative work is, of course, much older than current concerns about strategic environmental assessments and sustainability appraisals (see, for example, Lichfield, 1996, pp. 193–200; Countryside Agency *et al.*, 2005), but increasingly the trend seems to be to see 'technical' appraisals as being available for public discussion and indeed as capable of being challenged at the public inquiry stage of the plan-making process. I participated during 2004 and 2005 in the panel reviewing the sustainability appraisal work being undertaken as part of preparing a new development plan for Sheffield, where the approach adopted was to look at draft plan policies by a 'traffic light' methodology – green for positive, red for negative, and yellow (and various other symbols) for in-between or unavoidably qualified positions. This method, which is a fairly common approach to this task, is very effective as a method of communication because it enables the judgement that is being made to be grasped very quickly, but it turned out to be quite difficult to apply in practice because relatively few draft plan polices could be unambiguously assigned to the red or the green categories – and even then, it was possible to see where and how other interests might contest these assessments. The development of work of this nature, and of the guidance that supports that work, will be a very interesting test of this balance between technical planning work and work which has much broader community/political dimensions to it. My guess is that what is genuinely accepted as technical (and therefore as not open to being contested by most people) in this might turn out to be relatively limited, and that increasingly the material in analyses of this nature will come to be seen as the very stuff of local debate.

There isn't the space here to write in any detail about all the technical aspects of development plan-making, but a few points about the 10 steps in Box 2.1 to close this discussion of some of the technical aspects of development plan-making may be helpful.

• *Context and existing situation.* The key technical question here is the extent to which it is necessary to commission further work so that the planning team has an appropriate level of understanding of where it is starting from. It is always a temptation to do this because knowledge is rarely perfect, but the test should always be whether the improvements in understanding that would arise as a result of commissioning new work are necessary for the process to commence. Often, they are not. Often also, the issues that do need to be the subject of further study don't become clear until the process has unfolded somewhat, and then they can be carried out in parallel with other steps if necessary. As far as possible, therefore, it is often best to start with what is already known, and to make sure as part of this process that good communications are established where they don't already exist with sources of local knowledge, so that the process can be plugged into these as a speedy and effective way of overcoming limitations at the start of the process. An interesting illustration of this problem has arisen during my time as a member and subsequently as Chair of the Sheffield First for Environment Partnership (later renamed the Sheffield First Environment Partnership). Like all the elements of the Sheffield First 'family' of partnerships (which is reviewed in more detail in Chapter 7), SFfE had to develop a strategy as quickly as possible after it came into being, but it was faced immediately with a very difficult issue. What did we know about the existing state of Sheffield's environment, since if we were going to shape a strategy dedicated to improving it we would presumably be well-advised to know where we were starting from? There were three problems with this, however. The first was that there was no comprehensive study of this kind in existence, and indeed the available evidence was in scattered fragments rather than collected together in one place. The second was that changing this situation substantially would be an expensive process, and SFfE did not have a budget from which it could fund such an activity. The third difficulty was that assembling a reliable 'state of the environment' report would be a time-consuming exercise, and given the pressure to produce a strategy relatively quickly time was not available for an activity of this nature. So the decision was taken to rely on the knowledge of partnership board members and on the feedback gained from consulting on the draft strategy, and to work towards improving the partnership's knowledge about the state of Sheffield's environment by increments over time. This was an entirely pragmatic decision, but it made it possible to make some progress rather than being immediately stalled.

• *Trends and possibilities.* There are various forecasting and analytical methods of looking at what trends and possibilities may affect an area (Bracken, 1981; Field and MacGregor, 1992), and more generally various disciplines offer a very wide range of views about trends that will shape the future (see, for example, Cooper and Layard, 2003). There are also more consultative methods available, which essentially involve tapping into informed opinion. The essential point about all of these, however, is that they are as good as the framework of assumptions that goes into them and the data that is available for them. It is increasingly being recognized that these are not neutral activities, but are bound up with the political and policy frameworks to which they relate and indeed the values of the people carrying out forecasting work of this kind. Field and MacGregor (1992, p. 197) put this as follows:

> When using planning models, there is rarely a correct answer. In general, therefore, it is better to produce a range of values when making forecasts and to test the sensitivity of these to changes in the underlying assumptions of the model in question. This presupposes a well-defined set of such assumptions, and implies a degree of objectivity in their formulation. Unfortunately, politics and policy are difficult to disentangle from the purely technical aspects of forecasting methodology.

These words suggest that techniques of this kind are useful up to a point in being able to illustrate what the consequences of a particular raft of assumptions (some of which have been stated, and some of which almost certainly will have remained unstated) may be, but at the end of the day the choices in question will be social, economic and political rather than technical. Perhaps the classic example of this in recent times has been the widespread change in the way road traffic growth forecasts are perceived, from being guides to policy which were open to the charge that they became self-fulfilling prophecies to being figures that show what might happen if necessary policy and behavioural changes don't take place (see, for example, this debate in the report of the Royal Commission on Environmental Pollution, 1995, ch. 6).

• *Aims and objectives.* These are fundamentally about political choices. There is a very useful technical job to be done, however, in trying to frame possible aims and objectives in ways that facilitate these choices, and then in trying to express the objectives that flow from these choices in ways that enable measurement of progress towards them to take place.

• *Broad strategy packages.* Identifying what might be done to move in the broad directions desired involves looking at policy packages with as open a mind as possible. One of the dangers with this sort of process at this early stage is that the full range of possibilities isn't looked at, because minds become set fairly quickly on the area within which the appropriate package will be found and alternatives in practice become relatively minor variants of this broad theme. Over three decades ago, for example, I criticized the work of the Commission on the Third London

Airport, which had carried out the largest cost-benefit analysis done in Britain to assist with a public policy choice, on exactly these grounds (Kitchen, 1972); its processes of getting down to a shortlist had been relatively crude, as compared with the degree of sophistication involved in comparing four shortlisted alternatives, three of which in practice were very similar to each other.

- *Test promising strategic packages*. There is technical work to be done at this stage in evaluating what appear to be promising strategic packages, but again it is important to make the point as with forecasting that evaluation techniques are not policy- or value-neutral. The literature on planning evaluation techniques is quite large, but work in this field is usefully drawn together in Lichfield (1996). Three issues always likely to loom large in any evaluation process are:
- *Objectives* – How well does this package meet the stated objectives?
- *Resources* – Are we capable of implementing a package of this nature, in terms of financial and human resources?
- *Environment* – What is the environmental impact of this package? What kind of environmental quality will implementing the package achieve?

This latter point in particular has come in for a considerable amount of attention in recent years as world concerns about environmental issues have grown (see, for example, Bartelmus, 1994; Satterthwaite, 1999). This has led to the development of techniques of environmental impact assessment, including in terms of how development plans as a whole can be subject to such appraisals (Wood, 1992), and this latter notion has now gone so far as to become a requirement in Britain in respect of fresh development plans. As noted above, at the time of writing this is all being turned into a more holistic requirement for sustainability appraisals of plans at both regional and local scales. This process in turn spawned a growing literature; for example, Gilpin (1995) takes an international perspective, while Glasson *et al.* (1994) emphasize the British situation with a focus on techniques, methodology and case-studies. Research appears to show nonetheless that the introduction of these new concerns into professional practice in British local government was initially very patchy (Wen-Shyan *et al.*, 1995), and it is clear that one of the issues in relation to developments of this nature is always likely to be how quickly and how effectively it can be rolled out to the profession at large. The aesthetic dimension of all of this has arguably not been developed as fully, however, with the skills and appreciation of planners in this area being the subject of considerable criticism (Porteous, 1996, ch. 5).

- *Outline proposals and projects*. The importance of developing project ideas for early implementation alongside the process of working up policies and proposals in the preferred package is based upon two related ideas. The first is that most plans achieve a measure of recognition with the wider public on the basis of the specific actions they set in train rather than their general policies, and thus the early implementation of key projects is important in ensuring that a plan achieves some impact in these terms. Planners often talk about this as achieving some 'quick wins'. The second is that, because plans begin to decay even while they are being drafted, a plan which puts all its emphasis on things being done in the long term is a plan which is at risk of doing very little.

• *Consult.* This has already been discussed in this chapter, and it is returned to at some length in Chapter 5. There is less material available on how to carry out successful public consultation, however, than there is more critical material on the failings of the process in terms of its approach and context and also sometimes of technique (Hill, 1994; Greed, 1996, pp. 271–80). The key challenges for planning practice in this area are summarized by Darke (2000), and the broad principles of what the planning system ought to be trying to achieve are fairly straightforward (ODPM, 2004c). The operational challenges seen by planners who are in principle very positive to developments of this kind are nonetheless very real (Kitchen and Whitney, 2004).

• *Work up levels of detail and establish implementation methods.* The judgement about the level of detail that is appropriate in plans is a difficult one. Up to a point, detail can be helpful. Beyond that point, detail can be counter-productive in the sense that it can inhibit initiative, as well as because it can often be the detail that decays most quickly. This needs to be the subject of conscious thought, with as a general rule detail being excluded unless there is a demonstrable reason for it. The point about thinking particularly carefully about implementation at this stage is that it is important not to include in a plan policies or proposals that are in effect merely wishful thinking, and thus how one would set about implementing a policy becomes a useful test of its appropriateness.

• *Monitoring and review procedures and timetables.* Too many plans have had a last page entitled something like 'monitoring and review', which all too often gives the impression that this is an afterthought. If the concept of plan-making as a near-continuous process discussed earlier in this chapter has any validity, however, then monitoring and review are essential components of that continuity. This is one of the reasons I think that an effective model for this process is often the notion of an annual report on an adopted plan. This provides a regular focus for thought about whether change is necessary, without precluding the possibility of changes being made at other times if it becomes clear that this would be desirable. It also provides a known target date for data- and opinion-gathering activities which are designed to input into the process of review, which is necessary if one is to avoid the problem of several streams of this kind all producing results at different times and thereby making the job of looking at the plan as a whole very difficult. In England it has now become a requirement under the Planning and Compulsory Purchase Act 2004 for both regional planning bodies and local planning authorities to submit an annual monitoring report to the government, which is quite a large step down this particular road – although, of course, what might be monitored and reported on to the government may well prove to be on a smaller scale than what is needed for local purposes; and what the government is actually going to do with all of this material when it has got it isn't very clear, either.

- *Formal confirmation of acceptability.* This will be guided by whatever rules in a society govern the formal adoption of development plans. The main technical job is usually to ensure that all the correct procedures have been followed, to reduce the likelihood of subsequent challenges in the courts.

The processes of development control and of achieving area or environmental improvements

Chapter 3 deals at some length with development control (the British name for the process of granting or refusing permission to develop) in so far as it is influenced by system and procedural skills, as very heavily it is. This chapter looks at development control in terms of some of its technical content, and also looks at the processes of achieving area or environmental improvements. These two have been taken together because while they are different processes and often occur procedurally at different stages in the lifespan of a development idea, their technical content is often very similar. And there is another reason for taking them together. Development control as a process is often seen in fairly negative terms, and in one sense this is understandable since a local planning authority is not the instigator of most development but is usually reacting to proposals by others. But this should not prevent development control from being seen in what I believe to be its true colours, which is that it is one of the primary tools available to local planning authorities to enable them to implement their development plans (see, for example, Booth, 1996, pp. 3–5). The process of achieving environmental improvements on an area basis (be the area small-scale or very large) is another of the tools available to planners to enable them to implement development plans. So, these are two of the key means whereby the contents of development plans can be turned into reality on the ground, and taking them together in this section is intended to reinforce this positive view of their role.

It is not possible to cover comprehensively such a huge field, and so four representative issues with an environmental thread have been taken. It should be remembered, however, that development control is not just about environmental issues, but often involves balancing these matters against, for example, concerns about the local economy. The policies of the development plan should be the basis for these judgements. The four issues to be examined are:

- Design negotiations
- Achieving accessibility for disabled people
- Crime prevention through environmental design
- Brief preparation to achieve area or environmental improvements

Design negotiations

The extent to which the 'rules of the game' explicitly allow for or encourage negotiations about design quality in development control is one of the factors that will influence how lengthy the process of development control can become. It is clear that in a formal sense this is a variable commodity between the different parts of the world, although it also seems likely that planners commonly try to use the powers that they have got as part of the system in individual countries to engage in negotiations which are intended to achieve design improvements; see, for example, Wakeford (1990, pp. 90, 91) on design considerations in development control in the USA. Thus, while powers may diverge, intentions may converge.

There is some very difficult territory here. There is no doubt that there are some elements of the design process which can be about matters of personal taste or fashion, and many people would doubt whether this is an appropriate use of development control powers. Historically, this sense of the planning process stepping where it was not wanted dominated the advice given by the British government, albeit at a time when the Conservatives (who are probably more naturally predisposed to this position than parties further to the left) were in power. Annex A to the Department of the Environment's Planning Policy Guidance Note 1 (Department of the Environment, 1992b) put this matter as follows in para. A3:

> Planning authorities should reject obviously poor designs which are out of scale or character with their surroundings. But aesthetic judgements are to some extent subjective and authorities should not impose their taste on applicants for planning permission simply because they believe it to be superior. Authorities should not seek to control the detailed design of buildings unless the sensitive character of the setting for the development justifies it.

The annex did give some guidance on what it thought were important design considerations that should be taken into account when determining planning applications, however:

- The appearance of proposed developments.
- The relationship of proposed developments to their immediate surroundings.
- The wider setting of developments in relation to the character of the surrounding area.
- The appearance and treatment of the spaces between and around buildings, including hard and soft landscape as well as built form.
- Particular weight should be given to the impact of development proposals in environmentally sensitive areas (such as national parks, areas of outstanding natural beauty, conservation areas), and by extension in relation to listed buildings.

The overall attitude to what development plans or associated design guidance ought properly to say about design matters was summarized in para. A6 of the annex:

> Development plans and guidance for particular areas or sites should provide applicants with clear indications of planning authorities' design expectations. Such advice should avoid excessive prescription and detail and should concentrate on broad matters of scale, density, height, massing, layout, landscape and access. It should focus on encouraging good design rather than stifling experiment, originality or initiative. Indeed the design qualities of an exceptional scheme and its special contribution to the landscape or townscape may justify departing from local authorities' design guidance.

This cautious (some might even say minimalist) British government advice on the one hand established that there was a legitimate design function to be performed by the development control process, but on the other hand made it clear that this was about checking that broad principles have been satisfied rather than engaging in fully fledged debates about design detail. It might be said that it encouraged an approach which might be capable of filtering out really inappropriate designs, but that its role in promoting good quality design was less obvious. This has always been quite an important issue for planners, because the appearance of the physical environment and particularly of new development within it is one of the tests that the general public can and do use in making judgements about the quality of current planning activity (McCarthy *et al.*, 1995, ch. 2), even though as can be seen from the above there are clearly limitations to the reasonableness of this because of the limited nature of planning powers in these terms. Actually, we know very little about how effective over a period of time attempts at design control are, although there is a useful and interesting longitudinal study of this issue in relation to city centre office developments in Bristol by Punter (1990).

The question as to whether this formal view of the limited role of the development control process in influencing design was underplaying what was needed to achieve better quality development in urban areas was implicitly raised by the quality initiative launched by John Gummer as Secretary of State for the Environment in 1994. He put the need to improve the quality of urban development thus (Department of the Environment, 1994a, p. 2) in his introduction to this document:

> Quality affects us all. Architecture is the only art form which is inescapable. Most of our days are spent in or around buildings which therefore have a great influence on our lives and require careful thought.
>
> Good urban design can reinforce a sense of community, whereas anonymous grey and alienating surroundings isolate the individual. A depressing environment destroys local pride, attracts crime, deters investment and leaves people feeling powerless. Yet quality attracts quality, good design attracts life and investment and a strong community stands out against crime.
>
> We need to pay more attention to urban detail; whether in street signs and furniture, in the standard of local services, or in the thoughtfulness of design of the public space between buildings. All these contribute to our experience of the whole built environment, so if we improve our buildings and the streets and spaces which they define, we surely improve the quality of all our lives.

Perhaps not surprisingly, the above commentary implied the need for a review of the then current advice about design, to try to move it to a more proactive stance, and some moves in this direction can be seen in the version of PPG1 published in February 1997, just before a general election brought a change of government (Department of the Environment, 1997, paras 13–20 and annex A). Further impetus was given to this process by the report of the Urban Task Force (1999) chaired by Lord Rogers, which argued that good design was critical to urban renaissance. In subsequent years, we have seen a plethora of advice about urban design (see, for example, DTLR and CABE, 2000; DTLR and CABE, 2001; DETR and CABE, 2001) which does indeed reflect this more positive view of its role, and at the time of writing the extant government advice about the place of urban design in the planning process carries this forward (ODPM, 2005a, pp. 14, 15). Importantly, this advice not only seeks to promote the value of good design, but also argues that design is about much more than aesthetic considerations. Specifically, it argues that good design should:

- Address the connections between people and places by considering the needs of people to access jobs and key services;

- Be integrated into the existing urban form and the natural and built environments;
- Be an integral part of the processes for ensuring successful, safe and inclusive villages, towns and cities;
- Create an environment where everyone can access and benefit from the full range of opportunities available to members of society; and
- Consider the direct and indirect impacts on the natural environment. (Ibid., p. 14)

The point of all of this, therefore, is that the 'official' attitude towards the role of design negotiations in development control in Britain has changed in recent years towards a more positive and a less minimalist stance, although this cannot take away from the essential point that the primary responsibility for good design must rest with the designer and the designer's client rather than with the development control planner who takes receipt of their product. This debate, about the legitimate role of the planning process in intervening in the design approaches and details of development proposals, will not always have followed the British route in every part of the world, but its component elements are likely to have been the subject of fierce discussion in most countries with planning jurisdictions. At least five points follow from this:

- Planners who perform development control functions have got to be both confident enough and skilled enough to engage in design discussions with developers and their professional advisers from a position of strength. This means understanding what the legitimate role of the development control process actually is in terms of design negotiation, and being clear about the design objectives and issues that need to be raised from that perspective. For example, is a particular use essentially about 'fitting in' with surroundings or is it about something that in design terms is much more free-standing? And planners also need to think carefully about the circumstances under which design negotiations are likely to be worthwhile, in terms both of what potentially can be achieved and of the amount of time likely to be involved, because they will have to trade off the gains they might make in an individual case against all the other demands on their time. They will also need to know when they need more expert help, as may for example be the case with very complex design negotiations involving a listed building.
- Both the government and most local planning authorities in Britain encourage intending applicants to have pre-application discussions with the planning department. This is an excellent opportunity to convey what the design policy issues are likely to be in any particular case, and to discuss how they might be taken into account in a design before positions on this issue have become too rigid. This is a part of the development control process where there is a real opportunity to be proactive with a developer and agent, because there is scope to discuss how a

future application can be turned into one that is likely to succeed without the pressure of a statutory clock ticking which starts when an application has been registered. A key issue here for most planning managements in local planning authorities is the need to create the development control staff time and space needed to enable them to engage in activities in this nature.

• Increasingly, local planning authorities in Britain are looking to deal with this question of design policy through the preparation and publication of design guidance, tied in an appropriate manner into their development plan. The point of this is that it declares publicly what a local planning authority is trying to achieve in design terms in the area to which the guidance relates, and explains why these policy stances have been adopted. This is intended to encourage both development and general public interests to think about these sorts of matters, and perhaps in particular to think about the area as a whole rather than to focus immediately on a particular development site.

• Nevertheless, my experience of public (and political) reactions to new design proposals is that they often start from comfort with the familiar and discomfort with the new or unfamiliar. This can lead to a situation where new development proposals in some circumstances are almost inevitably going to receive opposition from some quarters. The planner has to try to understand what the basis of such opposition actually is, because there is an important difference between being opposed to something simply because it is new and being opposed to something because it is seen as inappropriate or lacking in quality in ways that can be described and understood.

• In conservation areas and in relation to listed buildings, there is a need to be particularly careful to ensure that development respects the character that caused these special categories to be identified in the first place. In Britain, the numbers of conservation areas and listed buildings are increasing all the time, as part of a growing interest in and concern for urban environmental history and heritage; and many countries throughout the world have similar legislation or practice. This is also likely to be reflected in the general level of public interest taken in matters affecting conservation areas and listed buildings, which in my experience is greater than on average happens with developments outside such areas and often comes through organized groups of various kinds. Conservation is a specialist field (Larkham, 1996; see in particular ch. 7), and planners often have specialists to help them with the detail of these matters. But what all planners need to have to make effective use of specialist inputs is a good feel for the basic historical or architectural character that the whole process is designed to retain and enhance.

This cannot possibly be a 'how to do it' text on design negotiations, but I hope enough has been said about the basic principles and issues for the importance and the potential of this part of the planning job to be appreciated. The need to avoid the traps associated with moving beyond what is legitimate in public policy terms and into fields of personal taste or prejudice on the part of the individual planner has also been touched upon. Many planners find design negotiations one of the most enjoyable and most rewarding parts of development control, because they can see a direct result of their input in terms of improvements to schemes. Customers of the planning process, on the other hand, can and do at times see this as the imposition of arbitrary and often personalized views rather than as a legitimate act on behalf of the public at large; and successful planners in this area have to be good at seeing the differences between these two things. The cumulative effect of all this in terms of environmental improvement can be considerable, although it is never likely to be seen by the public at large because they will only be aware of the end product with individual schemes and not of the various stages that led up to it.

Achieving accessibility for disabled people

Until relatively recently, it could be argued that the planning system (at any rate in Britain) took no or very little explicit account of the access needs of disabled people. One of the consequences of this was that planning applications would be approved which perpetuated the historic difficulty that many people had of gaining access to public buildings, to recreational facilities, to shops, to offices and to many other building types, and of moving around the streets of a town or city. This was despite the fact that it could easily be argued that over 10 per cent of the population have identifiable disabilities, and that providing facilities to meet their needs would also benefit many other groups in society such as elderly people and parents with prams or buggies. Today, planners would be expected as part of the development control process to check that a proposal was fully accessible for disabled people, and this would usually be backed up by a development plan policy requiring all development proposals to meet certain standards (ODPM, 2003c).

This is also helped by part M of the Building Regulations, which since 1985 have required developers in respect of many new buildings to meet some basic standards of accessibility. In addition, some local planning authorities publish their own advice about appropriate action to achieve accessibility. Thus, the system has come quite a long way in a relatively short period of time, although it is still far from perfect.

Perhaps one of the reasons why the British planning system was slow to pick up on such issues was that it didn't tend to have all that many disabled people within the system, and thus there wasn't much first-hand experience of coping with the environmental frustrations often suffered by disabled people. Nothing can bring this point home more forcefully than first-hand experience, and the absence of this experience can so easily lead people not to think about these matters. The importance of this was brought home to me in Manchester during the second half of the 1980s, when it had been decided that the city planning department would appoint an access officer who ideally should be a disabled person. The two occupants of that post between then and the mid 1990s were respectively a blind person and a person who relied for mobility largely on a motorized scooter. Their first-hand experience of access difficulties was invaluable in at least three ways: persuading developers that they knew what they were talking about when asking for changes to be made to submitted schemes; persuading the existing staff of the importance of taking access issues for disabled people more seriously; and helping to train staff who had not had their experiences in terms of what to look for when appraising submitted plans. Some of this is very simple; a dropped kerb or a gently inclined access ramp can make such a difference to the relative ease with which a road can be crossed or a building can be accessed. Some of this is more complex, however, such as when lift provision is involved. Very often these issues are straightforward when dealt with as an integral element in the design proposals for a building or a space, and only become difficult when they are tackled as an afterthought requiring changes to be made to a scheme to which a degree of commitment already exists; and the available research evidence suggests that many applications are still deficient in these terms (Imrie and Hall, 2001), which means that planners are too often involved in trying to correct faulty designs where changes can have significant consequences for the whole design approach.

In an ideal world, of course, the need for planners to play a backstop role of this kind would not be there, because all development proposals would take full account of the needs of disabled people. After all, anyone, even developers and designers, can find themselves in the position of being temporarily or permanently disabled, and so ensuring that the access needs of disabled people are met is potentially about helping with problems that anyone can experience. There is undoubtedly an issue in design education here that needs to be tackled, because schemes still come forward designed by architects which are not fully accessible. There is also an issue in terms of the consciousness of developers which needs to be tackled, because whether it is from ignorance or a desire to cut costs or for some other reasons, developers still table proposals that are not fully accessible, even sometimes for uses where disabled people would be welcomed as paying customers. But we are not in the position of being able to say that the development industry and the design professionals are fully aware of these matters as yet. So planners still have a useful role to play through the development control process in insisting as far as they can on adequate access provisions for disabled people, in publishing policy guidance on these matters ideally linked to their development plans, and in consulting representatives of disabled people about the development of access policies. They also have a key role to play in ensuring that the public realm more generally is as sensitive as it can be to the needs of disabled people, and in tackling any issues this raises via environmental improvement programmes and projects. Imrie (1996) looks more fully at the issues faced by disabled people in our cities, and at what can be done to improve their circumstances not just in the British situation but also internationally.

More generally, this is but one example of how the planning system seeks to cope with issues of diversity and equality. It would probably be fair to say that some planners have been rather dismissive of these arguments (perhaps because they have been unaware of the scale of individual need in this context), and have felt that since they aim to treat everyone in ways that are essentially the same they haven't discriminated against or disadvantaged anyone. Reeves (2005) argues that this approach ensures that planning does not achieve its full potential in terms of responding to diversity in society and helping to achieve equality of opportunity, and that as a consequence these issues should be approached actively rather than passively. She sees planning for diversity and equality as meaning:

- Planning that takes into account the needs of numerous different groups of people;
- Planning that takes a rights-based approach and that incorporates a duty to promote means to ensure that all groups can access and utilize their rights;
- Planning that engages people in a participatory way as equals rather than as passive target groups simply to be consulted;
- Planning that takes the social dimensions of sustainable development as seriously as it does its environmental and economic dimensions.

The application of these principles will undoubtedly affect the technical work undertaken by planners, but they are also four-square with the arguments in Chapter 6 about working with customers.

Crime prevention through environmental design

Crime prevention through environmental design (CPTED) has become a major growth area in North America in recent times (Fowler, 1992, pp. 90–8), traceable back in particular to the writing of Jane Jacobs (1964) and Oscar Newman (1973). Widespread interest in Britain is probably more recent, perhaps prompted in particular by the writing of Alice Coleman (1990), although again there had been advocates of this approach for some time before then (see, for example, Poyner, 1983). Both countries, and many other parts of the world, have seen a shift away from the historic view that crime is a matter for the police and the courts, and towards a view that deterring crime and helping to make its detection easier needs to involve a much wider range of agencies and approaches (Schneider and Kitchen, 2002, ch. 1). Interest in the role that the manipulation of the built environment can play in limiting the opportunity for crime can be seen as part of this process of broadening the approach. As a consequence, all the police forces in England and Wales now have an architectural liaison officer (ALO) or equivalent, who gives advice on these matters to development interests and who often acts as a consultee on planning applications. CPTED, in whichever of the various possible forms that it takes, appears to be here to stay, and thus its relationship with the planning process is likely to be of growing significance.

The formal position of police ALOs in the development control process was established in DoE Circular 5/94 (Department of the Environment, 1994b), where planners were advised to develop regular consultation arrangements with ALOs on planning applications to enable their input on crime prevention matters to be obtained. For many planners this was a new situation, because police officers (and the particular perspectives they bring to bear) hadn't traditionally been among the groups of fellow professionals with whom planners were used to working. The next step in this process of connecting crime prevention and the planning system was that for the first time section 17 of the Crime and Disorder Act 1998 placed a statutory duty on local planning authorities to take the prevention of crime and disorder into account in their work. The Urban Policy White Paper of 2000 made a commitment that crime prevention would become a significant objective for planning, and to this end agreed to review Circular 5/94, which by then was seen as being inadequate for these emerging purposes (DETR, 2000, p. 120). These commitments were discharged via Planning Policy Statement 1, which treats the public feeling that a place is safe as a critical feature of what planning should be seeking to achieve in helping to create sustainable communities (ODPM, 2005a, para. 5), and also through the publication of much more detailed good practice guidance to replace the generalities of Circular 5/94 (ODPM and Home Office, 2004). So, in a period of around ten years, crime prevention has moved from an activity with which the planning system (and planners) scarcely connected to one where the government's expectation was that it would make a significant contribution to the creation of safer places. This can be seen, therefore, as another example of the kind of large-scale and externally driven changes that planners can expect to have to cope with during their careers that were discussed in Chapter 1.

This journey has not been without its difficulties, however, because there is undoubtedly some controversy over the prescriptions here. To oversimplify, one school of thought would argue that the solution is better security measures, the minimization of escape routes, and a series of other measures that contribute to the term 'target-hardening'. The other main school of thought would reject this approach, and instead would argue that the solution to the problem is to emphasize urbanity as a natural deterrent. This would be done through relatively high-density living, with an emphasis on natural overlooking and on community life achieved by encouraging social interaction, and a focus on making the street and the public realm safe places because of high levels of activity spread throughout the day (Kitchen, 2002). This can in turn be related to debates about urban design, with the latter view being closely related to the design philosophy known as 'new urbanism', which in turn challenges in some ways the police advice that typifies the former view – notably in relation to issues such as the permeability of layouts and the extent to which they encourage/discourage some human activities (Kitchen, 2005). This is an oversimplification because there are elements common to both approaches, such as an emphasis upon good-quality street lighting and on the elimination of ready-made hiding places. Nonetheless, the two broad schools of thought do have many points of departure, and it is important that the adherence of true believers to their particular points of view doesn't obstruct the process of learning more about these differences both from what actually appears to work on the ground and from public reactions to what is done.

There are three other points worth making about what can be seen as still quite a young field of planning activity:

- While each school of thought is fiercely defended by its protagonists, it is far from clear from the available research evidence that one approach is 'right' and the other is 'wrong'. Indeed, it may well be that both would be able to lay claim to being effective by their own lights, simply because each in its own way pays attention to issues that had previously been neglected. That having been said, there is some research evidence which seriously questions the effectiveness of permeable layouts in terms of crime prevention (Taylor, 2002).
- While crime prevention through environmental design would be a very important prize to be won if it could be achieved, the desirability or otherwise of most designs is a function of several factors and not just this one. So a critical issue which needs to be understood is how the crime prevention dimensions of design relate to all their other aspects. My experience has been that this factor explains one of the difficulties that has commonly been experienced in the process of developing

effective working relationships between planners dealing with planning applications who try to look at them 'in the round' and police ALOs looking at those applications solely from a crime prevention perspective.
• Social choice needs to be acknowledged as a factor in all of this. People may consciously choose for perfectly good reasons to live in residential areas that don't meet CPTED standards, and in a democratic society this needs to be recognized as being a right that people have. This is a right that can only really be exercised on the basis of a good level of public awareness of what the crime experiences of particular kinds of layouts are, however, and there is a distance to travel as yet before this position will be reached.

Overall, this is a field of planning activity where a considerable amount of development can be expected in the years to come, and where planners will have an opportunity to contribute to making places better for people in ways that previous generations of planners would scarcely have considered.

Brief preparation to achieve area or environmental improvements

Often, one of the most important tasks a planner has the opportunity to perform in relation to the ultimate quality of a development or of an environmental improvement is the process of preparing a brief to guide the design process when such work is anticipated. The purpose of a brief is to guide design professionals (usually architects, landscape architects or engineers, but other professions may be involved as well) on behalf of the client as to the sort of outcome that should be aimed for and the principles that should be followed in doing this. It is not a design itself, and it is important that the process of brief-writing should not be so detailed as unduly to constrain the designer's skill. At the same time, it is important that the aspirations of the client (be this the person who is paying for the scheme to be undertaken, or with a public scheme the local authority acting on behalf of its residents) should be clearly set down. If the client is not the local planning authority it is also important that the planning policies and principles that the authority will use in making a judgement about the scheme once it is submitted to it for approval should be clear. These might well include, for example, a commitment to achieving full access for disabled people and a particular approach to crime and environmental design, to return to two of the examples discussed above.

The other basic function that briefs usually perform is the conveying of necessary information, or of guidance about how to go about acquiring that information if it is not readily available in a form that will allow it to be incorporated into the brief.

Information regarded as being necessary will vary according to the particular circumstances, but typically it would include information about the character, condition and ownership of the land in question and any important constraints acting on these matters, similar information about any buildings there may be on the land or in the area in question, and information about infrastructure services affecting the site such as highways, drainage, energy and telecommunications. Cost information will often be given as well, especially if there is a budget ceiling which the project must not exceed.

A brief needs to be drafted in such a manner as to enable the scheme that emerges from the design process to be tested against its requirements. For these purposes, it is important to be clear about what is essential and what is desirable, and then to make judgements about what emerges which recognize this distinction. The reason this is important is that the design process may well be capable of generating alternatives which had not been considered at the outset, and which may have real benefits associated with them which should not be discounted simply because they don't pass some of a large number of tests. There are frequently trade-offs to be made in this sort of situation, and a knowledge of what is a requirement as distinct from what might have been thought at the outset to be desirable is very helpful in this context. Indeed, it is common for there to be regular liaison between the planner preparing the brief and the design team undertaking the detailed work throughout the design process, not only to sort out any problems of interpretation as quickly as possible after they have arisen but also in acknowledgement of the fact that in reality the design process is an iterative one. All of this raises a very wide range of issues, and the selected extracts in two readers around the broad theme of urban design (Stein, 1995, pp. 178–227; LeGates and Stout, 2003, pp. 409–63) provide a useful introduction to many of the key debates in this area. For a more general discussion of the role of urban design in improving the quality of urban areas, see Parfect and Power, 1997.

Before leaving this topic, it is important to acknowledge that the task of environmental improvement is very often carried out by the public sector, although increasingly this is done in partnership with private sector and other interests, especially where complex tasks such as the remediation of brownfield land are being undertaken (Syms, 2004). Environmental improvement is often not the only task being undertaken in a development or redevelopment project, however, but is part of an initiative with a multiplicity of aims. If the planners involved in this process from an environmental improvement perspective are to make the most effective contribution that they can, it is important that they see their particular interest in the context of the development as a whole and the environment of the area in which the development will sit. To this end, they need to understand the development process fully and the interests of the various parties involved (Syms, 2002), and also how the environmental improvement dimension interacts with the other elements of the project. This is a good illustration of the ways what I have called synoptic and integrative skills (which are discussed in Chapter 8) need to be applied alongside more specific skills particular to the issue in question. In a phrase, the planner always needs to be able to see the big picture.

The application of topic-based expertise: the case of retail planning

Many development fields with which planning interacts involve a considerable degree of expertise in their own right. Planners cannot hope to be expert in all of these areas, although many planners choose to specialize in one or more of them and do develop a degree of expertise in these areas as a consequence. Even where this does not happen, planners will need from time to time to interact with specialists in many fields such as transport, housing, population forecasting and retailing, and thus need to develop the skills both of doing this and of evaluating what it produces. This section looks briefly at how topic-based expertise of this kind relates to the planning process, using as an example the field of retail development.

The retail field tends to be fast-moving. Because it also involves very large amounts of money both at the development end of the operation and then in the processes of trading, it has tended to be a field where there have been a large number of policy contests, for example between the defenders of in-town shopping interests and the promoters of out-of-town shopping. In the 1990s, for example, national policy about such issues was in a state of flux, moving essentially from a position of relying largely on the market to one which emphasizes the role of existing centres and puts in place a series of tests in this context. The flavour of such debates can be captured in contemporary writing (see, for example, Bromley and Thomas, 1993; Guy, 1994; Technology Foresight Panel on Retail and Distribution, 1995; Ratcliffe and Stubbs, 1996, pp. 362–401).

The planning process is likely to impact on the retail development process at five interrelated levels at least:

- At the development plan scale, where the issues are likely to be the broad scale and location of retail developments seen as being necessary over the period of the plan;
- Through the development control process, determining whether large- and small-scale proposals should be allowed and then negotiating over the form of that development;
- At the level of impact assessment, looking at what effects (quantitative and qualitative) large-scale retail proposals are likely to have;

- At the level of the individual centre, looking at what can be done to improve its competitiveness and its environment;
- At the level of community or area regeneration, looking at what role retailing might play in helping to meet the objectives of the exercise and at how to secure appropriate developments of this kind.

It should also be said (and retailers in particular often emphasize this point at planning inquiries) that access to a range of retail opportunities is an important element in all of our lives because we are all consumers. And so it is perfectly proper that, in addition to the above points, the planning process should give weight to the quality of retailing that is on offer to people in a locality.

Each of these levels has its own technical component to the necessary work and its own experts. Over the years, perhaps the most controversial aspect of this has been the process of trying to measure retail impact, and then of trying to reach a judgement about the significance of the answers that emerged from this exercise in terms of the vitality and viability of centres affected by those impacts. During the 1960s and 1970s, the interest in Britain in developing ever more sophisticated mathematical models as a means of performing this function was intense (National Economic Development Office, 1970), and groups of people developed a particular expertise in these terms. The difficulties with this approach included:

- It could be an expensive and a time-consuming process to build a model of this kind.
- Data were of variable quality, and the reliability of the model was sensitive to this issue.
- Many of the intangible factors that have an important effect on the success or otherwise of a particular centre (such as marketing, for example) are very difficult to model effectively.
- The behavioural assumptions built into models, for all the complexity of the models themselves, were certainly open to challenge.
- The answers produced were still open to a very wide range of interpretation, since for example an impact of 10 per cent on turnover might be a very serious matter for one centre but might be a level of impact that another centre could cope with relatively easily.

As a consequence, while retail impact modelling has not disappeared entirely, this approach has rather fallen out of favour in Britain, and by the 1990s had been replaced by a policy-led approach via the development plan coupled with an attempt to measure the 'vitality and viability' of town centres across a much wider range of measures than those conventionally covered in a shopping model. What was added subsequently to this package was the so-called 'sequential test', which in effect required retail applicants to demonstrate that if they wanted to develop on a site that was not consistent with this policy then this was only because it was not possible to do otherwise having tested these other options in sequence, starting with town centre locations. This approach is set out in PPS 6 (ODPM, 2005c), which also describes a series of technical tasks that local planning authorities would be expected to perform to maintain a planned approach to retailing in this context. This is set out in Box 2.4. The scale and complexity of what is involved in this series of tasks will be immediately apparent from reading this box – and rightly so, because this is a very important part of urban planning, involving major impacts on people's lives and investment on a massive scale. Realistically, most local planning authorities which undertake this work will require at least one member of staff to specialize in this field, and to develop both the expertise and the range of contacts needed to undertake it effectively. For many smaller local planning authorities (and

---

Box 2.4   Technical tasks that local planning authorities are expected to perform to maintain a process of plan-led retail provision

- Assess the need for new floor space, taking account of both quantitative and qualitative considerations.
- Identify existing deficiencies in provision, and the capacity of existing retail centres to meet these deficiencies.
- Identify centres in decline, where change needs to be managed.
- Identify existing centres where new development will be focused and any new centres needed.
- Define the extent of the primary shopping area for all centres, and how these relate to the town centre.
- Identify and allocate sites in accordance with a series of considerations:
  (a) Assess the need for development.
  (b) Identify the appropriate scale of development.
  (c) Apply the sequential approach to site selection.
  (d) Assess the impact of development on existing centres.
  (e) Ensure that locations are accessible and well served by a choice of means of transport.
- Review all existing allocations and reallocate sites no longer consistent with policy.
- Develop spatial policies and proposals to promote and secure investment in deprived areas which provide growth opportunities for centres within them and improve access to those centres.
- Set out criteria-based policies that enable new development proposals to be tested, including those on sites not allocated in the development plan.
- Carry out a series of monitoring tasks on a regular basis.
- Do all of these things in association with retail stakeholders and local communities.

Sources: Information from ODPM, 2005c, *Planning Policy Statement 6: Planning for Town Centres*, HMSO, London.

for some of the larger ones as well), this is beyond what can realistically be achieved with a relatively small staff cohort, and as a result they often use external consultants who specialize in this area of work.

Sitting behind all of this is a strong policy view that the stance ought normally to be one of being supportive towards existing centres rather than encouraging the large-scale development of new out-of-town facilities, as part of the emerging argument about urban sustainability. In this sense, the British planning system tries to operate in a more proactive way than has been the case in the more market-dominated societies of North America. The hope is that this will avoid some of the problems of the devastation of downtown areas that have been experienced in many American towns and cities (see, for example, the case-studies reported and the responses this has generated, in Wagner *et al.*, 1995). At the same time as looking for strong policy statements in development plans as a means of seeking to resist undesirable developments, however, it is clear that this essentially negative power needs to be supported by a major effort to improve the quality of what existing centres offer to their customers, otherwise they will vote with their feet or their wheels in favour of the competition. As a consequence, a great deal of interest has developed in Britain in physical and management actions that can be taken to improve the vitality and viability of town centres (URBED, 1994). Planners are likely to get intensively involved in such activities at all the levels of the shopping hierarchy.

This brief run-through of some of the key elements and issues in retail planning should be enough to illustrate the basic point, which is that planning involves making the best use of particular knowledge and expertise in the field while relating it to the needs and aspirations of the wider community through the development plan-making process, through development control, and through processes of area and environmental improvement. What planners do in these contexts is likely to be examined critically by at least four groups of actors, and therefore needs to carry conviction in all of these quarters if possible:

- Development interests, and their professional advisers;
- Retail trading interests, and their professional advisers;
- The general public, in its capacity both as shopper and as a user of centres;
- Government in its various forms, including in particular the process of testing development plans and refusals of planning applications at public inquiries.

The first two of these in their own different ways can be both powerful and well organized (see the general arguments of Adams, 1994, ch. 6), and as a consequence large-scale retail planning inquiries can be among the most bitterly fought of all planning inquiries. This reinforces the need for planners to be clear about both their policy perspectives and their wider responsibilities to the community if they are working in the public or the community sectors, and for there to be people as part of the

planning team who have enough expertise in this field to be able to negotiate effectively with development and trading interests.

Conclusions

This chapter opened with a quotation from Alan Altshuler about how
planning officials used the claim that something was technical in effect to
take power to themselves, since this argument implied that they were particularly well placed by virtue of their expertise to understand it and that
others without that expertise would inevitably struggle. This was an
important insight in the mid 1960s (the time when I was first coming into
planning as a student), because there is evidence that planners at that time
did often present their work in this manner (see, for example, Burns, 1967;
and for a contemporary critical perspective on the views of Burns see
Davies, 1972). My own experience of planning education at this time was
very much out of this same school. It was about finding the best technical
solution you could (which often meant particularly in urban design terms)
to the problems of a given locality, which was often a small place or a small
part of a larger place. In a sense, it was large-scale architecture. The
broader strategic element wasn't very strong; there wasn't much emphasis
on the raft of written policies we see today; and there wasn't much emphasis on public consultation, on the idea that many people might have views
about these issues often based upon long experience of living there, or on
the essentially political process that would be involved in obtaining
approval to the drawn solution presented. So, without wishing to suggest
that this necessarily encompassed the views of all planners, there was a
strong element in the planning armoury forty years ago that did indeed
emphasize the technical (and therefore specialist, and therefore restricted
to relatively small numbers of people) nature of the planning job.

Since then, I think it can fairly be said that most planners have come
quite a long way from this position, not least because they have had to
experience the large-scale trends discussed in Chapter 1. Very few planners
today would claim that their work is essentially technical, and most of
them would acknowledge that the issues they deal with are very often the
stuff of local debate, where technical issues have a role to play in shaping
those debates but where they are likely to turn on an essentially political
judgement about what the key stakeholders are aspiring to achieve in a
given situation. But we mustn't throw the baby out with the bathwater
here. This chapter has argued that there still are lots of complex and
knowledge-based tasks to be undertaken by planners as part of the
planning process, and I have chosen to describe these as 'technical'.
It is important that in so far as there are technical components to any situation that planners are expected to deal with, this is done well. So, for
example, there are real gains to be made in design negotiations with

developers and their agents on planning applications, especially if public views express clearly the direction that such negotiations should take; there clearly is scope to ensure that the public realm and the buildings fronting it are accessible to disabled people, and indeed in the contemporary world it is surely indefensible if a situation considerably less than this is accepted; the design and layout of the built environment can make a difference to the opportunity to commit crime, and planners and the police need to get better at working together to this end; and as we have seen in the particular example of retail planning, there is a large amount of technical work to be done in this complex field in order to shape public debates about the key issues. Underlying all of this is the importance of putting together a development plan that shapes the future of our places, and carrying out environmental improvement projects that help to move them in these directions. So, the technical component of planning is necessary and important, and needs to be done well. What we do have to accept, however, is that just because this work is technical (in the sense that it requires specialist knowledge and understanding in order to do it), that doesn't make it unchallengeable. Technical work almost always includes non-technical elements, such as value judgements which are really socio-political, and in any event in a participative society technical work should rightly be open to inspection and comment. It *is* still likely to be the case that what is presented as the technical advice of the planning officer is likely to carry weight in the process of decision-making because it *is* the view of the planning officer, but what has gone is the idea that a view from this source must be unimpeachable because it represents a higher order of knowledge and understanding than anyone else can aspire to. So, planners need to accept that their technical work is a contribution to debate; it should open doors to this end, rather than close them. Planners also need to accept that their technical work should be seen as sitting alongside lots of other contributions they need to make, rather than as being the dominant element, and these contributions are introduced in the following chapters.

Self-assessment topics

1. Take any development plan known to you where it is possible for you to have a discussion with someone who was involved in its preparation. How does the process of preparation of this plan compare with the generalized model in Box 2.1? What are the explanations for the main differences between the model and the case?
2. What are the spatial scales of all the current plans that seek to have an effect on the whole or a part of a town or city near to you? Are there any problems that may arise in trying to understand the relationships between these various plans? Are they all equally up to date? And do there appear to be any omissions from this hierarchy of plans?

3. Take any one stage in the process of preparing any development plan known to you. What technical work was undertaken for that stage? How was that technical work made use of in this stage of the process? And what effect did this have on subsequent stages of the process? To what extent was this actually 'technical work', and to what extent do you think it subsumed judgements that were really political, economic or social?

4. A typical design problem faced in the development control process is whether proposed new development 'fits in with' the development immediately adjacent to it and the street scene. Find an instance of recently completed development of this kind, and evaluate how well you think it 'fits in' in these terms. Ask yourself how such an assessment would have been undertaken at the time the planning application was considered, and if possible talk to the local planning authority staff involved in that process about how they undertook this task.

5. See if you can borrow a wheelchair, and with a companion (necessary both for safety and for information recording purposes) try to travel in it around the main streets of any area known to you and to enter the public buildings in that area that are open. Record and categorize all the obstacles and impediments that you find, including how difficult it was for you to overcome these problems. What do you think could be done by way of a systematic programme of improvements to tackle these difficulties? (I actually did this during my time as city planning officer of Manchester, and doing this directly is very different from trying to imagine what the experience of using a wheelchair must be like. So don't be afraid to try this; it will change the way you think about access for disabled people.)

6. Take any shopping centre near you. Evaluate from your impressions of the centre what you think are its main strengths and its main weaknesses from the perspective of its success as a trading operation, from an environmental perspective, and from the perspective of its role in providing services for its local or its wider community. To what extent can these evaluations be quantitative, and to what extent must they necessarily be qualitative? How would you set about converting your impressionistic evaluation into systematic studies that cover both the quantitative and the qualitative dimension? Were it to be decided that the centre needed to be improved to meet criticisms from any or all of these perspectives, what would the main features of such an improvement programme be?

Chapter 3

Planning System and Process Skills

Introduction

One of the distinctive characteristics of the planner is a good level of knowledge about the planning system of the locality where the planner practises, and a good level of understanding about how to operate effectively within the processes that planning system engenders. In a phrase, this is the procedural dimension of planning. Indeed, it could be argued that customer expectations of planners, whatever else they might include, would certainly be quite high in this regard. Many planners in fairly senior positions in public sector organizations, for example, have to be good at giving advice to all of their customers about how to get things done within the system within which they operate, and people go to them for advice with the firm expectation that they will be able to provide it (Healey, 1992). No society makes knowledge about planning systems and processes a precondition of public participation in planning; but most societies recognize that participation is likely to be more effective when views about the outcomes that participants are seeking can be related to the rules, regulations, practices and expectations of the planning systems extant in those societies. Planners need therefore to be able to add value in these terms, either directly through the ways in which they conduct their own business within the framework provided by planning systems or processes or through the advice they give to other intending participants in those processes. This present chapter and Chapter 7 are about all of this. This present chapter concentrates on the ways in which planning systems and processes work, and on how to advise and work with participants who wish to engage with the planning machine. It is thus essentially about the procedural aspects of planning; how things get done. Chapter 7 then looks at how the planner as bureaucrat, manager and worker with politicians can operate from the inside of such processes.

This may be one of the skills clusters described in this book where the differences between countries in various parts of the world are most marked. Not only will countries adopt planning systems and processes that relate to their particular forms of governance, but also there are likely to be elements of the ways in which these systems and processes operate that derive from cultural norms and values. Inevitably, therefore, the British examples I use in this chapter need to be seen in this context. But what doesn't change as between countries is the need for planners not merely to be expert at working within their own particular systems and processes but also to be good at guiding the customers of planning in the most effective ways of getting their needs taken into account by those systems and processes. Planners need to be good not just at giving substantive guidance ('this is what planning policy is') but also at giving procedural guidance ('this is how you should set about advancing your particular interest in the planning system here').

A simple example drawn from a regularly repeated set of circumstances during my own practice experience will serve to illustrate the importance of the kinds of skills being considered in this chapter. The British planning system does not acknowledge the impact of a development proposal on the value of a property owned by an individual as a material consideration in the determination of a planning application, and this has been a long-standing position. The advice about this during my time as city planning officer of Manchester was set out in paras 39 and 40 of the 1992 version of Planning Policy Guidance Note 1 (Department of the Environment, 1992b) as follows:

> The planning system does not exist to protect the private interests of one person against the activities of another, although private interests may coincide with the public interest in some cases ...
>
> It is often difficult to distinguish between public and private interests, but this may be necessary on occasion. The basic question is not whether owners and occupiers would experience financial or other loss from a particular development, but whether the proposal would unacceptably affect amenities and the existing use of land and buildings which ought to be protected in the public interest.

Notwithstanding this very clear guidance, it was a very familiar experience at that time (and, indeed, still is) for local planning authorities to receive representations about the adverse impact of a development proposal on property values when undertaking local consultations about a planning application for that proposal. A local planning authority refusing a planning application on these grounds, however, would be in very real difficulties at a subsequent appeal, precisely because the guidance about what it is material for that local planning authority to consider in these terms is clear; and in practice an authority would not normally contemplate such a course of action. Thus, an individual who felt very strongly about this issue, which would be very understandable if there was indeed a significant likelihood of falling property values as a consequence of development, would almost certainly be in the position of having no effect upon the decision-making process if they made representations solely on this basis. On the other hand, many of the elements that can cause property values to fall as a result of development in an area, such as increased noise and higher traffic levels, are of themselves perfectly proper and indeed everyday planning considerations in Britain. Representations about such matters would therefore usually be given very careful consideration when they are made. The knowledge that while one way of looking at this issue would have no effect on the decision-making process, another way of looking at this issue could potentially carry significant weight in that process, and then the understanding of how to make a case in these terms, is thus potentially very useful to the aggrieved party. But the ordinary citizen could not be expected to have developed skills of this kind (much less to have read a government planning policy guidance note!), especially if the instance in question is the first time that the individual has come across the way the development control process operates. A planner would certainly be expected to have knowledge of this kind, however, and a planner would also be expected to have skills in applying that knowledge to a particular process, which in the case of this example is the operation of the development control process in Britain. Thus, advice based upon this element of the planner's skills is potentially capable of making the difference for the particular customer of the planning service (in this case, the local resident) between a successful and an unsuccessful outcome. During my time in Manchester it was commonplace for staff to advise residents about how to make representations of this kind, irrespective of whether or not they personally happened to agree with the points being made.

Of course, as already noted, planning systems in their structure and in their detail of operation vary considerably throughout the world. The British system, for example, has been exported in various forms to many parts of the Commonwealth, although not always with the degree of discretion attached to local systems everywhere that has evolved in Britain. Indeed, this point about the degree of discretion inherent in planning systems is an important one, which is dealt with in more detail below (Booth, 1996). Other systems, for example that which operates in the United States of America, place more emphasis on the concept of zoning than does the British system (see for example, s. 6 of Stein, 1995; see also Mandelker, 1972). There is considerable variety within Europe, with for example the strong component of national and regional planning to be found in the Netherlands producing a very different type of planning product from the emphasis to be found in plans for Italian cities based upon fine-grained detail, down to the occupation of individual floors of buildings (Garner, 1975; Williams, 1984; Newman and Thornley, 1996). There are also considerable differences within countries, created by factors such as the extent to which such matters are determined through local or state powers (as in the USA) or through the legislative and administrative actions of central government (as in Britain). And even in this latter case, there is considerable argument about how systems of this kind can or should cope with the inherent unevenness of development needs and issues (Duncan and Goodwin, 1988). In recent years in Britain the gaps in these terms have tended to widen, in part because the government's programme of devolution has meant that planning in Scotland, Wales and Northern Ireland can develop differently from planning in England (Tewdwr-Jones, 2002). No attempt will be made here to cover this ground, beyond acknowledging this variety. The approach adopted here is that understanding planning systems and how to operate within them is a fundamental planning skill, which will always need to draw upon local knowledge of the particular system in question. Thus, the focus is on broadly common features of most planning systems, rather than on the detail of individual systems. And it is on common kinds of opportunities to interact with other customers of planning services, rather than on the particular ways in which this might occur within the systems of individual countries.

To this end, the chapter returns to the four major types of interactions between planners and their customers introduced in the discussion of the broad nature and purpose of planning systems in Chapter 1. So, it looks at how these processes of interaction can affect outcomes in relation to the making of a development plan, the determination of an application for permission to carry out a development, processes of public consultation, and adversarial processes like that of the public local inquiry in Britain or the public hearing in North America. The roles planners may play in these situations, either as staff of the planning authority or as independent planners providing services direct to the authority's customers, are considered throughout these sections. Finally, some self-assessment topics are identified to allow readers to explore in more detail some of the material covered in this chapter.

The process of making development plans

Chapter 2 has already discussed the basic steps involved in the process of development plan-making, with a focus as a consequence on the role of the plan-preparers who are usually working for the local planning authority. The focus here, therefore, is on operating effectively within this process to try to get a particular point of view to be taken seriously as part of that process, which is more usually the position of planners who do not work for the local planning authority. The critical point to understand about a situation of this nature is that while the process of development plan-making can stretch over quite a significant period of time, the opportunities to participate in that process from outside the local planning authority are likely to be episodic rather than continuous. Typically, there may be an opportunity to contribute at an early stage in the process when the planning authority is trying to discuss what the key issues that the plan should attempt to deal with might be (although not all local planning authorities choose to do this), and then an opportunity is usually available around a draft plan in some form. After that, at least in Britain, it is likely that the legal process will take over, and that 'participation' becomes about formal objections and case-making in the public arena at an inquiry or some form of hearing – in other words, the process becomes adversarial. This is different from the argument about planning as a process of continuous debate put forward by some theoreticians, which is discussed below in more detail; and it may well be that the theoretical process could be a better vehicle for effective public participation than the much more episodic real-world process we find today, if a way could be found to marry together the concepts of continuous debate and expeditious decision-making. But if planners are to work effectively with potential participants in that process then they need to understand it, to be aware of the nature of the different kinds of opportunities to pursue their client's interests during this process, and also to know how best to present that case at these very different stages.

The first thing to say about this is that the greater the emphasis placed on the development plan within a particular planning system, the more important it is to try to ensure that a preferred viewpoint has been incorporated into it rather than relying on subsequent processes to overcome difficulties that may be caused by this lack of development plan support. The changes in the British system in recent years have exemplified this very well. The Town and Country Planning Act 1947, which is the piece of primary legislation in Britain which created powerful local planning authorities, was clear about the place the development plan had in this new system. The broad level of understanding set out in that Act, to the effect that the development plan was the starting-point for making planning decisions, and that its provisions should be upheld in such processes unless there were clear and obvious reasons why this should not happen, such as the development plan being out of date, really stood largely unchallenged until the 1980s. During that period, a Conservative government, convinced of the view that planning was adversely affecting the economy through the imposition of unnecessary restraints upon the private sector (Thornley, 1991), changed this presumption to one where the development plan was just one of many material considerations in making planning decisions. This downgrading of the importance of the development plan was starting to have adverse consequences, in the sense that it enabled undesirable and unpopular developments in many locations to get through the system. Many of the people who regarded those developments as being undesirable were actually Conservative supporters; while the Conservative Party in government was seen as pro-development, many of its MPs represented constituencies with large Nimby populations. This led in turn to a further change that reasserted the primacy of the development plan (in the first instance, via s. 54A of the Town and Country Planning Act 1990); and while it can certainly be argued that this was a relatively small-scale change in the law which might not necessarily have had a major impact on the decisions ultimately made on planning matters in the courts (Keene, 1993), its symbolic significance was very important. What it also did was to send out the message that it was now more important than it had been before to get involved in the process of plan-making to get viewpoints established, rather than relying on subsequent arguments against the provisions of the development plan when development not in conformity with its policies was proposed. It may not be entirely a coincidence that the number of objections formally lodged to the deposit draft of the Manchester unitary development plan, which was prepared and went through its key processes before the effects of s. 54A were working their way through the system, was less than 10 per cent of those lodged a couple of years later to the deposit draft of the unitary development plan for another major city at the core of one of northern England's largest conurbations (in this case, Leeds), by which time s. 54A had been in existence for a while and was beginning to be well understood both by the development industry and by many active local residents. It may also be the case that an unintended consequence of s. 54A because of its role in encouraging formal involvement in the development plan-making process was that it might have prolonged still further an already elongated process (Kitchen, 1996); and certainly by the time of the Planning Green Paper (DTLR, 2001) the government saw the major challenge as being the need to put in place a plan-led system which retained and indeed extended the scope for public involvement in plan-making while at the same time it speeded the whole process up. There was considerable doubt in local government circles, however, about whether government targets in these terms could be achieved, because of the contradictory nature of some of these elements (Sykes, 2003).

Active and effective participation in the development plan-making process requires not only a firm commitment to a particular point of view about a planning policy or a site, but also an understanding of the plan's broad strategy, of how to relate arguments about particular cases to that broad strategy, and of the key opportunities provided by the pro-cedural steps in the process to make these points. In my experience, many participants in the process bring the first of these elements (a firm commitment about a particular issue) to the table, but far fewer bring the remaining elements. One of the major challenges in public participation exercises derives from this understanding; how can we communicate enough about the 'process' issues to participants to help them to put their points as effectively as possible without in effect setting a 'planning knowledge' entrance barrier to this process?

The best plans are based upon a clear and appropriate strategy for the place or places in question, and upon a good level of understanding of the needs and aspirations of the people who live in the area or who use it in various ways and who are in effect the development plan's major customers. An example of a strategy-driven 'plan' is given in Box 3.1, which is an extract from the Association of Greater Manchester Authorities' draft Economic Strategy and Operational Programme (1993) prepared for European Commission funding purposes. This was essentially about action to secure economic development across Greater Manchester (a process which would be assisted by European funding, and so one purpose of the plan was to be a basis for securing these resources), and thus its focus was very clear. A helpful, though not an infallible, test of whether or not a plan is strategy-driven is whether its essence can be expressed on a single page, as in this example. There ought to be a mutually reinforcing relationship between a strategy and local needs and aspirations, so that the strategy is clearly grounded in the needs and aspiration of the plan's customers, but at the same time the process of strategy creation has played a constructive role in clarifying those needs and in raising those aspirations. Put more simply, 'top-down' processes of thinking holistically about a place and its people and 'bottom-up' processes of working with local people to draw from them full contributions based upon their knowledge and understanding need to meet in the middle and to inform each other. At its best, this can produce a robust and a well-supported strategy; but this is likely to be an iterative process, and it is most unlikely to satisfy everyone's wishes in a pluralist society. Getting involved in these processes on behalf of a particular interest may well be time-consuming, therefore, but it can be one of the most effective ways of promoting views that get taken into account in plan-making. A plan that is strategy-led is likely to be tested in the first instance by exploring the appropriateness of the strategy, and if this is demonstrated it can be hard later on to argue for an individual detailed proposal which is inconsistent with that strategy but much easier if strategy conformity can be shown.

Not all plans by a long way are based upon strategies which would pass these tests, however, and indeed some plans seem to have relatively little strategic content but tend rather to be a collection of proposals and ideas about individual sites or policy issues that are only loosely related. A plan of this latter kind may well be much easier to argue against than a plan with a clear strategy that works its way logically through those sites and policy issues which impinge upon that strategy, because in effect there is no real strategic-level argument to contend with. In this type of situation, debate is likely to proceed in practice on a much more fragmented basis than with a more clearly strategy-driven plan. But the arguments presented about the individual interest are still likely to have more force to them if they are placed in some sort of strategic context, even if that has to pick up on clues in the plan that could become the basis for a strategy rather than on anything else.

Box 3.1   An example of a strategy-led plan

Summary: Greater Manchester economic development strategy and operational programme

VISION: Establishing Greater Manchester as a creative and distinctive European regional capital

By adopting the principles of:

- Strengthening the aggregate level of economic activity
- Rectifying structural and sectoral weaknesses
- Tackling disadvantage and areas of need and priority
- The diffusion of economic benefits
- Putting people at the centre of the process
- Taking a holistic view of the economy
- Strengthening the identity and integration of GM
- Recognizing the role of the environment
- Encouraging the development of partnerships

Supported by a strategy with 5 strategic priorities and 13 measures of activity:

1. *Strengthening the economic base*
   - EB1 Support to indigenous business
   - EB2 Stimulation of inward investment

2. *Developing human resources*
   - HR1 Improving the skills base of people in Greater Manchester
   - HR2 Support for businesses
   - HR3 Removal of barriers to employment for people who are unemployed and socially excluded

3. *Improvement of infrastructure*
   - I1 The provision and improvement of infrastructure within Greater Manchester
   - I2 Supporting the provision and improvement of infrastructure beyond the conurbation which provides linkages between Greater Manchester, the rest of the UK, Europe and beyond.

4. *Regeneration and the environment*
   - E1 Improving the environment
   - E2 Reclamation of derelict and vacant land
   - E3 Promoting better environmental practice

5. *Confirming Greater Manchester as the regional capital of the North of England*
   - R1 Raising the international profile of Greater Manchester through promotion and marketing
   - R2 The provision of regional facilities
   - R3 Tourism and cultural facilities

NB: This is a single page reproduced from the Association of Greater Manchester Authorities' 1993 draft economic strategy and operational programme produced to help secure and manage European Community funds over the period 1994–9. It demonstrates how it is possible to encapsulate the essence of a planning strategy in a single page.

That having been said, the formal opportunities to engage in debate of this kind may still be fairly limited. The idea of a process of continuous debate promoted by the 'communicative' planning theorists tends to come up against the procedural requirement faced by local planning authorities in Britain to get through the process of plan-making as quickly as possible, while still engaging effectively with the affected public. What this actually means in practice is that instead of a continuous debate there tend to be specific phases in the process when formal consultation takes place, and then in the later stages formal opportunities to object to proposals in a draft plan which may then, if unresolved, carry the right to be heard at a public inquiry or an examination in public. Some bold planning authorities do try to do more than the formal requirements of Government policy specify (ODPM, 2004a) in order to improve the opportunities available to local people and organizations to participate in the process, but at the same time they will still be aware of the desire to move as quickly as possible through that process. Perhaps the most important point to note in this context is that most local planning authorities one way or another do try to ground their development plan-making activities in the intelligence gained as a result of all their other ongoing activities rather than to regard development plan-making as an island. Thus, informal approaches to discuss issues and opportunities outside the formal procedures of development plan-making may well be welcomed, although not if this process becomes repetitive. The point here is that in Britain at least, local planning authorities are under a great deal of pressure to produce inevitably rather complex plans as quickly as possible via what can easily be long-winded processes, not just because the whip is cracked from time to time by central government but also because they know very well that they are dealing with a rapidly evolving world where some policies and proposals are likely to get out of date very quickly (Kitchen, 1996). In these circumstances, key planning skills that can be of real value to participants derive from a good working understanding of what the process of plan-making is and what opportunities it offers for participation, and also an awareness of the most effective ways to make points, be that to contest elements of the plan strategy or to argue that the strategy supports the points being made.

The process of development control

If the process of making development plans is relatively slow and more or less analytical, the process of development control (that is to say, the process whereby the state grants or refuses permission to develop) is one characterized by a large number of incremental decisions, each needing to be taken relatively quickly and often involving negotiations. These characteristics in turn affect the opportunities available for interested parties to participate in the process, where (unless the matter subsequently goes to appeal) there tends to be one chance at a fixed point in time. This makes participation in development control rather different from participation in development plan-making as discussed above. This section deals with four particular characteristics of this incremental system: the need for an efficient bureaucratic machine, the role of negotiations, the importance of the legal framework and the question of public involvement. Readers who wish to understand more about the development control process in Britain should see Morgan and Nott (1995), Thomas (1997), Blackhall (1998) and Bryan (1996) in respect of the appeals process.

To put this difference between development plan-making and development control into context, the process of taking the Manchester unitary development plan through all its stages from receipt of the commencement order at the end of 1989 to adoption in the summer of 1995 took Manchester City Council's planning department 67 months. If this seems like a very long time (which it is), some perspective on this might be provided by the fact that Manchester was the fastest of the ten Greater Manchester district councils to complete this process. During this time that it took to make a new development plan for the city, the city council received over 11,000 applications for planning permission, each of which had to be dealt with on its own merits within the framework provided by the development plan as it stood at that particular point in time. Inevitably, activity on this scale requires among other things an efficient bureaucratic machine if a planning authority is to handle such a workload effectively. And individual planners working within such a system have to recognize the need to meet the requirements such a machine will impose on all the members of the team if the system as a whole is to operate effectively. The strength of such a system, after all, is a function of its weakest link. It is also worth noting that the scale of public participation in that accumulated development control activity (measured by the number of formal representations received by the local planning authority in respect of planning applications) was several times greater than the scale of public participation in the making of the unitary development plan (measured again by formal representations received), despite major endeavours by the city council to promote the latter (Kitchen, 1997, ch. 4)

In recent years, information technology has been used increasingly to help to cope with this, particularly since (in Britain at any rate) this coincided with a period of reducing staff numbers as a result of public expenditure restrictions. As yet, computer systems have mainly focused on the mechanics of development control systems, recording each step of the process as it is undertaken and simplifying through their links with word processing systems the process of producing a report on the outcome of all of these steps; but as a new round of development plan-making gets underway in Britain in response to the Planning and Compulsory Purchase Act 2004, these same principles are likely to be found there also. The capacity to do more than this, and to use modern systems to help to focus on the quality of the decision rather than on the mechanics of the decision-making process, exists in the form of virtual reality technology, if its unit costs can be brought down to acceptable levels. And the history of technological innovation seems to suggest that within relatively short periods of time developments which have proved their value can indeed see dramatic reductions in unit costs leading to their widespread use. The ability to see a proposed development on a screen incorporated into the street scene of which it could form a part were it to proceed is clearly very helpful in the process of making a judgement about the quality and appropriateness of a proposal; and furthermore, this technology makes the opportunity to form views about matters of this nature available to a very wide range of interests, and not merely to planners and developers. In all probability, this would not stop the clamour that sometimes surrounds development proposals since there would still be disagreements about qualitative judgements, but it would perhaps help to make debates of this nature more informed. It would also improve the capacity to negotiate improvements to schemes to make them more acceptable to a wider range of people, through the ability to illustrate directly what the effects of possible changes to a proposal might be. Information technology in all forms seems likely to play an increasing role in planning practice in the future, and thus all planners will need sound basic information technology skills.

This concept of negotiation as an essential feature of the development control process seems to be common to many such systems throughout the world, although it takes different forms at least in part as a result of the degree of discretion available to planning officers (Booth, 1996, pp. 94, 95; see also Claydon, 1996 and the case-study presented by Tetlow, 1996). Developers recognize that negotiations with planning authorities are part and parcel of the real estate development process, and if they are sensible they try to organize themselves such that these negotiations are proceeding in parallel with other elements of that process so as to reduce the total consumption of time (and therefore of money) involved from the inception of a development idea to the commencement of construction work (Adams, 1994; Ratcliffe and Stubbs, 1996; Syms, 2002).

The nature of these negotiations may appear to vary between planning systems. For example, during July 1996 I engaged with colleagues in a fascinating discussion with a Toronto planner about how he made use of powerful codes typical of North American systems (see Wakeford, 1990, for a description of such codes, and of the variety to be found within them in the USA) which relate to individual aspects of the development process, such as density and daylight standards, as instrumental tools in a negotiation about the nature and quality of a proposed development. This negotiation had to be instrumental, because he would have found it difficult to have an attributable discussion about design quality with the promoter of a development in the absence of legal powers to support any negative recommendations he might make explicitly on this issue, as distinct from on the individual codes themselves. Nonetheless, the discussion about ways of meeting the requirements of these codes, which because of the legal powers behind them can be strong compliance tools, took place as far as the planner was concerned in the full knowledge of what the effects of suggested changes would be on the overall design of the scheme. The codes, in other words, as well as being ends in their own right were also used as means to a wider end; they provided an indirect vehicle which enabled a discussion about design improvements to take place in the absence of a direct vehicle. This was contrasted with the British practice situation, where in similar development circumstances a direct discussion about quality and appropriateness would almost certainly take place based upon the general support provided by broadly worded policies in a development plan and (where it existed) in published design guidance linked to that plan. Such a discussion, however, would probably have to start from a recognition that this policy guidance would almost certainly be open to some interpretation in terms of how it applied to that particular site, and at that time would have had to proceed in the knowledge (shared by both parties) that governmental advice about how far it was proper for planning officers to go in design discussions was not very encouraging; although as Chapter 2 has shown this advice has subsequently been rewritten to take a more positive stance towards the role of development control negotiations in achieving design quality. Arguably, planners in both of these situations are using the very different tools at their disposal in the best way they can to try to obtain broadly the same end; the best development that can be achieved in the prevailing circumstances. In one case, the tools were specific, powerful, but limited in scope, whereas in the other they were more general, potentially much more wide-ranging, but essentially discretionary in nature. It would be possible to argue endlessly about which of these systems is the better, or which combination from each would provide the best available package; but the real point is that the processes in each case are about doing the best that you can as a planner within the ground rules that are part of that particular system, to achieve what appear at that moment in time to be reasonable development solutions. In these terms, planners need to be effective negotiators not just in terms of their own opinions but also as far as possible on behalf of other customers of the service not present at these negotiations.

This example also seems to make the point that the development control process is heavily circumscribed by *a legal framework* (Morgan and

Nott, 1995; Heap, 1991; Ratcliffe and Stubbs, 1996, chs 2–6; Booth, 1996). Planners operating within any development control environment therefore need to understand the legal framework that applies in that environment, the practice issues that arise as a result of the continuous testing of that framework through negotiations, formal decisions and ultimately through the courts, and what room for manoeuvre they have (and can create for themselves, as the comparison between British cities and Toronto noted above hinted at) as a consequence. This is particularly true in relation to the planning enforcement system, where actions to deal with breaches of planning control may well end up in the courts. Planners also need to be aware of which other codes are likely to impinge on development negotiations alongside the development control regime. Examples here include the British building control system (which is separate in law from the planning system, and is essentially non-discretionary; it deals with matters such as some construction and safety standards which a building must meet), systems that deal with services for buildings such as traffic, waste and energy supply, and the increasing amount of environmental legislation that impacts upon development. Planners do not necessarily need to know the detail of these matters because they will usually have people with the requisite expertise in the relevant agencies to consult, but they do need to be aware of how these matters can affect development negotiations and of how by harnessing them in tandem with development control powers positive outcomes can be attained. It always needs to be remembered, however, that the legal framework is exactly that; it provides a series of tools with which the planner must work to try to achieve the ends of the planning system or of a particular customer of that system, but it does not actually determine the outcomes that planners are seeking to achieve in any particular case. Effective planners ought never to confuse this particular distinction between means and ends, otherwise they will be consumed by the minutiae of their system at the expense of remembering what it is actually there to try to do. As has already been said, the nature of these tools may well vary quite considerably from society to society, ranging from the codified and precise to the general and discretionary; but the planner's job is to use whatever tools exist as creatively as possible to try to achieve better places which improve the quality of life of their users.

A final, very important characteristic of the development control process is its emphasis to one degree or another (because this varies between jurisdictions) on *public consultation and involvement*. It is a common planning experience throughout the world that planners have generally found it very difficult to involve effectively other than a tiny minority of the population in the process of development plan-making, but have found that interest in specific development proposals either in the neighbourhood or in well-loved public areas of our towns and cities can mushroom. As a consequence, the development control process is often the part of the planning system that members of the public come into contact with most frequently. For example, the development control process in Manchester sent out in a single year towards the end of the 1980s over 50,000 consultation letters to households on planning applications in their areas, which with a workload of just over 2000 applications in that year meant that each application on average involved consulting 25 households. The range here was very wide, however, according to the nature of the application, with in some cases only immediate neighbours being consulted but in a small number of very major cases hundreds of consultation letters being sent out. With about 180,000 households in the city, this meant that the planning service was contacting the average household between once every three years and once every four years on a planning application. Again, however, the range was very wide, since there was little development activity in some parts of the city and quite intensive development interest in some other parts. As a consequence, some households would never receive a consultation letter from the planning service, whereas others would receive several over the three to four years period of the average. This level of actual contact with one of the major customers of the planning service, however, is greatly in excess of the effective levels usually achieved even in blanket consultation exercises for occasional development plan-making activities.

The demand for consultation of this kind appears to be growing in Western societies, as Chapter 1 has demonstrated. The idea that the governmental process at whatever level can be trusted to get on with making decisions about development matters without needing or receiving inputs of public opinion seems ever more to be a thing of the past. And public opinion can influence both political decision-makers and development interests, perhaps more at times than planners always acknowledge. For example, British planners in writing reports about development proposals for their committees need to recognize that one of the functions of those reports that is most valued by elected members is the process of recording the results of consultations, so that members feel informed about such matters when making a decision. Indeed, reports can still be useful to elected members in these terms even when the advice of the planning officer about the development proposal itself is rejected. There is, on the other hand, a critical literature about the extent to which processes of this kind still favour development interests rather than others such as those of local people (see, for example, Ambrose, 1994), and planners need to be aware of this while also being aware of the limits to their powers when faced with a planning application. Nonetheless, a trend-based forecast would undoubtedly be that the role and importance of public consultation and involvement in development control will continue to grow. The following section of this chapter looks at processes of public consultation and involvement in planning in more detail.

Processes of public consultation and involvement

The classic piece of writing about this subject in relation to planning is probably Arnstein's ladder of citizen participation (1969; the original American version from 1969 is reproduced in Stein, 1995, pp. 358–75). Its identification of eight levels of citizen participation arranged as ascending rungs on a ladder (see Box 3.2, which revisits Arnstein's concept) was important because it demonstrated that citizen participation was not a single idea but a concept containing a multiplicity of possibilities. It is certainly possible to criticize Arnstein's presentation of the ladder as being unashamedly normative, in the sense that climbing to the top of the ladder is seen to be inherently desirable, and as a consequence the worth of intermediate positions in appropriate sets of circumstances is undervalued. In particular, the 'contemporary analysis' column of Box 3.2 suggests that there are positive things that can be said about the worth of elements of Arnstein's middle cluster (which she described as 'degrees of tokenism'), with experience showing that there are valuable roles in appropriate circumstances for 'informing', for 'consultation' and even for 'placation' (a dismissive term in itself, which is really about various forms of selective representation), provided that these are understood for what they are and are not made out to be any more than this. Equally, not all citizens or communities would necessarily want components of her upper cluster (which she described as 'degrees of citizen power') in all circumstances, although in recent times the component of this that has come to the fore is 'partnership', to the point at which it is in danger of becoming so overused a concept as to be largely meaningless (Peck and Tickell, 1994; Bailey, 1995; Bailey, 2003). Notwithstanding these and other criticisms (see also Darke, 2000), which are made with the benefit of hindsight, Arnstein's paper was a landmark in the development of ideas about citizen participation, and together with Paul Davidoff's work on advocacy planning on behalf of the poor (Davidoff, 1965; reproduced in Stein, 1995, pp. 48–63) acted as a powerful stimulus to the emerging public participation movement in Britain. This surfaced in an official form via the report of the Committee on Public Participation in Planning (Skeffington, 1969), which tended to take an instrumental view of participation as a means of securing greater community support for plans (i.e., it saw public participation as a vehicle for generating improved levels of public support for plan proposals; see, for example, the cartoons on pp. 34 and 35), but which nonetheless started down a road which has led to the securing of statutory rights to public participation in planning processes in Britain.

Several other attempts have been made to model the various different types of public engagement with decision-making (not just in planning) that can be found, and one example of these is the so-called 'pyramid of

Box 3.2   Arnstein's ladder of citizen participation revisited

Contemporary analysis	Arnstein's original ladder	Arnstein's original clustering of rungs on the ladder
These pose challenges to the process of electoral democracy, by replacing in differing ways the politician elected on to the council with the idea of direct community representation in various forms. As yet, it is largely an area for experimentation rather than mainstream action.	**Citizen control**	Arnstein described these three as 'degrees of citizen power', which was the only level she regarded as being meaningful citizen participation. This illustrates very clearly her own view of her ladder, which is that it was for climbing - which of course is what ladders are for in the real world.
	Delegated power	
The importance of this area has grown tremendously in recent years, although who isn't involved in the process of partnership can be as important as who is.	**Partnership**	
This is really a process of selective response to active citizens (i.e. the ones who have made a fuss about an issue) rather than direct involvement of them all: and the critical issues here are around how representative these views might be and to whom are their holders accountable.	**Placation**	Arnstein described these three as involving varying 'degrees of tokenism', although she accepted that 'placation' involved some degree of citizen influence. Placation was the level that she felt most typified the USA's Model Cities programme at the time she was writing.
Many public bodies do this to inform their own decision-making activities, and as long as they are clear that this is what they are doing it is a legitimate part of political life.	**Consultation**	
This needs to be an element of most citizen participation activities, which is capable of coexisting with many of the others.	**Informing**	
These are rightly described as non-participation and are examples of how citizens can be manipulated by other parties to serve their own ends.	**Therapy**	These were dismissed as 'non participation', although she found ample evidence that both existed in various American programmes.
	Manipulation	

Source: Arnstein's original ladder was first published in Arnstein (1969).

Box 3.3   The pyramid of community engagement

Increasing community engagement

Empowerment

Involvement, participation

Consultation

Communication

Information

Source: The Improvement Network's website, www.improvementnetwork.gov.uk, consulted on 4 August 2005.

NB. The Improvement Network was established by four organizations working together, with a focus on how local managers (largely of public or quasi-public sector organizations) can improve service delivery to their customers in local communities. The four organizations are:

The Audit Commission
The Chartered Institute of Public Finance and Accountancy (CIPFA)
The Employers' Organization
The Improvement and Development Agency (IDeA)

community engagement' reproduced as Box 3.3. One of the advantages of this model is that it recognizes that there are many different ways organizations seek to engage with communities, and also different expectations about processes of this kind on the parts of communities themselves. Another helpful perspective of this model is that it acknowledges that the various layers of the pyramid coexist in various ways, with for example 'information' being a component of all the other categories but 'empowerment' (forms of decision-making exercised directly to one degree or another by communities) being a further and less commonly found development from the other layers. Each layer is seen as being of value in its own right, however; there isn't here necessarily the normative view that the pyramid should be climbed as there was with Arnstein's ladder. The model also recognizes that the five identified places on the face of the pyramid merely represent helpful ways of describing what is happening rather than fixed points in an ascent, so that (for example) 'involvement, participation' can represent a wide range of ways of operating which may well shade or grow into 'empowerment'. This is, therefore, a less normative model than Arnstein's, although no doubt it can still be argued that it carries normative implications.

Some of the general issues of public involvement in development control and in development plan-making activities have already been raised above, and in particular the question of the relative significance of development control activities as compared with development plan-making activities in these terms has been discussed. My own practice experience is that both of these work better if they are part of near-continuous processes of direct dialogue with local communities as customers of the planning service than if they are handled as one-off events (Kitchen, 1990). This has organizational implications for a public planning service, since in practice it is harder to do this if the service is organized on a conventional subject-specialism basis (such as development plans, development control, environment) than on an integrated area basis, but fundamentally it is about attitudes. Local people often have a great deal of knowledge about and 'feel' for their area, much more so than an individual planner could develop other than through protracted study, and thus quite apart from arguments about people's rights in a democratic society there is a clear pragmatic argument for planning services to try to find ways of tapping into this base of knowledge and concern. As I have argued elsewhere (Kitchen, 1997, p. 30), during my time as city planning officer of Manchester 440,000 Mancunians to 110 planners created odds of 4000 to 1, and it was clearly sensible to try to reduce those odds by working as closely together as possible rather than by operating at arm's length and only making contact at points of conflict. Consultation carried out occasionally around an agenda determined and driven by planners can be a very arid activity for people on the receiving end. A consultation process which is part and parcel of an ongoing relationship, and which both draws on and contributes to the development of that relationship, is likely to be a much more productive process, as the experience of preparing the Manchester Unitary Development Plan demonstrated (Kitchen, 1996).

It would be possible to write at considerable length about techniques for public consultation and involvement, and quite a literature is now building up on both the theory and the practice of this (see, for example, Hampton, 1977; Hill, 1994; Atkinson, 1995; Booth, 1996; Albrechts, 2002). My experience is that there aren't any right answers here, but there are a multiplicity of choices which can produce better or worse outcomes. This partly depends on factors such as whether these processes were imposed or whether they were negotiated. The role of government at all levels can also be critical in this, with the emphasis in the USA with its fragmented governmental structures tending to be more on the need for 'bottom-up' approaches which are citizen-led as compared with the 'top-down', public-agency-led approaches still commonly found in Britain. (See, for example, Hastings and McArthur, Hambleton, 1995; see also Savitch, 1988, for an American pers͵ ͏ on these sorts of comparisons, and Bennett, 1997, for an interesting direct comparison from first-hand experiences of British and American approaches.) These concerns are in turn claiming more attention from theory writers, who increasingly see citizen interests and movements as a major factor in urban politics (see part III of Judge *et al.*, 1995) and who emphasize the need to promote communication and collaborative action as a basis for the development of planning in increasingly fragmented societies (Healey, 1997; Brooks, 2002, ch. 9). Thus, whatever the precise nature of the planning system in operation in any location, and the formal role ascribed within it to citizen participation, planners will need to develop a strong community basis for their work. They will also need to handle any tensions there may be between this attitude and their role as bureaucrats when employed in the public sector as best they can.

Adversarial processes

Most planning systems, no matter what emphasis they put on citizen participation and on negotiation, also have built into them formal adversarial processes where unresolved disputes go for adjudication, and also (but usually less frequently exercised) ultimate rights of appeal to the courts. In this situation, a planner could be on either side of the argument, may well have to produce a written statement of one kind or another, and can expect to be cross-examined by representatives of other points of view. While it is often possible to resolve some difficulties by continuing negotiation almost up to the opening of the inquiry (in Britain) or public hearing (in North America) itself, there are many that will not be amenable to this approach because they reflect deeply held interests or feelings or because one or more parties wishes to take advantage of the platform provided by the event itself.

My personal experience of working in the British inquiry system (which is described in general terms in Allinson, 1996; see also Bryan, 1996, chs 4, 5) is that the single most important component is usually making sure that a good written statement is prepared as basic evidence. Without denying the importance, and sometimes the drama, of cross-examination, on the whole it didn't usually seem to weigh so heavily with inspectors at inquiries as a good proof of evidence. This is thus the component of the process where the planner, whatever viewpoint is being represented, needs to concentrate the greatest amount of effort in advance of the inquiry proceedings. It is also, of course, the part of the process over which the planner has the greatest amount of control. When preparing for large inquiries, which are likely to be complex and protracted, the planner is likely to be working as part of a team, which usually includes the advocate who will be presenting the case at the inquiry. In these circumstances, it is common for the outline of a proof of evidence to be prepared well in advance of the date of the inquiry as part of the process of shaping the case as a whole, especially where this will involve several witnesses from different backgrounds who all need to be pulling in the same direction and who all need to avoid giving hostages to fortune that could embarrass other witnesses from the same team. Proofs are often finalized after consultation with the advocate, and in my experience advice from this source about the most effective presentation of planning arguments is usually most helpful. Advice can also be given about the likely lines of cross-examination that other parties will adopt in relation to that evidence, to help the planner prepare for this part of the process.

Cross-examination is usually the part of the process about which planners feel the greatest trepidation, especially when they know that some of their points are not particularly strong. Very often, advocates seemed to me to start cross-examination with what they regarded as the weakest elements of my proofs, and the recognition that this was likely always made me think hard about whether to include weaker points at all. Sometimes this is unavoidable, because some cases are simply stronger than others; but it is good practice not to include a weak point that is not essential to the case being made, because this is an unnecessary invitation to other parties to the process to probe. And being cross-examined for a lengthy period of time can be uncomfortable enough without self-inflicted difficulties of this kind! Different people react differently to the process of cross-examination, and over time planning practitioners work out for themselves the methods that suit them best. There really is no substitute, however, for a good quality proof of evidence, which is well-reasoned and factually correct, as the basis for an appearance at a public inquiry, because this is also the basis for cross-examination. After that, the best advice I was ever given about being cross-examined was, 'Stick to your proof, and don't engage in verbal gymnastics with their advocate because he'll be better at it than you are.'

One feature of public inquiry work that has grown in scale over the years is the involvement of citizens groups as third parties. Planners representing either the local planning authority or a development interest that has submitted an appeal in a sense have a relatively straightforward role to play, because the broad line that their side of the argument represents is fairly clear-cut. The range of potential involvements on the part of citizens groups is very large, however, and the roles played by the planner in working with or on behalf of such groups can also be wide-ranging. This range may include acting as advocate, helping to develop the case from a reaction (a group is against something) to a reasoned set of arguments (a group can present a convincing case as to why its opposition should prevail in this instance), and advising the group on procedures and tactics. Many inspectors at inquiries will give citizens groups more latitude than they would the local planning authority or the developer, because they recognize that these 'big guns' can both 'out-resource' and 'out-knowledge' a citizens' group. But it is also true to say that many groups develop a considerable expertise in the inquiry game over a period of time simply by virtue of experience; and this knowledge can be a valuable commodity, as an action guide for community groups prepared in the 1970s by the Shelter Community Action Team (undated) vividly demonstrates. As well as this kind of pooled knowledge which is available, community groups also tend to have one other attribute which they often undervalue: local knowledge. In Britain in recent years, the process of helping citizens groups and individuals in these kinds of situations through planning aid has become of growing importance (Royal Town Planning Institute and Planning Aid for London, 2005). This works on the principle that planning expertise is available on a voluntary basis, and provided that planners can avoid the obvious conflicts of interest issues to which this could give rise, it is a very valuable way of reducing the disadvantage that community groups and individuals can and do experience in planning situations as compared with the resources available to local planning authorities and to development interests. To give an idea of the scale of this, in 2004/05 the planning aid system in England dealt with just under 3000 enquiries, just over half of which were in respect of planning applications (ibid., pp. 3, 4). The planning aid system is being expanded with public financial support because of the resource it provides for community groups and individuals, and so these figures for 2004/05 represent both a significant increase on the previous position and a baseline from which further growth is expected.

Inquiries and hearings take many different forms, with some being less adversarial and more inquisitorial than others, and some being less formal than others. The rules and procedures that apply to each need to be understood, and taken into account in deciding how best to present the case in this particular situation. This also needs to be thought about in terms of the attitude of the planner during the inquiry process itself. There is little point, for example, in being very formal and sticking rigidly to the precise terms of a case at a relatively informal hearing where it becomes clear that a resolution to a difficulty may be capable of being found via a degree of accommodation on either side. An unwillingness to be helpful when a point of principle is not at stake is unlikely to go down well, and may even cause the loss of a point that is more damaging than a partial concession. The thrust of this is that an inquiry or a hearing is a public event, and planners need to take into it a well-prepared case and to behave at it in a manner that is appropriate to the situation.

A particularly problematic situation for planners working for local planning authorities can be where they are defending through the formal process a decision taken by their authority which went against the written advice given in the name of the chief planning officer. There are different views about how planners should respond to this situation, including the view at one extreme that they shouldn't attempt to defend decisions of this nature at all and that the politicians who have made the decision should have to defend it in this formal arena. My own view, however, is that unless the decision that was taken is so perfidious as to be indefensible (and that can very occasionally happen in political situations!) the local planning authority's position is entitled to a defence. This has to start from a recognition, however, that the written report of the chief planning officer which made a different recommendation will be a matter of public record, and therefore the individual planner should not attempt to depart from its analysis and its advice. The line that should be taken is that this was what was in front of the committee at the time it made its decision, but that it took a different view of the balance that should be struck between the various issues (hopefully with some evidential indication as to why this was the case) and decided accordingly. This may not very often be a successful line of defence, but properly presented it should at least avoid the award of costs against the local planning authority (which can happen in Britain in certain circumstances), which certainly is a matter of concern for a local planning authority because of its potential impact on the budget for the planning service. Occasionally, this line of defence is successful because the inspector taking the inquiry accepts that it is a legitimate task for politicians to balance the various issues (rather than simply accepting their chief officer's advice about this), and that the balance they struck in making their decision was a reasonable one. This kind of 'win' can be much prized by both politicians and planners because it underscores the legitimacy of decision-making as a political act. To keep this in perspective, Manchester City Council, during the ten years or so when I was senior assistant city planning officer and then city planning officer, had three adverse costs awards made against it at appeal, in each case as a result of a decision by elected members which was made essentially on political grounds and against the advice of the city planning officer. While I have no reliable way of counting the number of occasions when decisions by elected members taken against professional advice (because they took a different view of the 'balance' of issues) were upheld at appeal, this must have been several times that number.

Conclusions

This chapter has been not so much about what planning is trying to achieve but about how it sets about doing it. The emphasis, thus, has been upon the procedural dimensions of planning activities rather than upon their long-term goals, and in particular it has been on how potential participants in planning processes can be helped to navigate their complexity in order to make their inputs effectively. I would argue that these two elements (what planning is trying to achieve, and how it sets about doing it) are closely linked, however, because if one of the things that planning aspires to is working with communities to achieve their ends rather than those of planners, then helping people and organizations to navigate the system is an essential part of this activity. My own experience was that planning processes were often seen by non-planners as impenetrable, and that what they really wanted was sound advice about how and when to access them and how to get across their own points of view in the most effective ways possible. Their expectation, as a consequence, was that I would be able to give them essentially procedural advice of this nature, irrespective of whether or not I happened to agree with the points they wanted to make, and so that was what I tried to do.

Of course, one of the ways of tackling this issue would be to try to make planning systems and processes less complex and therefore more accessible; and that indeed was what the British Government's Planning Green Paper argued for (DTLR, 2001, paras 2.5, 2.11). There is very considerable scope to debate, however, whether the English planning system after the Planning and Compulsory Purchase Act 2004 has actually achieved this objective, or whether it has simply replaced one form of complexity with another. In complex modern Western societies it seems to me to be inherently likely that planning systems (which, after all, are a product of those societies) will also be relatively complex, and also that the scope for reducing this complexity no matter how desirable this might be is likely to be fairly limited. That being so, one of the things that planners should be if they are to relate effectively to their customers is expert interpreters of that system, and this is also likely to be one of the things that their customers will expect of them. Indeed, while I argued in Chapter 2 that the technical skills of the planner are not today seen in the same unconditional sense in which they were often presented some forty years ago, the role and importance of system and process skills has arguably grown over that period as planning has sought to be more customer-oriented and less impositional in its approach. I see no reason to argue that this process of change has now come to its natural end, and so I would expect the significance of system and process skills to grow still further as planning continues to journey down this long road.

Self-assessment topics

1. Find a local example of an adopted development plan. Chart the various procedural steps that it went through and how long each of

these took. Try to discover the degree of change that took place in the content of the development plan as a result of key procedural steps such as public consultation on the draft and a public inquiry to hear objections.

2. Imagine yourself acting on behalf of a development interest wanting to change aspects of that development plan, for example those relating to the location of new residential, retail, office or industrial developments. There are plenty of examples of these sorts of phenomena all the time, so it should be possible to base this on a current issue in your locality. How would you set about trying to convince the local planning authority that such changes would be appropriate? What form might such changes take? And what sort of case would you make to this end?

3. Now look at that development plan from the perspective of a local community group worried that in practice the plan is allowing too much development of the wrong sort to take place in their area, such that the group feels that the area's character and qualities are being eroded. This is not an uncommon situation, so it should be possible to find a live example of such an occurrence. How would you set about trying to convince the local planning authority that tightening the development plan in response would be appropriate? What form might such changes take? And what sort of case would you make to this end?

4. Find a local case of a controversial development that has recently been granted planning permission. Try to chart the key stages in the process, from the submission of a planning application to the granting of a planning permission; it should be possible to do this kind of reconstruction relatively straightforwardly from publicly available documents such as council reports. What was it about this case that made it controversial? What do you think were the key elements in this instance that led to the grant of permission? What consultations took place as part of the process of determination, and how influential do you think these were in the outcome? What was the relationship in this case between the decision and the provisions of the approved development plan?

5. Find a local example of a public consultation exercise in the planning field that has occurred recently. Why was it undertaken? Did it have any stated objectives, and if so what were they? What was the form of the consultation? Over what area and on what issues? Who decided these matters? What was the response, both in numerical and percentage terms and in terms of the points raised by consultees? How were these results reported, and to whom? What happened as a consequence?

6. Now find a local case of a partnership arrangement that is said to involve the community in some manner. What form does this partnership take and what resources does it command? What are its

objectives, and what does it actually do in practice? Who decided these matters? How is the community represented in this arrangement, and how in turn are those representatives accountable to their wider community? Who isn't involved in this partnership who maybe could or should be? What is the relationship between this partnership and the local council?

7. Get hold of an example of a planning proof of evidence or witness statement from a recent public inquiry. This can be any kind of planning inquiry, and it can also be a planning proof that is presenting a case on behalf of any of the parties to that inquiry. What was the purpose of the inquiry? What is the line of argument being presented in the proof in this context? How well do you think this particular case is presented in the proof? If you were a supporter of the line of argument in the proof, how do you think the presentation of this case could be improved? And if you were an opponent of this line of argument acting on behalf of one of the other parties to the inquiry, how would you try to show the weaknesses in the proof?

Chapter 4

Place Skills

Introduction

One of the strongest demarcating characteristics of planning in practice is that it is to varying degrees place-specific. Fundamentally, it is about trying to manage change in places or localities for the benefit of their citizens and their users. The cutting edge of planning can usually at the end of the day be reduced to a simple question: 'What do we do here?' Even planning at the broadest of spatial scales (for example, thinking about spatial policy at the Western European, national or regional scales) has some sort of boundaries to it; it is intended to be about some places but not about others, although of course it may well take into account issues that relate extensively to areas outside its areas of coverage, such as the degree of competition that may exist between two cities and the broader ecological footprint of action proposed in a specific locality. Thus, the characteristics of places matter a great deal to successful planning activities, because planning involves (or ought to involve) the application of policies and proposals designed to be effective in the particular situations to which it relates rather than the use of standard prescriptions irrespective of these local circumstances.

This chapter is about the development of skills which relate to this understanding of places. The history of places, the factors that have forged the way they are today and that have shaped the ways people use them, the forces that are already at work shaping what they will be like tomorrow, their natural and built environments at both the macro and the micro scales, and things about localities that people value; these all contribute to the kinds of place-based understanding which is essential for effective planning. A doctor who tried to prescribe medicines for a patient's complaint without knowing anything at all about the patient would be at high risk of achieving an unsatisfactory outcome, and the patient would be at even greater risk. The same is true of the planner and the place or places the planner is trying to improve. While the effect of a failure to understand the dynamics of places in planning policy development may not be as dramatic or as immediate as the effect on an individual of inappropriate medicines, the long-term consequences can nonetheless be severe. The focus of this chapter is therefore on understanding and applying place-based knowledge in planning-relevant ways.

The main sources of information about places in these terms can be broken down broadly into five classes: the written record, oral sources and other forms of direct customer feedback, the ongoing process of drawing understandings from the output of the local media, the capacity and (even more) the potential of information technology, and the first-hand experiences of planners. These in turn are discussed in the following pages, with the exception of the capacity and potential of information technology, which is discussed fully in Chapter 5 (although much of what is said there links with the content of this chapter as well). The discussion in the following sections ranges very widely, because while these are the main sources of information for planners about places they are also of considerable importance in terms of the development of many of the other types of skills discussed in this book. The chapter then discusses what might be involved in the process of 'place-making', returning to the dimensions of place-based understanding discussed above, before closing with some self-assessment topics designed to help readers explore some of this material more fully in their own local circumstances.

Written sources of place information

Most written material is to a degree already out of date. To oversimplify, something has to have happened before somebody can write about it or record it. To give a very common example, one of the most comprehensive sources of information about places in much of the world is the national census. In Britain, these are carried out once every ten years across the whole country, as a common activity at household level backed up by the force of law. They provide invaluable information at local level about a very wide range of matters, and to varying degrees they also enable very useful analyses of change across time to take place. But by the time that census material other than headline results emerges in printed or even machine-accessible form, three or more years may often have elapsed since the date the census was carried out. At the time of drafting this chapter in the summer of 2005, for example, material from the UK 2001 census was still being released, while in parallel with this process consultations were taking place about the preparations for the next census in 2011. This isn't in any way to disparage the value of the census as an information source, of course; it is simply to make the point that data from this source can already be out of date by the time it emerges, with the likelihood that this problem will grow in importance the further away from the original date one moves.

In many ways, the gap between the date when the census was carried out (to which the information in it relates) and the date when it becomes available for use in a planning office matters hardly at all, because the uses to which it will be put are not often especially sensitive to this sort of passage of time. But sometimes this may matter a great deal. An area experiencing significant inward or outward migration over the intervening period, for example, or one which has experienced planned change on a considerable scale, may not be well described in terms of its population structure by what the census has to say. In these sorts of circumstances it clearly is very important to understand the date to which data relate and what has changed in the intervening period. A practical issue deriving from these considerations may well be the question of what to do about a census database that is significantly out of date because of changes of this nature, given that the process of undertaking a fresh local survey can be both expensive and time-consuming. Often, the response to this question has to be that planners have to make the best use of what they have already got, because putting something better in its place is not a feasible option in the circumstances no matter how desirable that may appear to be. Planning practice is often like this; it is about doing the best one can with imperfect information, because although it is not too difficult to see how the information base might be improved the practical opportunities to do so can be very limited.

As well as the question of the date on which data was gathered, the 2001 UK census illustrates another characteristic which is vital in understanding the reliability of written sources of place information. That is the question of how accurate the data are. It is most unlikely that something like a national census could ever be 100 per cent accurate, but generally UK censuses are regarded as being very accurate when looked at in the round. The real difficulty in their use comes when there is a suspicion that under-enumeration may have occurred on a more concentrated scale in some localities. As the UK government's Office for National Statistics puts it:

> Under-enumeration in the 2001 census did not occur uniformly across all areas. The patterns of census response were as expected, that is response rates were lowest for inner city areas where characteristics known to be related to census non-response are most prevalent such as multi-occupancy and higher proportions of non-English speaking population. (Source: www.statistic.gov.uk/census2001/methodology.asp, consulted on 4 August 2005)

This can be a particular problem for planning activities in the larger cities, of course, because the areas where under-enumeration tends to be at its highest are those where the social conditions that cause it are also likely to be part of the reasons why planning and urban regeneration initiatives tend to take place. More generally, it can also be a problem when administrative processes rely on census figures as a trigger for action, for example in the UK in terms of annual financial allocations from the government to local authorities. At the same time, it is important to keep such problems in perspective, because the census remains a hugely important source of data which it would be very difficult for others to replicate in a locality with anything like the rate of return that the census achieves. It is important, though, to be aware of limitations of the kind discussed above.

One of the greatest attributes of written material is its ability to help us with our understanding of the history of how we got to where we are today. It is also true to say that an understanding of history in these terms can be absolutely fundamental to effective planning; we need to know how we got to where we are today if we are to be able to plan effectively how to go forward from there to a better tomorrow. My experience was that many of the customers of the planning service expected this kind of knowledge of the head of the planning service; it was almost as if respect for the advice being offered was dependent upon how well grounded it was seen as being in these terms. Nevertheless, the written record can be maddeningly incomplete, and of course what is there can also be very partial in the sense that it reflects the views of whoever wrote it. This isn't just a problem of history in the sense of the distant past. We are far too often very careless with our con-temporary history, in the sense of recording recent and current urban change and how and why it happened (but see Manchester City Council, 1995b, for an attempt by a local planning authority to do this), and also in the sense that the quality of the case files in the planning office can be very dependent upon the commitment of the case officer to main-taining this kind of record. These problems with the written record are also very frequently replicated in relation to the pictorial record. I was able to play a part in Manchester in securing a pictorial record of the process of urban change in relation to two very major projects in the city centre (Grant, 1995 and 1996), but these two instances are much more notable for their scarcity value than for the regularity with which they occur in our towns and cities.

Notwithstanding these points, the written and pictorial records clearly represent a very valuable starting-point for learning about places. Their incomplete nature, and the partiality that typifies much of the material contained within them, suggest that caution always needs to be exercised in using them, but not that they should be ignored. Without going so far as to endorse the old saw that those that don't read history are condemned to relive it, planning proposals that are not grounded in an acute understanding of the history of the places they are seeking to influence may well prove to be deficient, and so a specific understanding of urban history is central to the planning process. Planners who share this view often find that they develop a fascination with the detailed urban history of places with which they have an association, and of course this needs to be kept in perspective, although it can of itself have some direct practical applications (for example, in Britain in rela-tion to conservation areas and to buildings listed as being of historic or architectural importance). But a focused knowledge of local urban history, that seeks to understand the processes that have made a place what it is today and that are continuing to have an effect on it, is a vital planning tool, and the written record is usually a good starting place for developing this particular implement.

Oral sources, and other forms of customer feedback

As noted in Chapter 3, my starting point for thinking about this during my time as city planning officer of Manchester was that the detailed knowledge that 440,000 Mancunians had of Manchester and its locality must by a factor of many times over be greater than that of the city council's 110 planning staff, even if perhaps not at the ratio of 4000:1 that these numbers might suggest. The clear conclusion from this self-evident observation was that it must be in the best interests of those planners to try to tap into this knowledge source as fully and as effectively as they could.

Of course, the problems with this knowledge source are many and various. It is not always easy to access, since it exists in many forms rather than one. Its reliability is likely in practice to be unknown at the level of what any individual may say, although often this is capable of being checked. There are likely in practice to be a large number of contradictions in the views that are expressed, not necessarily because people will deliberately lie (although occasionally this may happen) but much more usually because people's memories are selective and imperfect. And much of what people will say will not be disinterested; it will be coloured by their own particular views or aspirations. It would be a great mistake, however, to believe that these manifest problems disqualify this kind of information source from serious consideration by planners. To do so would be to throw away a vast amount of potentially valuable experience and knowledge, much of which is very difficult to acquire in other ways. It would also take away a great deal of awareness about public opinion that is absolutely fundamental if the planning process is to achieve the objective of helping to create the kinds of places that people want, as distinct from the kinds of places that planners tell them they ought to have. So the question becomes one of how to obtain the real gains that are to be made here without being misled by the problems.

The way a planning service is organized can of itself make a contribution to this process. Most people's urban experiences are of particular localities; where they live, where they work, where they shop, where they go for entertainment and recreation. Much of this is very local. My experience of working in Manchester, for example, was that many Mancunians had an intimate knowledge of the area where they lived, quite a good knowledge of the city centre because it was an area of shared experience, but quite a limited knowledge of much of the rest of the city. A planning service organized on an area basis, as the service in Manchester was at that time, has the potential to tap into this area-based knowledge, especially where liaison with local communities is explicitly made part of the job of the individual planners working in area teams. This isn't, of course, the only factor to be taken into account in trying to decide how to structure a planning service for a city, but it is worth remembering in those discussions that forms of organization that relate naturally to the ways that people live a large proportion of their lives may well be more effective at tapping into local knowledge sources of this kind than forms of organization that are not congruent in these terms. It is also worth remembering in this context that local people are probably more likely to be willing to share their knowledge and experience with staff they know and see on a regular basis than with individual subject 'experts' who parachute in and out of their lives.

Another way the planning service can access local sources of information of this kind is through the kinds of customer feedback processes to be discussed in Chapter 5. Some of these will take the form of formal exercises designed to elicit public views, such as public consultation on draft plans or on planning applications, but the vast majority of feedback processes that operate, provided that they are recognized as such, will be as a result of the normal day-to-day relationships that the service has with its customers. Potentially, every such interaction is a source of customer feedback, provided that the planner is able to reflect on what is happening, what has been said, and also in some situations what has not been said when it might have been expected to have materialized. This kind of constant learning is not just about effective practice in the sense of trying to tune the service to meeting customer needs, but is also about customers' knowledge and appreciation of place and what is happening in it. A very good example of this phenomenon is the role that civic societies often play in drawing the attention of the planning department to what may turn out to be a breach of planning control which might justify enforcement action being taken. To the best of my knowledge, no English local authority planning department in the modern world has the staff resources for people to be constantly out on the street 'on patrol' in these terms. Indeed, informed feedback suggests that most local planning authorities don't even have the staff to check consistently that the conditions imposed on planning permissions are being properly implemented. In these circumstances, enforcement tends to be a reactive process, relying on complaints to identify the need for something to be investigated (see, for example, Bryan, 1996, pp. 83, 84). But local civic societies are often happy to be the 'eyes and ears' of the planning department, as long as they can be assured that if a potential breach of planning control has occurred it will be investigated and that if it is justified action will be taken to deal with the matter. This kind of relationship can pay dividends for the service in all kinds of ways, because it can turn a very resource-expensive job into one that is highly focused and at the same time can deliver a good measure of customer satisfaction.

The sorts of relationships discussed above tend to work best when they operate on quite a long-term basis. It takes time, for example, for an area-based planner to build effective working relationships with people who represent organizations and interests in the area where the planner works. Similarly, it takes time for those interests to get to know and to trust the individual planner, and to see that working relationship as being a continuous one that can survive the ups and downs that will inevitably arise from the fact that individuals will almost certainly not agree with every decision that the local planning authority takes. One of the potential drawbacks in this situation is that the area-based planner can be seen by colleagues as being so close to this set of community contacts as to lose any sense of judgement about the weight that should be attached to the views of those contacts; and it does need to be acknowledged that, notwithstanding the importance of the community dimension of planning, not every view from such a source is equally appropriate or equally capable of being translated into effective action through the planning process. This potential problem needs to be set against the intrinsic value to a planning service of receiving this kind of community-based feedback, however, especially since the richness of this is often hard to capture via conventional public consultation exercises. Another potential drawback is that it is in the nature of a planning career that people do move around, and that indeed they need to do so if they are to gather a full range of experience. As a result, the desirability of long-term working relationships with community interests being argued for here has to be tempered by this recognition of the realities of planning career patterns – and indeed, by a recognition that community activists move around as well. Nevertheless, my practice experience was that the experienced area- or patch-based planner brought a huge amount of knowledge and understanding into the planning service from having an ongoing set of local relationships, and in turn was seen as the 'face' of the planning service out in the local community in a way which is very difficult to replicate through other forms of organization.

I talk more in Chapter 7 about working relationships with local elected politicians, but it is also worth recording in this present context that my experience was that elected members who had served their wards for some years were often a mine of useful local information. Planners are sometimes unwilling to tap into this particular source, perhaps because they think that local councillors will relate their observations to what they currently want to see done in their area rather than present a disinterested view, or perhaps because they feel that they may be laying themselves open to the accusation of political bias if they liaise with individuals from a particular political party. But I found generally that elected members were very willing to talk about the locality they represented when asked to do so on an informal basis (that is, away from the cut and thrust of political debate), and often were able to do so both knowledgeably and informatively. It is probably true to say, however, that it is helpful to know the individual concerned, at least to the extent of being able to judge whether this is a case where my 'generally' from above probably won't apply, before travelling down this particular road. Nevertheless, this is an information source that should not be neglected, because the experienced local councillor can add real value to the planning process through such contributions.

This approach needs to coexist alongside other more formal ways of gathering community views. Sometimes it is necessary, for example, to know statistically what the balance of local views about a particular issue might be, and while informal and ongoing discussions with active members of that community might convey the general shape of this, they won't do so with the precision that a representative formal survey would. And, of course, it is possible that the views of active members of communities won't always reflect the views of the less-active majority, simply because (in my experience) people usually become community activists because they have firm views; they are not prepared simply to be neutral gatherers of the views of others. As a consequence, it is quite helpful from time to time to obtain more formal sets of community views via consultation exercises of various types, which can act as a check on the views being received from community representatives on a more ongoing basis. But my experience was that planning proposals affecting a locality tended to be much better received by the residents of that locality if they had already been shaped by taking into account the known views of active community members than was the case when this had not happened. This was a very important element, for example, in shaping the work on the area-based dimensions of the Manchester Unitary Development Plan (Manchester City Council, 1995a) in the early 1990s, and the accumulated understanding that this provided in turn contributed to the broader policies in the plan (Kitchen, 1997, ch. 4).

Using the local media

My experience was that the local media, and particularly local newspapers, were very often the places where people got their views about planning issues and the planning process. This experience is very similar to the much more formal finding of McCarthy *et al.* (1995, p. 11) when exploring the sources of knowledge about planning that members of the general public said they had used; in Britain at any rate, the local media appear to be the most commonly used source of information about planning, and by some distance. Paragraph 2.41 of that study (ibid.) is summarized in Box 4.1.

Box 4.1 suggests not merely that the local media and particularly the local press were the dominant source, but also that this was so by approximately five times the second most commonly cited source, which was the direct experiences of respondents. Planners ought to be very conscious of this when thinking about the local media; they are the main method the general public at large uses to form views about what they are doing.

The subject matter of planning (the fact that it is essentially about managing change in order to try to achieve a better future) makes it intrinsically interesting to the local media. It also means that people's reactions to proposals of this nature will be of interest to the local media, and since people are often uncomfortable with change this can at times lead to some fairly negative stories about planning. It would be wrong to give the impression that local media interest in planning is usually negative, however, because in my experience this was far from being the case. In particular, the local press generally gives quite a sizeable amount of coverage to the ongoing work of the local authority in its area, and planning is very much part of this process. My experience was that the journalists who did this kind of work were frequently quite knowledgeable about local affairs, and that they very much appreciated informal background briefing about the specifics of a planning issue to help them to relate that knowledge to the particularities of the case.

Box 4.1   General public sources of understanding about planning

NB: Because respondents could identify several sources the numbers add up to more than 100 per cent.

1. The local media, and particularly the local press (approximately 67 per cent of the 2000 households questioned).
2. Direct experience of the planning system, on the part either of respondents (13 per cent) or of people known to them (11 per cent).
3. The national press (11 per cent).
4. The local council (4 per cent).
5. Being affected in some way by development in the locality (6 per cent)
6. 39 per cent of respondents (virtually 2 in 5) said either that they couldn't identify a source for their knowledge about planning or that they didn't know about it.

Source: Data from McCarthy, Prism Research and Harrison (1995, para. 2.41).

I always found them in this context to be scrupulous about what was 'on the record' and what was 'off the record', perhaps in part because journalists doing this kind of work would expect to be discussing it with the city planning officer or another senior officer on several future occasions. Very often, the starting-point for discussions of this nature is a press release from the local authority, and while the authority will almost certainly have professional staff who deal with matters of this nature my experience was that I was frequently and extensively involved in the drafting of such documents. Press releases are very different from full professional reports, and they need to be drafted accordingly. The basic principle here was usually to be as clear as possible about what it was you wanted the local media to pick up from the press release, and then to produce a document that did this job simply, straightforwardly and in non-professional language. Background briefing material could be attached and was sometimes useful, but very often the journalist in question preferred to deal with this as a face-to-face or telephone discussion. I always felt that it was best to work with local journalists on the basis that they were essentially allies, notwithstanding the fact that they would sometimes produce items that presented the planning service in a less positive light than I would have wished, and to try not to let disappointment over one story interfere with discussions about the rest. This is a counsel of perfection, and I am sure that my own behaviour didn't always match it, but the objective here was to gain the reputation of someone who could be trusted and who was relatively easy to work with because of the longer-term dividends this would produce.

Of course, if the local media see what they regard as a news story then they are likely to pursue it (because that is their job), especially when local politicians are involved. This can at times be difficult for planning and other officials, since they need in these circumstances to leave the politics to the politicians (see, for example, Kitchen, 1997, pp. 159–65). But generally my experience was that journalists were quite prepared to present stories in positive ways, because, I am sure, they often felt that they were genuinely positive stories; that is to say, irrespective of any spin that the local authority was trying to put on the story via its formal and informal briefing processes, or that politicians were attempting for their own purposes, they could see positive dimensions to this for the city and its people. There was another dimension to this process as well. During my time in Manchester I generally felt that the local media had a strong interest in and a strong commitment to what could be described as 'the good of the city'. They were part of the fabric of the city's life, and they in turn were dependent upon that life. So promoting the city was something to which they were committed and in which they had a clear vested interest. In this sense, their position was very like that of the city council, of which exactly the same things could be said. They were also fairly dependent upon the city council for news (they would have had a lot of empty pages without reporting the business of the council) and to an extent also for advertising. All of these things meant the interests of the local media and of the city council often coincided, and that undoubtedly helped when it came to having planning stories treated as positively as possible, although it didn't prevent the appearance of more critical stories when that was felt to be appropriate.

The thrust of the above argument has been around the importance of strong working relationships with the local press, recognizing that since this is the most important single means by which the public at large gets to form views about planning it is sensible to treat the local press as an ally and to try to work positively with the journalists who report on planning issues, irrespective of whether or not individual stories have been reported in the past in ways that the planner would wish. But the local press aren't the only form of local media. Local radio and television too can be interested in planning matters, and can see opportunities for dealing with planning issues in news and current affairs programmes (in particular). My experience was that this interest didn't tend to be as continuous as that of the local press, but nevertheless intermittent opportunities to communicate about what the planning service was trying to do, to discuss current initiatives, and to try to present the planning service positively to the listening or viewing public did present themselves. I suspect that the scale of this will grow in future, and that in particular the interactive nature of opportunities of this kind will have an increasing part to play not only in the delivery of planning services generally but specifically in securing public feedback. Planners who find themselves in this kind of position with any regularity would be well advised to take advantage of whatever professional media coaching is available to them, because these are media where first impressions of the individual can be very important. My own experience of this was that radio opportunities tended to be longer and more discursive whereas television opportunities tended towards the sound-bite end of this spectrum, but in their different ways they all represented opportunities to be positive about the planning service and communicate with some of its key customers, potentially in quite large numbers. And if from time to time the price to be paid for these opportunities was the need to do some fending off of some difficult questions, I felt that a few uncomfortable moments was a price well worth paying.

The first-hand experience of planners

Notwithstanding any of the above, in my view there is no substitute for planners getting to know the areas to which their work relates intimately by experiencing those areas at first hand as frequently as possible. Such experience can take many different forms, like walking the streets regularly, undertaking frequent site visits, attending events in the areas at different times of the day, using the facilities of areas such as shops and restaurants, and having meetings with local groups and individuals at venues in the area where they feel comfortable and at times of the day or evening that are convenient for those groups or individuals. A big part of such processes involves talking with local people in order to try to understand how they experience the area, what they value about it, and what they dislike and would like to see changed. This kind of knowledge builds up over time, which is one of the reasons why I strongly favour organizing public planning services in ways which include staff with patch-based responsibilities (Kitchen, 1999). While it is possible to gain a great deal of very valuable information from a single well-organized site visit (and many people working in the field of consultancy, whose job by its very nature often involves working in several different localities each for relatively short periods of time, are very good at this), that cannot be the same thing as the kind of working knowledge built up over time by a planner regularly undertaking the kinds of activities in an area described above. It is worth remembering in this context that the kind of fine-grained understanding of localities being argued for here is exactly what many of the residents of those localities bring to the table, albeit not in a professionally tutored form, and if planners wish to win the respect of this type of customer of the planning service then they need to be seen as having not merely a good working knowledge of the make-up of an area but also an empathy for it and for the quality of life it offers. My experience also was that local elected representatives often thought in similar ways, and several times I have seen experienced councillors take great pleasure in tripping up planning staff at varying levels of seniority by exposing the relative lack of local knowledge and understanding sitting behind the points they are making.

Of course, this again is a counsel of perfection. There are good practical reasons why a planning service might not be organized in this way in the first place (like, for example, that it may not be seen as such an efficient way to organize a service faced with targets such as those related to the speed of decision-making in development control), and even where area-based organization is part of the structure of a planning service events such as staff turnover will inevitably mean that there will sometimes be people responsible for areas who have not yet acquired the first-hand understanding of their patch and of the people who relate to it being argued for here. Nevertheless, it seems to me that this is the direction in which public planning services should always strive to be moving, if they are indeed to meet the aspirations of their customers. The UK Government's Planning Green Paper (DTLR, 2001) captures this idea well when it talks about engaging local communities in planning at the neighbourhood or other local area scale as follows:

> Action plans should form a new focus for community involvement in developments affecting neighbourhoods or other local areas. Local authorities will have the opportunity to seek direct participation from local people in shaping the future of their communities, taking their view on the type of development they would like to see and how it is to be laid out. Our concept of action plans is very much one which encourages planning to be undertaken close to the people who it most directly affects. (Ibid., para. 4.24)

How can a local planning authority expect to achieve this aspiration unless within the team undertaking work of this nature it has people who can engage with local people to discuss 'the type of development they would like to see and how it is to be laid out', based upon a good level of local knowledge and understanding? My answer to this question is that it cannot.

More generally, it seems to me that the recent thrust towards 'spatial planning' in Britain must by definition require of planners an intimate understanding of the spaces they seek to plan.

The Royal Town Planning Institute (RTPI, 2001) defines this approach as follows:

> Planning involves twin activities: the management of the competing uses for space; and the making of places that are valued and have identity. Our focus is on the location and quality of social, economic and environmental changes. In developing a *New Vision for Planning* we therefore use the term 'spatial planning'. We do so to emphasize that planning is as much concerned with the spatial requirements for, and impacts of, policies – even where these do not require a 'land use' plan – as it is with land use zonings. The interrelationships, for example, of governmental policy can only be properly demonstrated by consideration of their aggregate impacts for specific places. 'Spatial planning' operates at all the different possible scales of activity, from large scale national or regional strategies to the more localized design and organization of towns, villages and neighbourhoods. (Ibid., p. 2)

The implications of this approach, according to the RTPI, are set out in Box 4.2 in terms of three broad propositions:

- Successful spatial planning is sustainable.
- Successful spatial planning is integrated.
- Successful spatial planning is inclusive.

Box 4.2   The dimensions of spatial planning, according to the Royal Town Planning Institute

Successful spatial planning is sustainable

Sustainable planning integrates the objectives of economic development, social justice and inclusion, environmental integrity and integrated transport. There is often conflict between short-term economic and fiscal benefits and the longer term environmental and social implications arising from development. There is often no natural equilibrium between them. Planning must offer a means to mediate consciously between these competing objectives.

The resolution of these matters will require:

- Planning for the *long term* in order to effect the strategic shifts necessary to ensure change and to meet growing needs. As a corollary prudence requires us to take account of possible longer term consequences of action even where there is not yet unequivocal proof of adverse impacts. Planning decisions therefore cannot be based exclusively upon an open-ended presumption in favour of development.
- Planning for the *medium term* to ensure the careful consideration of social inequalities and wise use of natural resources. This must be based upon social as well as economic and environmental assessments to enable development impacts and requirements to be considered over their whole life-span.
- Planning for the *short term*, action orientated and responsive to changing circumstances and available opportunities, negotiating the directions of change set out in the longer term visions. This requires plans and planning to be integrated with delivery mechanisms, and to carry a genuine commitment to monitoring and review.

Successful spatial planning is integrated

Too often plans are made and planning decisions are taken on a restrictive land-use basis, without proper integration with other policy objectives. Planning needs to be developed on a more consistent, cross-cutting and collaborative approach.

- Spatial planning should take account of a much *wider set of issues* currently excluded from statutory systems of land-use planning, for example, inequalities in health and education, energy policy, the rural economy and urban design;
- Spatial planning should integrate and be an integral part of the *full range of public, corporate and community strategies and initiatives*;
- Spatial planning should be carried out according to *coherent, functional areas* and at local, regional and national levels, rather than being constrained unnecessarily by artificial administrative areas; and
- Spatial planning should be *linked to delivery mechanisms* through the expenditure programmes of all relevant government and corporate agencies.
- Spatial Planning should bring together a *wider range of professional skills and disciplines*.

→

Successful spatial planning is inclusive

The engagement of individuals and communities and regard for their respective rights have always been an integral part of planning processes. Public engagement in policy-making and action should engender partnership and collaboration, and enhance 'well being'. To achieve this, changes in the formal planning processes are required if we are to meet the expectations and aspirations for greater influence over the impacts of development and the quality of the environment.

Successfully negotiated outcomes carry a greater commitment from the parties involved and create a greater likelihood of implementation. We need to recognize however that effective planning cannot always be achieved through consensus. Where hard choices are required, clear and equitable decision-making frameworks are essential.

We also need to understand that conflicts are often resolved through the established power structures in ways which disadvantage those most in need. Planning as a truly societal activity must seek to give a voice to those excluded communities – those with a direct interest in creating a better 'world' but little power to influence it.

Planning processes, policies and outcomes therefore need:

- to embrace more fully a *respect for differences*, notably of gender and ethnicity; changes should be considered to guarantee the rights of all to be included in the process;
- to reduce *social and spatial inequalities* and not create new ones;
- to be negotiated through a process that is first *transparent* and second subject to *independent scrutiny and arbitration*; and
- to result in a *shared commitment* to act upon the agreed outcomes of discussion, and to review and update plans.

Source: Reproduced from RTPI (2001).

As we saw in Chapter 1, the British government takes a similar approach in describing the plan-making process:

> Spatial planning goes beyond traditional land use planning to bring together and integrate policies for the development and use of land with other policies and programmes which influence the nature of places and how they can function. (ODPM, 2005a, para. 30)

To repeat the style of rhetorical questioning used above, how can plans 'influence the nature of places' and how they can function without an intense understanding of the character of those places and their potential as a starting-point? Again, my answer is that they cannot, and in my view this has major implications for the kinds of skills that need to be present in the planning teams that are undertaking this type of work. In saying this, I acknowledge that there is still a lot of work to be done to be clear what exactly spatial planning is in various situations, and how in practice it will differ from (and be superior to) what are often described as the narrow land use planning approaches that preceded it. The critical literature, for example, suggests that there is still considerable scope to define and refine the ways in which people and organizations think of space, and that spatial planning approaches need careful thought in terms of the different scales at which they are expected to operate (Harris and Hooper, 2004; Shaw and Sykes, 2005). But nevertheless, if what this is about is place – looked at from spatial scales ranging from the international to the very local – and about modifying the ways in which various forms of policy-making activities impact upon place so as to emphasize the place at least as much as the policy, then planners need to start from an understanding of what characterizes places not just in terms of their own perceptions but from the perspectives of their users. And if the task of planning is to integrate and modify the impact of a range of functional policies upon place, planners' title to speak to the authors of those functional policies must surely be that they bring to the table an intimate knowledge of the very thing those functional professionals are not likely to have – namely, place.

The nature of place-making

As Heather Campbell asks in her introduction to the discussion in the Interface section of *Planning Theory and Practice* in its June 2003 edition (Campbell, 2003), is there more to the process of place-making than urban design? My answer to this question would be an emphatic yes, but it is an important question to ask because in recent years in Britain this space does seem to have been extensively colonized by arguments about and proponents of urban design. That comment is not made in any way to disparage the process of urban design or to suggest that it isn't really very important, but comes from an experience of how people respond to and feel about places that suggests strongly to me that this is not only a function of the process of physical design. At the beginning of this chapter I identified five elements which in my view all contribute to developing place-based understanding, and these are worth repeating here just to underline the point that place-making isn't just about urban design. The five were:

- the history of places;
- the factors that have forged the way they are today, and that have shaped the ways people use them;
- the forces that are already at work shaping what they will be like tomorrow;
- their natural and built environments at both the micro and the macro scales;
- the things about localities that people value.

A fairly brief inspection of that list will demonstrate that while urban design dimensions can be identified in each instance, there are many other components as well to each element. Of course, a very broad definition of urban design could be seen as encompassing much more than the manipulation of buildings and spaces in order to create a physical environment, and this appears to be the approach that the Urban Task Force chaired by Lord Rogers was working towards in its report (Urban Task Force, 1999). Lord Rogers in his introduction to that report puts this as follows:

> We need a vision that will drive the urban renaissance. We believe that cities should be well designed, be more compact and connected, and support a range of diverse uses – allowing people to live, work and enjoy themselves at close quarters – within a sustainable urban environment which is well integrated with public transport and adaptable to change.
>
> Urban neighbourhoods must become places where people of all ages and circumstances want to live. We have to increase investment in our urban areas, using public finance and incentives to steer the market towards opportunities for lasting regeneration. And we must all take responsibility for the process of change, combining strengthened democratic local leadership with an increased commitment to public participation. (Ibid., p. 8)

So, a strong approach to urban design is needed, but in turn it needs to be set within a wide ranging set of other initiatives if the process of regenerating existing run-down urban areas is to be successful. This theme is continued further in Richard Rogers's subsequent book with Anne Power, where as part of the discussion of these issues (Rogers and Power, 2000, pp. 226–35) there is an attempt to define what design means in this context, what problems it faces, how to organize this kind of work, and what problems that in turn faces. These views are summarized in Box 4.3.

It is possible to see many of the approaches to urban design that were adopted in the twentieth century in very critical terms, however, and in particular to see these various strands of opinion as a push to tackle problems when the cure was often worse than the disease; see, for example, the polemical approach to this issue of Jane Jacobs in *The Death and Life of Great American Cities*, which is sub-titled 'The Failure of Town Planning' because she sees planning as seeking to impose new orders which are not grounded in the virtues of what already exists (Jacobs, 1964). The seductiveness of the grand vision rather than the incremental approach to change is also easy to understand, and yet it may often be the incremental approach that is much more grounded in a careful understanding of the way places work and

---

Box 4.3 Urban design in the regeneration of urban areas, according to Rogers and Power

- Rogers and Power take a very broad view of what constitutes design. They see it not merely as a process of ordering the built environment, but also as a process of manipulating the physical environment in order to achieve social ends.
- They see many of the problems of design as being not merely about limitations in the availability of design skills themselves but also as being about the limits to the relationship between physical design and social order, which they see as being exacerbated by a lack of public participation.
- The key process points they identify are around seeing urban design as a problem-solving activity, which needs to engage effectively with all the stakeholders in the process and also to link with funding and other resource-allocation processes, including those that are political in nature.
- They see management structures as often getting in the way of urban design processes, by too often being (among other things) top-heavy, insufficiently supportive and overly bureaucratic.

Source: This is a summary of the views expressed in Rogers and Power, 2000, p. 232.

---

people utilize them than is the grand vision, especially when it is imported from the outside and is conceived not from the particularities of the place but from the personal beliefs of the designer (see the discussion in Schoon, 2001, pp. 218–23). Debate about such issues will probably never end, but certainly in my experience (which was mainly in the management of incremental change in urban Britain) urban design was an important part of the process of place-making but by no means its sole component. At the same time, there was undoubtedly an element of negative public reaction to some of the things done in its name in the past, and so we shouldn't be too surprised that this track record breeds suspicion in some quarters rather than an open-armed welcome.

It seems to me that the nature of the place-making task must inevitably be dependent upon the circumstances in which one is working. The five elements mentioned above will be present in each location, but their nature and characteristics will vary substantially. For example, the construction of what are in effect new suburban communities as part of the continued attraction of retirees to Florida must in these terms be a very different proposition from the fine-grained construction of single buildings and the refurbishment of others in a complex urban place like Manchester City Centre. And equally, the process of redeveloping an inner city location with a substantial amount of brownfield land, as was experienced in much of East Manchester in the 1980s and 1990s, is a very different one in many ways to the process of managing change in a popular suburb such as Didsbury, where market forces at the same time were all pushing in the same direction and a lot of local residents were unhappy about what they saw as the consequences of over-development caused by this market interest. The common threads linking all these situations are the need to understand the five elements that I have described as shaping place-making in those particular circumstances, the need in particular to understand the characteristics of the locality well, and the need to work with the people who are active in that locality or (in their absence) to understand the needs of those likely to be in that position in future.

One of the things from my own experience that I think helps planners the most in these terms is the lessons available from living with the consequences of past decisions. It is too easy, and too common, for planners to be involved in making decisions at one point in time but to have moved on by the time the developments permitted have been built and occupied. Sometimes this is unavoidable, but where things can be organized so as to permit this to happen it is one of the best learning experiences available to planners. In particular, the views of occupiers, neighbours and users of new development come together to create a sense of what it has achieved, and in turn to offer lessons about the management of change in that locality which it is difficult to create by other means. This is another of the reasons why I am strongly in favour of a patch-based system in the organization of the delivery of public planning services, and also why I support keeping staff in those sorts of positions (other things being equal) for significant periods of time. I think it is also helpful in these terms from time to time to undertake site visits with elected members to look at the consequences of past decisions and not just (as is common in British local government) to look at the sites of current controversies.

That having been said, there is a great deal of material to help planners with their own contributions to the process of place-making, be this by incremental change or by larger-scale developments, and it is far from being the case that the only tools available to planners are the (sometimes hard) lessons gained from their own experiences. In Britain in recent years, for example, the work of the Commission for Architecture and the Built Environment (CABE) has produced several useful pieces of advice (see, for example, DTLR and CABE, 2000; DTLR and CABE, 2001; DETR and CABE, 2001). More generally, there are several valuable reflective volumes which provide helpful advice and raise important questions about elements of the process of place-making (see for example Parfect and Power, 1997; Punter and Carmona, 1997; Fyfe, 1998; Imrie and Hall, 2001). But none of this is a substitute for understanding the nature and character of places, understanding how people experience them and what they think about them, and learning from the experiences (good or ill) of previous planned interventions in them.

Conclusions

This chapter has ranged far and wide, but at its heart is a simple point. Planning is about making places better for people, and to do that it is necessary to develop both an intimate understanding of how places work and of what people think about them. There are many sources for developing understandings of this nature, as this chapter has discussed, but in my view it is likely that such understandings will be best built up over a period of time rather than being instantly acquired from a single site visit, useful though this can be. It is worth remembering in this context that this will also be the experience of many of the customers of the planning service – they will have got to know the places where they live, work or undertake other activities over a significant period of time, and will often react badly to proposals to change these places when they see them as being uncaring about the things they value or not being grounded in an understanding of the fine grain of those places. Sometimes this may reflect innate conservatism, because my experience was that people were often comfortable with the familiar and hostile to the unfamiliar. But often opposition of this nature reflects a knowledge and understanding which is capable of making a positive contribution to efforts to improve the locality, and is simply not being taken into account. If planning really is about working with people to improve their places, and not imposing views on them based upon a feeling of professional superiority, then it is important that planners find ways of tapping into this wealth of public knowledge and of working with it. If planners could do this more successfully, it would have the potential to close some of the gaps between the planning process and the general public that have been referred to elsewhere. The starting-point for activities of this nature must be a detailed knowledge of places and of what people think about them, and in this context there is no substitute for deep immersion over quite long periods of time. As Gert-Jan Hospers put it, when reviewing the contemporary relevance of the views of Jane Jacobs, particularly in a Dutch context:

> Vision, creativity, an eye for what exists and common sense are, according to Jacobs, indispensable. Thus, her message to present day planners and city authorities is simple: put your tennis shoes on, get into the city and take a fresh look! (Hospers, 2003, p. 211)

Self-assessment topics

1. Identify a part of a place that you really like. Why do you like it? What can you understand about other people's views about that locality? How might it be changed for the better?
2. Now identify a part of a place that you really don't like very much. Why do you dislike it? What are other people's views about this locality? In particular, are there people who value it, and if so why? Is it possible to change the things you don't like about it while retaining the things that others say that they do like?
3. Find someone who has lived in an area for a long period of time and who is willing to talk to you about that experience. Try to get them to tell you what living in the area was like at various points in their lives, what they liked and what they disliked about that experience at each of these points in time, and how they have reacted to any significant physical changes in the area during this period. Try to understand what are the main forces that have shaped their views of the area over this period, and the extent to which and the ways in which these have changed over time.
4. Find any development issue that has received significant coverage in the local media over a reasonable period of time. What form did that coverage take? What factors appear to have shaped that coverage? Does this portray a positive or a negative view of the planning process, and do you think that in the particular circumstances that is a reasonably fair view to present?
5. Identify any locality of your choosing, and try to assemble a portfolio of material of various kinds which captures the essential character of that area. Identify the ways in which the planning process should tackle the key issues facing that area in the light of your assessment of its character.

Chapter 5

Customer Skills

Introduction

This chapter treats planning as an activity that has customers whose needs providers of planning services set out to meet, in many of the same ways that apply to the customer relationships of many other services and activities. This has always been the case for the consultancy sector of planning practice, of course, but for the public sector this is a more recent idea which in some circles was resisted because planners saw themselves as being responsible for a general public interest which was by definition superior to individual interests (see Kitchen, 1991). That particular argument (that planning is about an overarching and superior public interest) was linked in some minds to the idea of planning as a technical process discussed in Chapter 2, with part of the technical skill of the planner being to understand and to articulate this interest. While there are (entirely properly) still lots of debates about whose interests planning serves (see for example the discussion in Rydin, 2003, ch. 7), this idea of an overarching public interest identified and operationalized by planners has largely been replaced by a more conditional view of planning as a process of pursuing articulated and agreed goals which have emerged after (quite intensive) public debates. Individual and group interests can thus be seen within this context, one hopes on the basis that they have played a part in shaping the agreed direction for the locality in question.

This chapter is thus mainly about planning as a public sector activity with a range of conflicting customer demands to attempt to satisfy. Many of these customers may well in turn be helped to pursue their interests within this framework by their own planning advisers, be these in-house members of staff, consultants, or planning aid volunteers working with community groups.

This issue of the conflicting views about whose interests ought to be served has been a particular problem for planning as a public sector service for a long time, as the classic study of Chicago by Meyerson and Banfield (1955) vividly demonstrated. In Britain, the radically different views of the planning process in Newcastle in the 1960s presented by Burns (1967), writing as city planning officer, and by Davies (1972), writing as a passionate advocate of those on the receiving end of that service, reflect a fundamental divide between a public sector planner convinced that he and his team were working for the greater good of the city as a whole and a community-based researcher equally convinced that this process was not actually operating in the interests of many of the poorest people in the city. The problem of defining interests has not been anything like such a difficult issue for most planners who have worked outside the public sector, however, since planners who act as consultants or who work for community groups and organizations are in practice working for particular and usually well-defined interests, which it is their job to represent. The enormous divide reflected in the stances of Burns and Davies is not an inevitable consequence of the different positions of public sector planner and community-based critic, however. It is possible, for example, for a chief planner of a large city to acknowledge that the operations of the development process can all too easily work in favour of wealthy property-owning interests and against the interests of the urban poor, and to set about as a consequence with tacit or explicit political support trying to use the planning process to achieve benefits for deprived communities that they would not otherwise have obtained. Norman Krumholz is explicit about adopting this stance during his period as the city of Cleveland, Ohio's, planning director throughout much of the 1970s, and his book with John Forrester (Krumholz and Forrester, 1990) reflects this approach (which he calls 'equity planning') in its title. I suspect that approaches to issues of this nature might be culturally specific, but in principle there is no reason why planning officers in many parts of the world could not adapt this way of looking at their task to their own local circumstances.

The stance taken by this chapter is that planning services irrespective of their sectoral location have identifiable customers, and that as a consequence it is a basic part of the skills package that planners need in order to operate effectively that they should understand who these customers are, what their needs are, and how to begin to relate to them. Indeed, there is some evidence from a recent British study which suggests that in some quarters at least the communication skills associated with working with customers are regarded as being among the most important skills that planners will need to possess in the future (Durning and Glasson, 2004b). Since the definition of customers appears to be at its broadest in relation to planning as a public sector activity, it is this definition that will be used for the purposes of this chapter. For these purposes, it is important to acknowledge the point that the term 'customer' is not used here to imply someone paying for a service, but rather is used because it denotes a well-understood relationship of entitlement between customer and provider. For some planning services, for example that of consultancy, the customer–provider relationship may be directly franked by the making of a payment. For many others, particularly in relation to public sector planning services, the issue of entitlement to service will be settled through the political process. Here, the resource levels made available for service provision will usually be accompanied by explicit and implicit guidance about how and for whom such services should be provided. Even in this case, however, it should be noted that the service still has to be paid for via the taxation system (plus, increasingly in Britain, what the planning service can also raise through its own income generation activities), and thus customers are paying indirectly as well as through charges for specific services such as fees for planning applications. The relationship here is not such a direct one as is the case with consultancy; the payment of local taxes, which among many other things contributes to meeting the costs of running a public sector planning service, does not carry with it an entitlement to a specific quantity of service. There is a terminological debate that could take place about the use of 'customer' as distinct for example from 'user', 'client' or 'stakeholder', and when writing about this in the early 1990s my preference was to use the term 'client' (Kitchen, 1991). But rather than enter into this debate here, the term 'customer' has been used because it conveys best the nature of the service relationship being described in language that is well understood, since everyone has extensive experience from their daily lives of what entitlements arise from being a customer irrespective of how the particular relationship with providers gets paid for.

This is not to argue that planning as a public sector activity is only about meeting the needs of a series of sectoral customers. To argue that customers can be identified and that their needs can be met is not to deny that public organizations charged by law to act in the public interest cannot and do not identify stances and policies that override sectoral interests, even if only because in democratic societies this is what governments at all levels are constitutionally responsible and politically accountable for. But it is to say that appeals to a wider public interest are not a substitute for thinking hard about who the customers are who constitute this interest and how they are affected by it. And it is also to say that the claim to be acting in a wider public interest needs to be subject to proper scrutiny, because it can be a cloak for sloppy thinking rather than a stance of transcending virtue. Thus, the recognition that, for example, development plans should be about how a locality can be helped to change physically, in ways that meet the objectives agreed for it by the responsible political authorities and in response to the needs of its communities, is not a substitute for thinking about the customer needs that will arise throughout the operation of the planning service in that locality; rather, it is a starting-point for thinking about how best to meet these needs. There is no more space in this book for debating the theoretical arguments surrounding this stance, but for some of the debate on these matters see Ross (1991), Taylor (1994), and Brooks (2002, pp. 53–8). For a review of some of these issues in the context of strategic planning as a public activity see Kaufman and Jacobs (1996).

After this introduction, the chapter examines the major customer clusters likely to be served by planners. This identification of the main customers is followed by a discussion of their needs and aspirations and how as a consequence they may well behave in planning situations, and of how the planning service can best meet customer needs in these circumstances. The need to seek and to interpret customer feedback on the quality and quantity of planning services available is also discussed. Finally, because developments in the use of information technology have the potential to change quite radically the nature of the interactions between planners and their customers, the discussion in this chapter also reflects on some aspects of this potential. The chapter closes with some self-assessment topics designed to help readers to explore some of the issues raised herein for themselves.

The customers of the planning service

I have elsewhere (Kitchen, 1997, ch. 2) defined the customers of the planning service from the perspective of someone who worked for a long time in British local government. This definition is repeated here in Box 5.1, because it represents a broad basis for seeking to understand who the customers of the local government planning service in Britain actually are. But it is not a substitute in any given situation for thinking carefully about who the customers of planning services in that particular set of circumstances might be, and it is certainly not offered as an all-encompassing definition of planning customers. It may well be the case, however, that to one degree or another these broad groupings are represented in most planning systems.

It is important to note that not all of the customers listed in Box 5.1 will automatically present themselves to planners wherever a planning situation arises which impinges on their interests. It is often necessary for planners to go out and seek views or responses from their customers, rather than sitting back and waiting for those customers to come forward. This is one of the reasons why it is important to identify and to think systematically about the needs of customers in planning; if this does not happen, and if planners and their employers take a passive view about the people who present themselves, there is a real danger that important views and interests will not be on the table when planning decisions are taken. And this is not likely to be randomly distributed across the community either, as a simple example from my own experience in Manchester will illustrate. It was a commonplace experience in handling the development control process in the city that consultations in the relatively affluent wards of its southern area would attract a much higher level of public response than would equivalent consultations in many parts of the inner city. This did not necessarily mean that local

> ## Box 5.1   The major customer clusters for planning services in British local government
>
> 1. Applicants for planning permission
> 2. Local residents affected by planning applications in an area
> 3. The wider general public in an area
> 4. The business community
> 5. Interest or pressure groups in the community
> 6. Other agencies whose actions impinge on the development process
> 7. Other departments of the local authority
> 8. The elected members of the council
> 9. The formal control mechanisms of central government
> 10. Purchasers of planning services

people cared less about planning and environmental issues in one part of the city as compared with another, although sometimes that might have been true. Nor did it necessarily mean that people in the inner city were more acquiescent towards local developments that had adverse consequences for their immediate living environments than were people in the more affluent suburbs, although again this might sometimes have been true. It certainly did not mean that because they made less noise about these sorts of issues, people in the inner city were less entitled to the protection afforded by the planning service from the adverse consequences of development than were people in the suburbs. What this experience actually reflected, in my opinion, was a much more societal phenomenon than any of these explanations. For reasons both of education and of life experience, many inner city residents simply do not participate in consultative exercises of this kind, and they do not join the kinds of civic and amenity groups often to be found in more suburban areas that frequently orchestrate (and often very effectively) the process of getting views expressed about these sorts of matters. A failure to recognize that there are significant differences of this kind within individual cities could easily lead planning services and individual planners to form quite erroneous conclusions from the presence or absence of views in response to planning consultation exercises.

It is clear that these customer clusters are of very different types, and that they are likely in many cases to be pulling in different directions from each other. Indeed, this may well be one of the distinguishing features in these terms between the position of the public sector planner, who is trying to satisfy as many customer needs in any given situation as is practicable, and the position of the planner working for a particular sector among these clusters or working as a consultant to a defined cluster. Even in these latter instances, however, the planner in giving advice about how the customer organization or individual may best secure its ends in any particular situation will need to be aware of how the operations of that particular customer will fit into the overall decision-making process. Thus, even for the planner working for say a developer, or a community group or a public sector quango, knowledge of how that organization's concerns will relate to the totality both of the issues to be addressed and of the interests likely to be represented will be an important component of the process of giving effective advice to the customer about how to influence the outcome in its own best interests.

Note that organizations or individuals at the same or at different points in time can fall into more than one of these clusters of customers. For example, applicants for planning permission may also be part of the business community and at times may also be purchasers of planning services. Similarly, local residents affected by planning applications in an area may also be members of interest or pressure groups in the community, and in a small number of cases may also be officials working for departments of councils or indeed elected members of those councils. This list of the major customers of local government planning services in Britain is thus an analytical construct linked to the roles that are played in planning decision-making, rather than a list of organizations and individuals separated out into watertight compartments. Remember as well that in any planning situation there are likely to be a series of multilateral relationships at work, rather than just a set of two-way relationships between planners and each cluster of customer. For example, local residents affected by a planning application may well try to make direct representations to applicants about changes they would see as desirable, as well as making representations to planners consulting them about the application; and in some instances developers are encouraged to consult informally with local residents before submitting a planning application so that the submitted scheme can take residents' reactions into account. Equally, both the business community and local interest or pressure groups often have very good contacts with councillors, and frequently seek to make use of these links to raise points about planning issues, especially matters that are controversial, before they are formally presented to elected members to enable decisions to be taken. Thus, planners' relationships with customers form but a part of a complex web of interactions likely to be taking place at any rate on the most controversial planning matters, often in turn fuelled by the publicity provided as a result of local media coverage. The complexity of such processes needs to be understood as the context within which planners develop their customer relationships.

The key characteristics of the main customer clusters

At the risk of stating the obvious, *what applicants for planning permission* and their agents want ideally from the planning service is a positive decision taken as quickly as possible. A relatively high proportion of planning applications are fairly straightforward and not particularly contentious, and thus this objective can often be met as to the outcome even if perhaps not always at the speed developers would wish. Most planning authorities in Britain end up approving at least 80 per cent of applications, and so while it is not always possible at the outset of the process to tell whether an individual application is likely to fall into this group, other things being equal statistically the odds are very much in its favour. Research on the experience of applicants with the development control process suggests that their main concern is the time the process takes rather than the fairness of the process (McCarthy *et al.*, 1995, ch. 3), and this may reflect the statistical probability that in most cases their applications were approved.

By 2001, when the government had concluded that radical changes needed to be made to the English planning system if its performance was to be improved, the inability of the system to determine a sufficient proportion of applications within statutory target time periods was seen as one of the main problems of the development control process (DTLR, 2001). The solution adopted was a combination of sticks and carrots – a more intensive targeting regime and some quite sizeable financial incentives via the Planning Delivery Grant mechanism. In its own terms this appears to have worked well, in the sense that the measured performance of the system as a whole improved and that of some of the previous worst performers improved spectacularly (Addison and Associates and Arup, 2004; 2005). At the same time, this kind of target-driven regime has given rise to criticisms from people acting on behalf of development clients to the effect that perverse behaviour is taking place in order to massage the figures, and that the real interests of those clients are actually being prejudiced by these processes (see, for example, Halman, 2004). In other words, this obsession with speed of decision-making as a measured end was not necessarily shared by development clients if it resulted in actions which harmed their interests.

Notwithstanding this recent focus on the time taken to determine planning applications, sensible developers and agents who know the system have always been able to mitigate the adverse consequences of a delay in decision-making to an extent by ensuring as far as possible that the process of getting the planning application determined occurs in parallel with other components of the development process rather than as one in a sequence of steps where unanticipated delay can hold up every other step (Syms, 2002, ch. 9). The position starts to become more complicated when a submitted scheme is not straightforward or proves to be controversial, because short of an outright refusal what usually happens is a process of negotiation. My experience in these situations was that within certain limits most developers would prefer to negotiate with the local planning authority for one or any combination of a least three interrelated reasons:

- If an approval is probably capable of being secured, attempting this is usually judged to be preferable to relying on the uncertainties of the appeal system.
- Time often does literally mean money for development interests when they have borrowed at market interest rates to fund their developments, and thus a satisfactory negotiation with the local planning authority, because it can be much quicker than the successful outcome of an appeal, can be financially the more attractive option.
- Most developers recognize that their development will have to live alongside its immediate neighbours for a long time, and thus a negotiation process which can help resolve problems of this kind can actually be beneficial for the development. It should be remembered in this context that a very high proportion of property development is actually on a relatively small scale and is undertaken by owner-occupiers, who have a clear and direct interest in reaching a sensible accommodation with neighbours, rather than by the rapacious property developers much beloved of the media. Occasionally, developers whose intention is not to occupy the property but to sell it on to other end-users don't think about the consequences for those users of needing to live in long-term harmony with their neighbours, but that seems to me to be a sign of poor market awareness on their part which might return to haunt them when it comes to finding future owners or tenants.

This gives planners quite a powerful opportunity to achieve improvements to schemes in the interests of their other customers. But it also raises suspicions in the minds of many people who are not directly party to these negotiations that planners may in fact be favouring development interests at the expense of others. My experience was that the only way to respond effectively to these very understandable kinds of suspicions (and planners probably need to recognize that it will not eradicate them completely) is to make sure that the reports that are written for decision by elected members, which are public documents, cover both what the intentions behind such negotiations were and how much they actually achieved.

Local residents affected by planning applications have two primary requirements:

- that the planning system should protect them from what they see as the adverse consequences of development; and
- that they should know about development issues that may affect them, be consulted about those matters, and have the opportunity to have their views taken into account as part of the decision-making process.

There are clear difficulties with the first of these requirements, because the planning system both in Britain and in most other parts of the world cannot act as a kind of all-encompassing local environmental policeman, even though in my experience that did at times appear to be the expectation of some members of the public. In Britain, for example, certain types and scales of development do not require planning permission at all, and although generally speaking these do not have significant consequences for neighbours occasionally they can have; and in any event, perceptions of these matters can often be distorted, for example if a neighbour dispute is involved. Even in cases where planning applications are needed, local planning authorities cannot simply refuse them because neighbours object. Generally speaking, the planning system is not an effective tool for resolving neighbour disputes, and of course it was never designed to perform this function. Similarly, planning is not intended to be a local head-counting exercise, but rather is meant to be policy-led so that applications which conform broadly with current planning policies can expect to benefit from that conformity. It can be very difficult to explain to an irate neighbour that an application for a house extension next door meets all the local planning authority's policies for such developments, and therefore that there is no scope for refusing it on the basis of that person's objections, but this is nonetheless what will need to be done in this situation. This underlines the importance of having policy packages in development plans which offer a fair balance between the rights of local people to a reasonable degree of protection (and indeed improvement) of their quality of life and the recognition that land and property development is an essential and often beneficial component of urban living, and also of having as good a level of publicity and consultation about these policy packages as can be achieved. The point about knowing about development issues in the locality and having the opportunity to comment on them should be relatively straightforward, in the sense that it is about the efficiency of a bureaucratic machine in identifying the need for such consultations and then in carrying them out. Even here, however, when local planning authorities carried out such activities by a letter of consultation or by posting a site notice, it was a common occurrence to find after the event that people said that they had not been consulted, even when the planning authority had undertaken its standard tasks. This really could not be taken as evidence of a massive failure of the postal system (because in my experience non-delivery rates in some areas would have had to be very high to account for all the claims people made about non-consultation), but often reflected the fact that people do sometimes ignore letters from their local council when they arrive and do not realize later on when the claim about non-consultation is made that the letter thrown in the bin on arrival was in fact the consultation letter. One frequent problem with this approach was that the local planning authority defined the area within which it consulted relatively narrowly, and in my experience another of the explanations for non-consultation was that people living outside this defined area nevertheless expected to be consulted. This is one example of the phenomenon of rising public expectations discussed in Chapter 1, and the response to it during my time as city planning officer of Manchester was a steady widening of consultation areas – which didn't seem to stop the complaints of this kind. Similarly, site notices can be removed or vandalized, and in any event it is not clear that people always spot or read a site notice that has been posted, especially when it is written in fairly legal language (as many still are). In the electronic age, many of these difficulties should be more easily handled by open electronic forms of consultation, but even here it is not clear as yet that this will achieve 100 per cent penetration of local publics; and the likelihood must be that those least likely to access and use electronic means of consultation will be the poorest and most socially excluded sections of society.

A particularly problematic issue in this context, which I certainly experienced from time to time, is the relationship between development control consultation and the development plan. Objectors to specific proposals sometimes have to be told (or become aware) that the application will be determined in accordance with a policy in the development plan, and what becomes clear fairly quickly is that what they are really objecting to is that policy. The problem can be that the policy was settled through a process that happened a while ago, and in my experience the typical response to this tended to be a complaint to the effect that the objector should have been consulted on that policy at that time and wasn't. Very often, the explanation for this state of affairs was that the specific policy was buried in a raft of material in a plan of which the objector took no notice at the time. Again, my experience was that many people found local policies of this kind written into plans very difficult to relate to, and didn't really register planning issues until they took the form of a firm development proposal, despite the fact that the basic principle of the system is that policies are settled via the plan-making process and then implemented via the development control process. This kind of problem is likely to become more common the more the planning system genuinely becomes 'plan-led', and so the challenge to planners is to get people to engage more effectively in plan-making processes by explaining clearly what policies are likely to mean in terms of the kinds of applications they would support. The potential payoff for this is that it might rebalance public interest more towards plan policies (where arguably it should be anyway) and less towards their implementation in the form of specific development proposals, although there is no prospect that this would eliminate representations about the latter, especially around matters of detail.

Where it can be established beyond doubt that an error of this kind has occurred, this can be the territory of a reprimand from the local government ombudsman; and in Britain planning cases are the second most common source of cases after housing cases. Seneviratne (1994, pp. 83–120) describes the system of operation of the local government ombudsman in Britain, and shows that housing over the period 1987–92 accounted for 39–41 per cent of all complaints and planning a further 28–30 per cent. The main complaint types listed are failure to consult neighbours about a proposed development, failure to take proper account of objections made to a proposed development, giving incorrect or unclear advice about the need for planning permission, and failure to enforce planning conditions. Thus, while it is clearly the operation of the development control process that is responsible for most of the planning complaints to the local government ombudsman, it should also be noted that these areas of complaint are often also areas where the development control system exhibits the discretionary characteristics that are a hallmark of the British system (Booth, 1996).

The reason why *the wider general public in an area* is such an important customer cluster for the planning service is not merely because the planning process is supposed to operate in the interests of the communities it is designed to serve. It is also because the quality of the planning service itself can be improved by tapping into the information and local knowledge base that this wider general public represents. As noted in Chapter 3, during my time as city planning officer of Manchester we had a ratio of one planning staff member to every 4000 people. Most gamblers would regard odds of 4000 to 1 as being very poor. It is possible dramatically to improve these odds, however, by seeing the knowledge and understanding that people have about their localities as an asset which most planners could not hope to match except by living in a particular location for a long period of time, and thus by trying to work in partnership with local people. In practice, this will tend to be via active members of the local community often organized in civic societies or residents' associations rather than with the general public at large, but such linkages can provide a very valuable 'eyes and ears' service for planners that can be very helpful for example in spotting potential planning enforcement matters.

My experience of the *local business community* was that it was often characterized by a desire for stability. In this sense, it is important that it is not confused with the cluster of applicants for planning permission, the vast majority of whom in any event – as has already been said – will be householders or local small businesses rather than large-scale property developers. In addition, of those who are developers, some will be 'out-of-town' rather than local, and some will be undertaking development to sell it on rather than retaining a long-term stake in it (and therefore in the community in which it sits). The reason why, generally speaking, the local business community wants a sense of stability from the planning system is that many (although not all) of its members see themselves as long-term participants in the community, with an important relationship between the health of their business and the general health and welfare of the community. Thus they expect the planning service not to take action which will prejudice their business operating environment, and they would certainly expect to be fully consulted about any matters of this nature that might arise. Local planning issues of this kind that would typically be the subject of discussion would be matters to do with the local transportation network and the servicing of their premises, matters affecting employee welfare, and matters of local environmental initiative or regulation. It should be acknowledged in this context that many members of the local business community have good political contacts, both directly and through their employees, and that their interests often chime with a local political desire to avoid job losses and to see existing companies expanding where that is feasible. These connections in Britain have probably been strengthened from the early and mid-1990s by the growth of local partnerships as the vehicles for many forms of regeneration, which very frequently include local business people among their private sector representation (Bailey, 1995).

The importance of *interest or pressure groups in the community* has already been referred to above when talking about the common mechanisms of contact between planners and the wider general public in an area. As well as civic societies or residents' associations, however, I have seen throughout my career a flowering of groups with a focus on issues or topics rather than with the kind of area focus taken by the former types of organizations. Within this, the most common is probably the wide range of environmental groups which now exist, although many others can also be found across a broad band of cultural interests and backgrounds. An example from my Manchester experience is the Peak and Northern Footpaths Society, which was very diligent in pursuing matters relating to public rights of way. Typically, such groups will have a clear focus, some knowledgeable members drawn from many walks of life, some good political contacts with elected members who share their interests, and quite often also an effective publicity machine. Just as civic societies or residents' associations can be effective allies for the planning service, so too can many interest groups; although planners need to be careful about this, because the agendas of many such groups may be in conflict and planners cannot afford to be seen to be 'in the pocket' of one such group at the expense of their relationships with all the others. By their nature, many such groups will be looking to relate to the planning service through the development of policy approaches or packages which reflect their interests, and will be arguing for these from an (often quite strong) local information base as well as from the convictions that have brought them together. Commonly, this sort of local information base can be a very valuable asset to the planning service, whether or not it agrees with all the policy prescriptions that may flow from this source.

The cluster of *other agencies whose actions impinge on the development process* covers a wide range of public or (in Britain) privatized former public agencies responsible for providing services that typically make them consultees on planning matters. Examples include statutory consultees such as English Heritage; utility providers in fields such as gas, electricity and water; major public services such as health, the police and transport; higher-education institutions such as universities or colleges; quangos established by the government of various kinds; and neighbouring parts of the local government structure. Characteristically, such organizations have a statutory basis for their existence, and a professional staffing structure. Very often also, they undertake in respect of their own functions policy planning activities that are recognizably close to the kinds of things that planners do when they prepare development plans, and typically planners are consulted on these documents just as planners consult these organizations on draft development plans. All of this gives organizations of this nature both status and respectability in their own fields, and they expect their inputs to the planning process to be taken seriously. Equally, they tend to look to the planning service to provide them with an appropriate level of support for their own activities, and this tends to lead to a premium being placed upon the development of effective formal and informal working relationships between such agencies and planning organizations. Such professional cosiness can look from the outside like a conspiracy from which people feel excluded, and as far as possible planners need to guard against giving this impression in the interests of all their other working relationships. At the same time, it is clearly essential that relationships of this kind do operate effectively. For example, local authorities within a conurbation clearly do need to work together on planning matters which affect the future of the conurbation as a whole, and the development of cooperative working arrangements between the planning staff of those authorities can depend at least as much on informal linkages as it does on the formal structures that exist to this end.

Linkages with *other departments of the local authority* are really very similar to those with the immediately preceding cluster, save for the important point that they are achieved within the framework of a single organization rather than between organizations. Most local councils are at one and the same time both a single organization (because that is often what the law says, and it is also likely to be what the political and officer leaderships of the authority will want to achieve) and a series of competing bureaucracies (because resources and political influence given to one can often be at the expense of another, and because in any event they reflect different interests and responsibilities). That is often very difficult for people outside the local authority to understand, in a sense rightly so because local authorities ought to be capable of behaving coherently rather than in fragmented or contradictory ways. But the reality is often that within councils there are both competitive and coop-erative elements in an uneasy set of relationships with each other, reflected in both the practices of officers and of elected members. There is also considerable variety in the arrangements here. For example, in some parts of Britain where unitary local government is in operation, highways engineers' comments on planning matters will come from another part of the same organization, whereas in other parts of Britain where two-tier local government is in operation these comments may well come from an organization that would fall into the previous clus-ter of customers. This should really make little difference, except per-haps in the sense that other authorities will not necessarily sign up for sets of corporate objectives or policies that departments of the same authority will share once these have been approved by the council. Often in practice one of the most difficult problems that planning services face is in dealing with development proposals emanating from other depart-ments of the same authority, especially when those turn out to be con-troversial and particularly when it transpires that those departments have done little or no public consultation before submitting an applica-tion. Consultees can find it very difficult to believe that a consultation exercise carried out by the planning department on a development pro-posal emanating from another part of the council is anything other than tokenism leading to a forgone conclusion; and really, since this is under-standable, planners have to try to do their best through informal and separate processes (difficult though this can be) to stop these kinds of situations from arising in the first place if they value their reputation for fairness.

The *elected members of the council* are covered quite fully as a cluster in Chapter 7 of this book, and so will not be dealt with separately here.

The *formal control mechanisms of central government* can at times be difficult to regard as a customer of the local government planning service, because the essence of the relationship is not the same as it is with the other customer clusters. Planning is by its nature about specific localities; it is about managing physical changes in places in the best interests of their resident and user communities. As such, there is a strong argument for planning services to be as diverse in their nature as are the places being served (Kitchen, 1996). This makes the role of national perceptions about the need for uniformity problematic, beyond basic provisions in law in terms of powers and responsibilities and per-haps some default provision. This description mirrors the relatively devolved approach that exists in some countries such as the USA, where the federal role relates more to the securing of funding for particular programmes than it does to anything else. In Britain, however, there has been some tension in these terms between the top-down view of plan-ning that appears at times to have been held in what is at the time of writing the Office of the Deputy Prime Minister (although the ministerial title with responsibility for planning changes frequently) and the essentially bottom-up view which is being argued for here, the consequence of which is that Britain appears to experience a more influential role for central government in local planning than is the case in many other countries. Certainly during my professional career in planning, one of the clearest trends has been the growing influence of national policy and the growing amount (and volume) of national planning policy documentation. Whatever people feel about this debate, however, there are probably at least three central government functions to which the local government planning service in Britain will need to continue to relate:

- The national and regional policies and programmes of government. While there is a debate to be had about how far these should go, there can surely be no argument that insofar as governments have national and regional policies and programmes local development plans should take them into account, hopefully as part of an iterative process rather than as an unchallengeable imposition.
- Funding programmes, especially where bidding is on a competitive basis, as is more frequently the case now in Britain. Local government, whatever it feels about this process, cannot usually afford to ignore funding opportunities of this nature, especially when its mainstream funding has been reducing in real terms.
- The appeals and plans inquiries systems, which (via the Planning Inspectorate, as a devolved arm of government) determine several thousand appeals each year against refusals of planning applications or the imposition of certain conditions on consents, and which deal with various forms of development plan inquiries as a stage in the statutory process between deposit and adoption.

Purchasers of planning services became a more serious component of the work of local planning authorities in Britain during the 1990s as an ever greater proportion of planning budgets got funded from this source rather than via local taxation. The trigger for this was the (related) reduction in real terms in the mainstream funding of local authorities and the growth in the scale of the income generated by the imposition of fees for planning applications; the relationship between these two is that they were both deliberate acts of policy by central government. One of the worries when planning application fees were originally introduced was that they might be seen by applicants (and, for that matter, by other parties to the process) as the purchasing of a planning permission. This does not appear to have materialized as a general phenomenon, since most developers simply regard the fee as a development cost which is on a small scale when compared with the other costs of development. What it did, however, was to create quite a sizeable income base; for example, income from all sources in Manchester in 1994/95 (my last full year as head of the planning service there) covered approximately one-third of the cost of delivering that service, and planning application fees were about 70 per cent of this income total. The other elements of income were funding for providing a development control agency service for Central Manchester Development Corporation (a central government quango which operated from 1988 to 1996 in the southern part of the city centre; see Deas *et al.*, 1999), and income generated by the sale of publications and information services of various kinds. The importance of these income streams to the budget of the service, from a position ten years previously when income had been negligible and five years previously when all income had gone into the council's central exchequer rather than being offset against the costs of the services generating it, meant that considerable attention had to be given to protecting and if possible enhancing this source. And this inevitably meant thinking about the needs of the customers that produce that income, and giving those customers a degree of priority. The significance of earned income as a means of funding public planning services has waxed and wained over the years, partly in response to different political views about this issue, but the weight attached to planning application fees, and therefore the fee levels that central government sets, as a component of the resource base for local planning authorities remains a major issue (Arup Economics and Planning and the Bailey Consultancy, 2002).

Relating to customer needs

The most important recognition in the task of relating to customer needs is an understanding of who customers are and what their needs are; this has been introduced in the previous section of this chapter. The second most important recognition is that these needs will often be in conflict with each other; it is not possible to satisfy all of the people all of the time. This is not an argument for not trying, however. It is an argument for thinking carefully about what planners are setting out to do and how they are setting out to do it.

I have certainly seen three sorts of strategies applied to this kind of situation by public sector planners that I would warn against:

• The first of these is a *minimalist stance*. This in effect says that trouble is usually caused by trying to do things, and therefore the best way to avoid trouble is to do as little as possible. There are some seductive aspects to this view, which is often held by very experienced administrators who have learned the strengths of this position through the school of hard knocks. One of these is that 'do nothing' is properly one of the options that ought to be examined in a situation, and it is sometimes a better option than any of the more action-oriented possibilities that might be canvassed. At the very least, the costs and benefits of action ought to be compared with those of inaction, rather than jumping in with both feet without considering first whether this will cause more problems than it will solve. Another argument in favour of a minimalist stance is that the process of change is usually disruptive, for example, in the sense that a smooth administrative machine that has been operating efficiently on well-worn tracks for a long time is likely to be less efficient at least for a while if it is required to change tracks. Arguments for change therefore need to be able to show not only that the gains to be achieved from the new stance are worthwhile, but also that the disruption caused by the process of getting there is insufficient to destroy this equation. I would argue, for example, that the mania for local government reorganization that has afflicted Britain since the 1960s, with structural changes affecting sizeable parts of the country carried out in each of the five decades spanning the period from the 1960s, has quite forgotten to take into account the disruption and inefficiencies caused by the process of change in itself in the pursuit of a holy grail that does not exist: the 'right' local government structure. Thus there are undoubtedly some useful warning notes to be picked up from considering minimalist strategies. At the same time, the reasons why minimalist strategies will not do as the answer to the problem of meeting as many customer needs in planning as possible are compelling. Much of the Western world has accepted planning as a desirable function of whatever local government arrangements exist because it offers the prospect of making our places better for their residents and their users than would be the alternatives in its absence, and thereby of improving the quality of people's lives. This sense that it is possible through the planning process to achieve worthwhile improvements is the driving force behind a great deal of planning activity and is the prime motivation of many planners, and the excessive caution that minimalist strategies can breed puts these attributes at risk. The second reason why minimalist stances are insufficient is that, while they might be valuable in terms of avoiding self-inflicted wounds, they are very poor at spotting opportunities and making the most of them. And the third reason is that what may appear to the cautious administrator as doing as little as possible in order to avoid trouble is not in fact a neutral act, but is a deeply conservative one that is likely to reinforce the existing balance of power in society. Planning is already open to the charge that the ways in which it operates tend to be reinforcing rather than redistributive in these terms (Ambrose, 1994), and planners adopting minimalist stances towards the planning function in local government are more likely to underline this criticism than are (for example) planners adopting the 'equity planning' stance argued for by Norman Krumholz and John Forrester described above, irrespective of the arguments that could be advanced about how successful such approaches have been. Thus, without denying that minimalist stances sometimes have a role to play as part of the planner's armoury, a minimalist strategy has severe limitations as a response to the need for public sector planners to try to achieve as much customer satisfaction as possible.

• The second strategy I have seen adopted in public sector planning, and would caution against in terms of the desire to achieve as much customer satisfaction as possible, is *the attempt to be what might be described as 'all things to all persons'*. The form this often takes is that, apparently as an exercise in good public relations, customers of the planning service go away from contacts with it believing that they received a sympathetic hearing and that the planners appeared to agree with their points of view. In a very short-term sense, this may appear to work; it can, for example, turn what would otherwise have been a very difficult meeting into a much easier occasion for all concerned. The difficulty with it over any period of time is that it simply does not stand up to scrutiny. There are two ways in particular in which this is likely to happen. The first is that, on issues ultimately requiring a decision by elected representatives, the planners will have to write a report which analyses the situation including the views of consultees and which gives advice. It is very difficult to maintain a position of being 'all things to all persons' in these circumstances, especially since reports of this nature in most Western societies usually become public documents by one means or another. The second is that, as has already been said, many customers as well as talking to planners also talk to each other on a regular basis, and those exchanges may well include commenting on dealings with planning staff. Behaviour of the all-things-to-all-persons type is therefore likely to come to light from these exchanges, and once planners develop a reputation among their customers for behaving in this way such a label can be very difficult to remove. In particular, it can adversely affect the perception that the planners that customers are working with are people of integrity, and this ought to be one of the strongest assets that planners take into these relationships. That said, there is an important difference between the all-things-to-all-persons stance and a position which says, 'We have come to this meeting to discover and to explore your views, as part of a process of gathering information and comment, and until we have completed that process among all consultees we aren't going to make any commitments to any particular set of views.' This latter perspective is an essential part of the process of gathering information, but unless it is carefully explained to customers that this is what is being done it can seem to those on the receiving end of it to be very similar to the all-things-to-all-persons stance. The key here is the need to explain what is being done in unambiguous terms, so that no false impressions are created.

• A third, and in some ways the most destructive, strategy to be avoided in looking at approaches to achieving customer satisfaction is what I would term *the 'middle-ground' strategy*, which I have seen adopted quite frequently in reporting on the results of public consultation. That in effect says, 'There are some views on one side of this argument and some views on the other side, which shows that probably we got it just about right.' This is seductive because it is a natural human reaction to look for self-justification, and also because on some occasions the search for the middle ground may be the best of the available solutions. But it is dangerous because it can so easily become a self-fulfilling prophecy. The fact of the matter is that in pluralist societies there usually are arguments advanced on all sides of the issue when public policy choices are up for discussion. Confirmation that this is the case is not at all the same thing as claiming justification thereby for the particular way the matter was expressed in the first place by planners. What this approach can also do is to discourage careful thought being given to what has been said by consultees, almost as if the only thing that matters is demonstrating that a range of views exists in order to point up the virtues of a middle-ground position. This can quickly reduce consultation exercises to mere tokenism, and ignoring people's comments on the grounds that they are balanced by someone else's opposing comments is an effective way to lose people's confidence. Finally, this approach can sanctify the middle ground, when the mere recognition of a status somewhere towards the middle of the spectrum may well be insufficient by itself to demonstrate that this is the most appropriate policy choice in all the circumstances. It is of course true that pluralist democracies do sometimes tend to go for this sort of position on the basis that it will be supported by (or disliked the least by) the greatest number of people, but planners serving democracies of this kind should not assume that this will automatically be the outcome and therefore steer towards it. Even where the adopted stance is to be found in this middle ground, there is often considerable scope to look at the ways in which policies are expressed and to find ways of accommodating a range of viewpoints and interests; but this is not likely to be achieved unless planners look carefully at what is being said, and do not discard it merely because it demonstrates that a range of views exists.

Elements of all three of these strategies can quite commonly be found in planning activities and documents. And as has been said, in each case there is something to be said for the stance, and sometimes part of it or something very close to it has a role to play among the range of responses that planners can adopt in seeking to achieve customer satisfaction. But none of these three strategies, or for that matter any combination of them, seems likely over a period of time to be successful in these terms, although the reasons this is likely to be the case offer several clues as to the sorts of stances that may be more effective.

Before going on to itemize what seem to me to be the essential features of an effective public sector planner committed to achieving as much customer satisfaction as possible across the range of customers to be served, however, it is important to discuss what can be the greatest stumbling-block in all of this unless it is handled carefully. This is the question of the planner's responsibility to the local planning authority. Part of this is the relationship of the employee to the employer. Planners are part of a public sector bureaucracy which is ultimately controlled by its elected members, and that is as it should be in a democracy. Not only should planners never forget this, but they should never allow this responsibility to be omitted from their relationships with all their other customers. There are many matters that should be determined via the political process, the basic structure of which is in turn dependent upon the ballot box, and planners should never try to pretend that they can do what is properly the prerogative of these processes. Even in the fragmented democracies of North American cities, where coalitions sometimes have to be assembled in order to get anything done and where a very high premium is placed as a consequence on planners working efficiently with various community groups, this point about the ultimate respect for the democratic process that one of its employees must maintain remains valid (Benveniste, 1989; Brooks, 2002, ch. 12). But the other part of the planner's responsibility to the local planning authority that adds complexity to this question of customer relationships is the matter of what local planning authorities are actually charged to do. In Britain, most planning decisions are actually taken by local planning authorities acting in what they regard as the public interest, whatever theoretical and practical difficulties there may be in defining what this is, and one of the tasks of planners employed by those authorities is to give them advice about what these decisions should be. This means that planners have to give their authorities the best advice they can about these matters in the prevailing circumstances, and then do their best to implement the decisions of the council, whether or not their advice was taken on any particular matter. Indeed, this position is encompassed within the classic definition of the roles of a local government chief officer in Britain, which are (my wording):

- To give the best advice possible to the council in all the circumstances, without fear and without favour.
- To implement the decisions of the council loyally and in the most effective ways possible.
- To manage the resources made available for the service by the council efficiently and effectively, so that the highest achievable standards of service are attained within the council's policy and financial frameworks.

Such responsibilities may not sit easily alongside the notion of trying to achieve as much customer satisfaction as is possible across the range of customers identified in this chapter, but nonetheless this is the balance that the effective public sector planner must attempt to strike. That individual is helped considerably in this task by a recognition of three points:

- Councils would normally want service delivery to operate on the basis of achieving as good a level of customer satisfaction as possible.
- Councils usually acknowledge that they can make better decisions when armed with good quality information about people's views, attitudes, needs and wishes than they can in the absence of such information.
- Councils would usually expect their officials to be helpful to the customers of services, and to be open and honest about the council's decision-making procedures and responsibilities.

Drawing all of this together, I have argued elsewhere (Kitchen, 1997, pp. 37, 38) that there are at least seven characteristics of effective planner behaviour for public sector planners who wish to pursue the objective of achieving as much customer satisfaction as possible. These are summarized in Box 5.2. The contexts of Box 5.2 can be boiled down to seven key words:

- competence
- integrity
- fairness
- listening
- flexibility
- opportunism
- relationships

It will be noticed immediately that these are not unique to planners, and they are not offered on the basis that they are peculiar to that particular group of people. Many of them, for example, draw heavily on communication skills, which are an essential component of the skills packages of competent professionals in many walks of life. What is important about them is that they constitute a package, each element of which reinforces the others. None of this can be seen as a guarantee of success, or indeed as an assurance that customer relations will always be smooth if planners display these behavioural characteristics continuously. Nor is it being pretended that these characteristics are easy to maintain as a package in the long-run job of relating to customers. It was said to me after I had covered this ground in one conference presentation that I had omitted the possession of a thick skin from this list of planner characteristics, and in the sense that public sector planners are inevitably in a difficult position in trying to operate effectively in a system where planning decisions often create winners and losers out of the customers of the planning service this is a very understandable

Box 5.2 The characteristics of effective planner behaviour by public sector planners

1. We have to be seen as competent professionals by the people we relate to. This means being able to bring both substantive and procedural knowledge to the table which adds to what is already available to our customers, and being able to communicate that knowledge in ways that are intelligible across the range of customers to be served. If we cannot carry conviction in these terms it is difficult to see how we could be successful in other ways.

2. We have at all times to be seen to be behaving with integrity. If we say something we have to mean it, and not to change it simply because we think somebody else would like to hear something else. Similarly, we have to be open and honest about what we can and cannot do. If we do not behave in these ways we will eventually be found out, and a reputation for integrity is important to everything we attempt. This must therefore include the ability to maintain confidences which are properly given and accepted, not allowing them to spill over from one set of customer relationships to another.

3. We have to give everyone a fair crack of the whip, and be seen to be doing so. This means searching out people's views and not merely waiting for them to arrive, trying to understand those views and then thinking seriously about them, taking account of them in our analyses, and reporting them fairly.

4. We have to be both willing and able to listen. We must accept that we don't necessarily know best merely because we are planning professionals, and that other people coming at things from their perspectives and their life experiences can make immensely valuable contributions. The subject material of planning is not esoteric, but is about matters that are parts of everyone's daily experiences; and we need to recognize this for what it is. Without a willingness to listen, we will never gain inputs of this kind.

5. We have to be flexible in our thinking and in our behaviour, and to recognize that our own frames of reference can be limiting without developing flexibility of this kind. This is an essential requirement of the process of turning other people's inputs to constructive advantage.

6. We must constantly be looking for opportunities to help meet customer needs and aspirations wherever possible. The skill of being able to help people clarify their needs and then to translate this into possible ways of achieving them is a very important part of delivering valued services to customers.

7. We must always be looking to build relationships with customers on the basis of a degree of continuity. Whatever views may exist about individual cases, many customers of planning services are likely to remain customers over periods that outlast those cases, and long-term relationship-building needs to be able to transcend difficulties over individual instances.

Source: This summarizes arguments initially presented in Kitchen, 1997, pp. 37, 38.

comment. On the other hand, if it is accepted that effective planning cannot be an ivory-tower activity dominated by planners because of their superior knowledge and understanding but must be seen as an interactive process between planners and the customers of the planning service, then there is a great deal of job satisfaction to be obtained from developing relationships that are seen as being valuable by both sides on an ongoing basis and that contribute fully to good-quality decision-making. From my own experience, the positions offered in Box 5.2 seem to provide a firm basis for doing this.

Securing customer feedback

In the light of everything said in this chapter, it is clear that customer feedback about planning service delivery issues needs to be sought on a more or less continuous basis, and to be thought about very carefully once it has been received. There are fundamentally two different ways of securing customer feedback:

- in the normal course of business, through the day-to-day operations of the planning service;
- through purpose-constructed exercises of various kinds.

The first of these two sources can easily be overlooked by organizations not geared up to thinking about customer service in these sorts of terms, but in fact feedback of this type is available on a large scale once this is recognized as such; I have already discussed the value of feedback of this nature in Chapter 4. As well as via the workings of the local political process and the coverage of local planning issues in the media, a great deal of input of this kind can be obtained through the ongoing processes of customer contact that are an inevitable part of so many planning jobs. This kind of feedback can be particularly useful for individual planners looking to improve their own professional practice, because it can be obtained on a one-to-one or one-to-small-group basis which is rarely possible via the purpose-constructed exercise discussed below.

The structures of planning departments themselves can either aid or hinder these processes of securing feedback from day-to-day operations. Basically there are three different approaches that are commonly taken to structuring planning departments in British local government (Kitchen, 1999):

- Functional groupings, which can cover fields such as development plans, development control and environmental improvement, as well as more specialist areas such as design and conservation, transportation and minerals. This is probably the single most common approach that is adopted.

- Area groupings, which pull together functions that are place-specific and locate them in multi-purpose groups which take responsibility for a particular patch. The focus of such groups is therefore the area that they serve.
- Project groups, which focus on a particular major task that needs to be done, often to a timetable, and pull together into an integrated team the skills needed to carry out that task. Such teams may be disbanded once the task has been completed, or they may continue as multi-skilled teams moving on from one related project to another.

Most planning department structures reflect combinations of these approaches, reflecting both the job to be done and no doubt also the preferences of senior managers and relevant politicians. Each of these arrangements offers the possibility of developing congruent sets of customer relationships, but to my mind the most-purpose area team approach has the greatest amount to offer in these terms because of its patch focus, especially when establishing and maintaining contact with active groups and individuals in the community is emphasized as being an important part of the jobs of area team members. For this reason, I was responsible in Manchester for arguing strongly for and then maintaining throughout a period of staff cuts area teams as a primary focus of service delivery for the City's Planning Department. One of the problems with this approach, though, is that its relative lack of functional specialization can inhibit performance. So, for example, development control performance when measured by speed of throughput may not be as efficient in such structures as it would be with specialist teams constructed with the purpose of achieving high levels of performance in these terms. I would argue that choices here depend upon what is seen to matter most. Whatever structure is adopted, however, it will both provide extensive opportunities for obtaining customer feedback from its day-to-day operations and create some barriers to flows by virtue of the way the structure operates; groupings of people do in practice create some barriers around the dividing lines between groups (the 'not my job' phenomenon) despite the essential management rhetoric about the service as a whole. Managers and staff alike will need to recognize that both opportunities and problems exist in these terms, and to gear themselves up accordingly.

More formal exercises can include opinion polls and questionnaire surveys of various kinds, as well as techniques such as focus group discussions with particular groups of customers. Of these, opinion polls can be very expensive to conduct, and where this is done at all it will tend to be across a council as a whole with feedback about the planning service being a small part of the total response. In addition, these kinds of surveys, because they are usually either household-based or involve stopping people in the street, can be very difficult to target on customers of the planning service. This is because, as already said in this chapter, in practice the customers of planning tend to be either people who fall into particular categories or people who choose to be active in their communities in various ways. Direct questionnaires to identified customers of the service, or focus groups which aim to have structured discussions with particular customers, have probably got more to offer in these terms, although they do raise the difficulty of the absence of any basis of comparison for the results except through the development of a time series of data of this kind. During my time as a senior manager and then as head of the planning service in Manchester we tried three of these structured feedback methods:

- A MORI poll of residents was carried out during the early 1990s, which included a limited amount of feedback about the planning service as part of its coverage of all the council's services.
- A follow-up postal questionnaire survey was carried out in 1993 about the operation of the development control process, using as a sample frame everyone who had received decision notices from the council within a defined period. Although the response rate to this was relatively low (about 600 questionnaires went out, with a 19 per cent rate of return), it generated useful feedback cheaply.
- A series of focus groups occurred in the second half of the 1980s around the theme of the development of equal opportunities policies and practices, with representatives of target groups. In practice we found it very difficult to get much feedback via this route, and the initiative was discontinued after a while in favour of more direct contacts over live issues.

This in no sense exhausts the range of what is possible here, and local planning authorities determined to think creatively about securing customer feedback have plenty of opportunity to develop ideas about this on the back of their service delivery processes. The real point about this is that formal exercises of this kind should not be seen as an alternative to the kinds of informal feedback that can be secured which were discussed earlier, but should be seen as occasional complementary activities which check and develop the feedback being received as a result of the day-to-day operations of the service.

Local planning services throughout Britain have some fragmentary national information against which they can compare their own customer feedback, as a result of a study of attitudes to the town and country planning system and service carried out for the Department of the Environment (McCarthy *et al.*, 1995). The main findings of this study are summarized in Box 5.3. Clearly, like any survey, it captured the opinions

Box 5.3   Attitudes to the town and country planning system and service in Britain: main findings of a national study carried out for the Department of the Environment

1. The general public has a good level of understanding of and a broad measure of sympathy for the development control process, but understands other aspects of the planning system (of which it sees property developers as the main beneficiaries) much less well.
2. Three-quarters of the sample of applicants for planning permission recognized the planning system to be valuable, and less than 5 per cent saw it as having no value. Generally, planning application costs, speed of decision-making and the fairness of the outcome were all regarded as being acceptable, although some individual sectors expressed concerns about one or more of these matters.
3. Business generally has a much more sophisticated understanding of the planning system than have either the general or the applicant publics, and a much wider range of views about it. Businesses tended to be more critical of the system as a whole than they were of its handling of their own applications, with a widespread view being that it is arbitrary, expensive, slow and unresponsive; although this tended to be a received view rather than a report on their own experiences.
4. Developers and landowners reported a very wide range of performance by local planning authorities, ranging from those providing very highly regarded services to those seen as obstructive, dogmatic and unfair. Great stress was laid on the value of early access to officers for discussion and negotiation, and overall these processes were seen as improving the quality of development.
5. Non-governmental organizations also reported a wide range of performance by local planning authorities, and also reported on difficulties authorities appeared to have in balancing the range of issues in cases and in handling the cumulative impact of individual case decisions.

Source: The above summarizes the key findings in McCarthy and Harrison, 1995.

held by respondents at the time they were questioned and these sorts of opinions may well change quite significantly over time, not least in response to initiatives that seek to deal with the problems they identify. In addition, like any national survey, this inevitably lumps together a very wide range of individual situations, and cannot as a consequence have an element of the particular characteristics of local services that one would expect to see reflected in local feedback surveys. Nonetheless, it provides some useful national levels against which individual local planning authorities can begin to look at themselves and their own performance in the light of their own feedback, and some benchmarking of this nature is a very useful part of understanding the customer responses on service delivery issues that are obtained.

The capacity and potential of information technology

Before leaving this discussion of how planners relate to their customers, it is important to reflect on what may well turn out to be one of the most dramatic influences on this relationship: the capacity and potential of information technology. We have already seen in Chapter 1 something of the argument around how information technology has the capacity to change the way places function, and also the ways in which planners think about this functionality. In all probability, we are still in the early stages of this process (see for example Castells, 1989; Graham and Marvin, 1996; Simmie, 1997; Fernandez Arufe and Diamond, 1998; Lautini, 2001). But it is also changing the ways in which planning services get delivered to their customers; and again the potential for this process to continue to develop is probably very considerable. In particular, electronic means of communication are changing the ways in which planning services interface with their customers, and as the capability of virtual reality methods (and the abilities of larger numbers of people to make use of them) continues to be developed this is likely to change the shared ways in which planners and their customers jointly understand and respond to proposals for physical change. This is a field which has developed from nothing during my own professional lifetime, and it is one of the differences between the capabilities young planners were expected to possess when they had finished their planning qualifications in the 1960s as compared with today. The current expectation is that young planners going into the planning system for the first time will take with them a wide range of I.T. skills. In response to this potential, the British government set a target that all planning services should be delivered on-line by the end of 2005. Early responses from local authorities suggested that achieving this target would be likely to be more problematic (Sykes, 2003, Table 25), but a survey carried out for the ODPM by Peter Pendleton and Associates in December 2005 showed that there had been major improvements since 2003 and that the povernment's target had very nearly been achieved (source: www.odpm. gov.uk/index.asp?id=1143331 consulted on 24 April 2006). The fields of planning where this is expected to have the most significant impact are illustrated in Box 5.4 (ODPM, 2004d). The vision for this initiative is as follows:

A World class e-Planning Service will deliver new, more efficient ways of enabling the community to engage in developing a shared vision for their local area, easier access to high quality, relevant information and guidance and, streamlined processes for sharing and exchanging information amongst key players. (Ibid, para. 2, Executive Summary)

What the diagram in Box 5.4 shows more than anything else is how comprehensive the e-planning initiative is seen as being. Not merely does it cover all the key aspects of service delivery (with plan-making and key area- or site-based initiatives being seen as part of strategic planning services), but also its cross-cutting elements – consultation, the provision of information and advice, performance management and monitoring – will impact on virtually everything local planning authorities do both in the ways in which they gather understandings about the characteristics of the places for which they are responsible (the subject matter of Chapter 4) and in terms of their working relationships with their key customers. This is also reflected in planners' perceptions of how the services they deliver will change in future, as the material summarized in Box 5.5 clearly demonstrates.

The traditional pattern of consultation is clear from Box 5.5, which is that most local planning authorities have been using a combination of consultation documents, exhibitions and public meetings. The dominance of this grouping of traditional methods is clear from the fact that the method that came fourth in this list (focus groups), just below this top cluster, actually scored only just over half of the score of the third method in the list (public meetings). But four points stand out from the

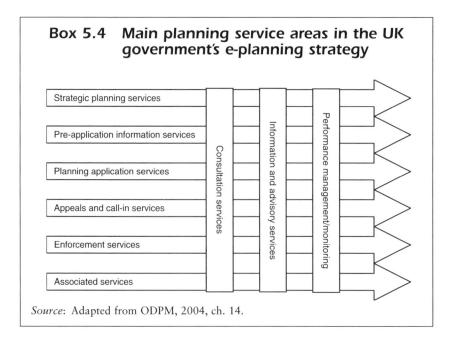

Box 5.4   Main planning service areas in the UK government's e-planning strategy

Strategic planning services

Pre-application information services

Planning application services

Appeals and call-in services

Enforcement services

Associated services

Consultation services

Information and advisory services

Performance management/monitoring

Source: Adapted from ODPM, 2004, ch. 14.

Box 5.5 Perceptions of changes in consultation methods used by planners in England

Consultation method	Used in the past		Used in the future		% change
	%	Rank order	%	Rank order	
Consultation documents	98	1	88	1	−10
Exhibitions	90	2	74	3	−16
Public meetings	87	3	65	5	−22
Focus groups	45	4	69	4	+24
Area/neighbourhood forums	37	5	62	6	+25
Interactive website	25	6	83	2	+55
Visioning exercises	17	7	36	7	+19
Planning for real	14	8	33	8	+19

This table is based upon returns from a questionnaire by 196 local planning authorities in England, or around 50 per cent of the total. N.B. Percentages don't add up to 100 per cent because respondents could indicate the use of several methods in parallel.

Source: Adapted from Sykes, 2003.

returns when planners were asked about their expectations about the future:

1. By a large amount the biggest percentage growth (+55 per cent) is expected to be in the use of interactive websites, which rises from rank order 6 to rank order 2 in the table. Interestingly, though, there were still 17 per cent (around 1 in 6) of responses that didn't indicate the use of this method in the future, even though respondents must have been aware then of the government's target for e-enabled planning services.
2. All three of the traditional methods of public consultation see an expected fall in usage, with the fall in public meetings being the largest (−22 per cent). Nevertheless, consultation documents remains the method occupying rank order 1, and exhibitions is still seen as a method in the top three places at rank order 3. Consultation documents do, of course, have the potential to become much more interactive tools when placed on websites (as is becoming common practice) and this combination might help to explain the continuing dominance of this method.
3. All of the other methods below the traditional top three see anticipated growth, with both focus groups and area/neighbourhood forums moving from minority to majority use positions.

4. The spread of results for future expectations is much narrower than in the past – the difference between rank order 1 and rank order 8 in the past was 84 per cent, but in the future it is 55 per cent. This taken together with point 3 suggests that we will see a much more varied pattern of consultation methods in future, with the traditional methods often accompanied by a wider range of other methods and website usage becoming the norm.

What all of this suggests is that the process of consultation should be designed to make things easy for consultees, and should in turn make the opportunities provided to local planning authorities to dip into the place knowledge of consultees much better. The traditional methods were often not very effective in these terms, mainly because they tended to be interactive in only quite limited ways. To use an example that many practising planners will be able to relate to, I have taken part in public meetings called about planning matters where the platform party (of which I was a member) was bigger than the audience, and where in any event the audience didn't really want to talk about the planning issue that was the ostensible purpose of the meeting but wanted to talk about the things that they saw as being problematic in the locality – which was actually very valuable feedback, if only the platform party members could ignore the fact that the meeting was supposed to be about something else and simply listen. So the rise in the more interactive methods – websites, area/neighbourhood forums, and focus groups (which are the three methods showing the biggest anticipated rises in Box 5.5) – at least offers the prospect of a more genuine dialogue about place and about what might be done to improve it than traditional methods, where in many ways the local planning authority controlled the agenda and the response options for consultees were quite limited.

As well as planning authorities responding to the challenges of e-government, which is essentially what the above discussion has been about, it should be remembered too that many of the customers of the planning service will also operate in e-enabled ways. So, for example, many developers in the future will be able to illustrate their development proposals on their own websites using virtual reality technology, which hopefully will show not merely their specific proposal but also how it fits into the immediately surrounding locality (at least). There is likely in many instances to be a promotional dimension to activities of this nature, and it is important that all parties should be aware of this and be committed as far as possible to accurate visual representation. This will mean that, as well as anything that local planning authorities might do to illustrate in this way planning applications deposited with them, it will often be possible to gain access to what may well be a wider range of material direct from the developer. This might prove to be especially valuable in encouraging developers to engage with local residents in the localities of their proposals before they are deposited in planning applications, rather than relying on the local planning authority's formal consultation on that application and in effect defending their proposals against negative responses to that consultation. This latter activity can easily give the impression to consultees that the process is in effect a fait accompli, whereas it is possible that the capability to engage interactively might also promote a greater willingness on the part of developers to make changes in the light of public reactions (and maybe also less of a Nimby reaction to development proposals, in some instances). Many local community groups and organizations will also develop websites and electronic communication as part of their regular operation, and this may well help them not merely to be more effective in their own terms but also to communicate more effectively with local people whose opinions they may wish to influence and whose views they may aspire to represent.

More generally still, the power and potential of the internet to provide information about planning and the things that it seeks to achieve seem to be increasing exponentially. This is a very difficult thing to illustrate, but a simple example might be helpful. On 24 April 2006 I typed 'sustainable development' (including the quotation marks) into the Google search engine, and got just under 5.1 million connections in 0.13 seconds. Readers are invited to try the same test for themselves (which will inevitably be at a later date than this), and to compare the results with those recorded above. My expectation is that the number will grow significantly year by year (although this is already a mind-boggling scale), and that the speed of the operation will continue to improve (although it scarcely seems possible for this to be much faster than 0.13 seconds). The potential inherent in this simple illustration should be clear; indeed, the problem is likely to be the human capacity to cope with this range of possibilities. Will there be anyone who looks at all 5.1 million of these connections, especially since by the time they have finished doing this the number is likely to have grown significantly? Nonetheless, the scope to create more informed debates about planning issues and proposals by using what is available on the internet is clearly very real, and this will certainly include the kinds of place-based issues and understandings which are the focus of this chapter.

There is a dimension to all this that needs to be understood before moving away from this topic, however. This is that access to this range of opportunities and the ability to make full use of it are unlikely to be evenly distributed throughout society. There will be several components to this, but one of them is likely to be debates around what in Britain is known as social exclusion (Social Exclusion Unit, 2001), which is the process whereby some people by virtue of their circumstances do not participate fully in society and don't as a consequence benefit fully from everything this has to offer in terms of the quality of their lives. It is vitally important that lack of access to information technology and/or limited ability to make use of its potential doesn't become yet another element in social exclusion, and there is clearly a risk that less-wealthy and less-well-educated people are more likely to be in this situation than those who have been more fortunate (Burrows *et al.*, 2005). As a consequence, this has been seen in Britain as an important area into which resources should be directed in order to support community leaders and organizations (Policy Action Team 16, 2000, ch. 4). This idea was subsequently incorporated into a learning framework for neighbourhood renewal, which sought to identify the knowledge, skills and behaviours that needed to be addressed in respect of all the major participants in the neighbourhood renewal process, including local community and resident organizations, if it was to become more effective (Neighbourhood Renewal Unit, 2002, ch. 3). This framework is reproduced as Box 5.6,

---

Box 5.6   Summary of the Neighbourhood Renewal Unit's learning framework, UK National Strategy for Neighbourhood Renewal

Building the knowledge base	• Building the knowledge base	Recognizing and understanding what works in housing, education, worklessness, crime and health, reviving local economies and improving quality of life.
	• Applying knowledge	Analysing problems, creating opportunities, designing solutions from the knowledge base, learning to learn.
Developing core skills	• Organizational skills	Project appraisal
	• Interpersonal skills	Community engagement, leadership, management of people, valuing diversity, communicating, conflict resolution, partnership, working, communication.
Changing behaviours	• Entrepreneurial	Problem-solving, spotting opportunities, taking calculated risks, a 'can do' philosophy
	• Reflective behaviours	Evaluating effectiveness, exploring reasons for success, learning from failure

Source: Reproduced from Neighbourhood Renewal Unit, 2002, p. 24.

where interpersonal skills such as those needed to make community engagement effective are seen as a key element in the core skills that are necessary. The perceived need for this kind of action, though, is clear evidence of the existence of a problem. And it needs to be remembered in this context that an emphasis on meeting the needs of leaders of local community and resident organizations to enable them to participate effectively in neighbourhood renewal on behalf of their communities still doesn't address the situations of many individuals in those communities. It is important as a consequence that planning organizations do not assume that the fast march to e-enabled governance will automatically pick up all of their customers, and thus that most other methods of generating engagement can be abandoned. The evidence in Box 5.5 suggests that there is a recognition that the approach to consultation in future needs to be based as broadly as possible and cannot rely solely or mainly on interactive websites, and there is also clear evidence from a small sample of senior planning practitioners that they see this as an important issue in achieving more effective public engagement (Kitchen and Whitney, 2004).

Conclusion

This chapter is essentially about relating to and working with customers because in my view this is one of the primary tasks of planning as a public sector activity. This represents a view that is significantly different from what would have been seen as the mainstream view of planners forty years ago, although there is certainly evidence of this beginning to change in the report of the Skeffington Committee (Skeffington, 1969). Today, however, it represents what is regarded by the British government as a necessary and desirable key aim of planning; to use the language of the Planning Green Paper, the planning system needs to engage with communities more effectively and to develop a much stronger customer focus (DTLR, 2001, paras 2.5, 2.6).

Of course, aspiring to this and delivering it can be two very different things, and one of the objectives of the culture change in planning initiative discussed in Chapter 1 is to look at the kinds of things that might need to be done to close the gap between these two elements. One of these issues is certainly the need to capture the hearts and minds of planners themselves for developments of this kind, although in a small piece of research in the Yorkshire and Humber region David Whitney and I found absolutely no problems of this kind among senior planning managers (Kitchen and Whitney, 2004). Another issue is undoubtedly the question of the resource base for the planning service, because the things discussed in this chapter are very staff-intensive, and staff time costs money. There is, in my opinion, no getting away from this; if we want public planning services that engage effectively with the public and that have a strong customer focus, we have to be prepared to pay for them by whatever mix of means is deemed to be appropriate in individual societies. In particular, there is a risk that when resources are inadequate and thus choices have to be made, the kind of work described in this chapter will lose out to more immediately tangible and measurable work such as speeding up the development control process. It is not surprising in this context that many of my discussions with British planners during 2004 and 2005, since the introduction of the Planning Delivery Grant regime which made more resources available for planning as a reward for performance improvements in specified ways, have suggested that this is exactly what has been happening; and at the time of writing the latest evaluation of the operation of Planning Delivery Grant does indeed suggest that local planning authorities have done what the government wanted in order to obtain extra resources (Addison and Associates and Arup, 2005). This regime rewards improved development control performance (measured by the percentage of applications determined within a set period of time), and thus it is a perfectly rational response on the part of local planning authorities to use their resources to this end in order to win more resources. But those discussions suggest that this has been at the expense of other things such as the development of better working relationships with the range of customers described in this chapter. It will be interesting to see whether what local planning authorities have to say about their intentions in this regard in their statements of community involvement (the requirement to produce these was introduced in the Planning and Compulsory Purchase Act 2004) is presented as being in any way resource-constrained.

I have not come at the issues discussed in this chapter from reading planning theory. My views about the importance of working with customers have come from years of planning practice, and from reflecting on the rich and varied experiences (both positive and negative) that this offers. But it is right to acknowledge that what I have said in this chapter chimes well with a strand of planning theory writing which has generated a considerable literature in its own right – the so-called communicative turn (see, for example, Healey, 1997). This also has its theoretical critics (see, for example, Brooks, 2002, ch. 9), and no doubt these debates will rumble on – see for example the exchange of views between Innes and Booher (2004) and Woltjer (2005) and then the further response by Booher and Innes (2005), which appear to be about the relative weight to be given to ongoing collaborative working as against more legally prescribed forms of participation in seeking effective community engagement in different cultures and situations. But my practice perspective is that the broad direction in which planning needs to move is clear; it is towards more and better working with its customers, while acknowledging the formal decision-making structures and rules that exist. As a consequence, the challenge to planners is to do the best they can in this situation given that the demand for this kind of work from many of the customers themselves (as we have seen in Chapter 1) is likely to be ever growing. As this present chapter has noted, there will always be lots of tensions in these situations, and the responses to these will not always be straightforward, but to my mind if the planning service moves continuously in this direction it will be improving its performance in the eyes of the people who matter the most – its customers.

Self-assessment topics

1. Get hold of a copy of a full planning officer's report on a recent large-scale or controversial planning application that has been determined by a local planning authority. Who appear to have been the customers of the planning service in this case? What sorts of views were obtained, by what methods, and how were they reported? Were there any customers that you might have expected to have been identified as part of this process, whose views appear to be missing from this report? How influential did the reported views of consultees appear to be in the framing of the final recommendations in the report?

2. Find a representative of a local community group which has dealings with a council's planning service, and who is willing to talk to you about such matters. What is the nature of the contacts this group has with the planning service, and how frequent and how extensive are they? How fairly does the group feel that its views and representations on planning matters are treated, and what improvements would it like to see in this regard? What other contact does the group have on planning matters, over and above its direct contacts with the planning service? What does it see as being the main strengths and weaknesses of that planning service?

3. Find planners who work for local councils who are prepared to talk to you about their relationships with the customers of their service. Who do they see as being their main customers, and where have these definitions of who their customers are come from? How do they try to handle such relationships? What do they see as being the most difficult customer relationships to establish and to maintain? What do they see as being the main benefits both to their customers and to themselves flowing from these relationships?

4. If a council asked for your advice on how it could set about evaluating its customers' views about its performance in relation to
   (a) its development planning activities
   (b) its development control activities and
   (c) its environmental improvement activities

how would you suggest that it should carry out such exercises? And if such studies suggested that there was scope to improve performance in these areas from customers' perspectives, what are the main changes you would suggest to that end?

5. Find an example of a council that has a published strategy for developing e-enabled planning services. Evaluate how effectively you think that strategy is being implemented from two sets of perspectives: the perspectives of service managers wanting to develop more efficient and effective service delivery, and the perspectives of a range of customers of the planning service wanting not only to find out what it is doing but also to influence it. Compare and contrast these two sets of evaluations, and think about how any contradiction between them might be resolved.

Chapter 6

Personal Skills

Introduction

It is a truism to say that, whatever else the planner brings to a particular situation, what is always part of the mix is the particular set of personal characteristics and human experiences up to that point which contribute to the make-up of the individual. No amount of argument about, for example, the distinctive technical skills a planner may possess can take away from the point that each individual also brings to the table a collection of personality features, good and bad life experiences, and preconceptions and even prejudices. Equally, there is no point in planners trying to pretend that this is not the case, any more than there would be for individuals in most other walks of life to make such a claim. Indeed, much of this can be a very valuable asset for a self-aware planner, because the lessons of experience are often among those most firmly learned. Over and above all of this, planners will struggle to be operationally effective if they haven't sorted out for themselves the basic principles that will govern their own behaviour in practice situations, which need to include the reflective skills that make learning from practice experience possible. In a phrase then, planners have to take responsibility for themselves.

This chapter is about some aspects of this mix that are inherently capable of being developed as part of the toolkit of the effective planner, aside from those aspects of personality which are more the territory of psychologists and psychiatrists than of planners. Four in particular have been chosen for attention: communication skills of various kinds; skills to do with awareness of and careful thought about issues of attitudes, values and ethics; the use of reflective skills as a tool of continuous personal development; and some of the interpersonal skills involved in being an effective member of a planning team. The chapter takes each of these in turn, before closing with some self-assessment questions designed to help readers to explore some of the issues raised in this chapter for themselves.

Communication skills

There are four skill areas that are likely to be the central elements of a planner's ability to operate as an effective communicator:

- Speaking
- Listening

- Writing
- Production of graphical material

As ever more planning work is carried out via the use of information technology, it may be that this should be seen as a fifth communications skills area, but for present purposes this should be seen as being particularly relevant to the third and fourth items above.

The central importance of the ability to communicate in these sorts of terms can be illustrated by thinking about the value that the customers of the planning service obtain from a plan. If that plan cannot be understood by its intended users, and if it cannot be interpreted unambiguously (except where ambiguity is intended as a means of maintaining flexibility), then it will fail the test of communication no matter how splendid its policy content may be. At the heart of effective documentation preparation in these terms are the skills of writing and the production of graphical material. So much of the output of the planning process is produced in written and illustrated forms of various kinds that this example could be repeated many times over in respect of the output of most planning organizations; it is not only true in respect of formal plans. Equally, the ideas in the plan will need to be explained and related to a large number of individual cases on countless occasions throughout its life, and this continuous process of interpretation is central to the implementation of any plan in a discretionary system. Very few plans are so precise in all their aspects that decisions about individual cases that will arise in the context of the plan can be made simply by looking up the appropriate page. Almost always, this is a process of explanation, discussion, and exploration of possibilities, and speaking skills are at the heart of these sorts of activities. In addition, experience shows that plans can often fail to carry people with them because they do not relate to the aspirations and needs of those people, and plans that do not succeed in these terms will probably not be successful in many other senses as well. At the heart of the process of grounding a plan in the views of the people intended to benefit from it is the ability to listen to the sorts of views being expressed, and to understand them in such a way that it is possible to relate them to the circumstances to be tackled by the plan. In this sense, listening is a very different thing from hearing; it is about trying to develop an acute level of understanding of what people are saying and what this might mean, rather than merely registering the words that have been used.

These very simple examples of how good communication skills of all four kinds are central to the success (or otherwise) of a plan serve also to make the point that communication skills do not operate in isolation, but can either reinforce or undermine each other. An all too common planning situation is one where it becomes clear that people have read planning documents and been to meetings to discuss them, but have come away from these experiences with different views as to what the planning policy stances actually are. Some of this, of course, may be because of difficulties at the receiving end of this communication process. It may well be the case, for example, that people will approach matters of this kind with their own preconceptions or strongly held views about their self-interest, and will try to read into what has been written and what has been said what they were hoping to find there. But in so far as the communication difficulty is at the planners' end, as at least in part it often is, one of its consequences for the planning organization will almost certainly be that it will have to engage in further work to try to sort out the tangles that have arisen as a consequence of its communication failing. And unless it handles this process in turn very well, there is a danger that, far from producing clarity, confusion will merely be piled on confusion. What this example shows is that, leaving aside entirely for the moment arguments about the extent to which effective communication is at the heart of good service to customers, successful communication is actually cost-effective for planning organizations. The search for effective communication by all available means and at all times is a sound strategy for a planning organization to adopt, not only because it helps the organization to achieve its stated objectives but also because it enables the organization to use its own resources as effectively as possible.

This can, of course, be a particular problem for the individual planner. While most organizations ought to be able through their processes of team-building to assemble groups of people tackling planning issues with a collective competence across this range of communication skills, it is very often not the case that an individual possesses equal (and equally high) levels of competence in all four of these areas. Most individuals, if they take stock of their own skills, and if they think hard about the constant feedback coming at them from their customers about how effective they are as communicators, would probably conclude that they are stronger in some areas than in others. While it is possible, through coaching and through practice, to do something about this in virtually every case, this almost certainly will not get people to the level of being star performers in all four areas of communication skills. Somebody who finds public speaking an ordeal, for example, may always struggle to get to the level of the 'natural' public speaker. What most people can do, however, is to achieve a reasonable level of competence, such that they can cope with the day-to-day demands of professional practice without skill deficiencies in one or more of these particular areas proving a major barrier to their effectiveness. It is undoubtedly worth the effort to achieve across-the-board competence at least in these terms, because as has already been said, good communication is central to so much professional practice in planning that its absence can be a major limitation (see also Brooks, 2002, pp. 190–2).

Speaking skills are taken first because of all the communications skills relevant to planning these may well be those that are used most intensively. As well as the relatively formal occasions of speaking to audiences of various kinds (and some planners do a great deal of this), there is a wide range of semi-formal events such as meetings or one-to-one contacts with customers of the service as well as informal discussions that take place with colleagues, particularly within team situations on a more or less continuous basis. This very wide range of circumstances makes generalization very difficult, but from my own experience three elements are common to successful operation in all of these situations:

- Know your audience. It is essential that all acts of spoken communi-cation are pitched at a level that the audience can understand, and are related as far as possible to what you know about the interests and concerns of that audience.
- Know what you want to achieve as a result of the exchange. Not only does this make the process more focused, but it also increases the likelihood that the speaker will not fall into the greatest trap facing any speaker, which is of talking too much and losing the attention of the audience in the process.
- Know your material, so that you come across to the people you are speaking to as a competent professional who can be relied upon in that capacity. This is particularly significant in relation to the kinds of one-to-one contacts with customers that were described above as semi-formal, because the planner in those situations (as well as in many others) may well be the only person from the organization with whom the customer concerned has such dealings, and thus the impres-sion formed of the planner may also be the impression formed of the organization as a whole.

Brooks (ibid., p. 191) lists nine common mistakes in the oral communica-tion of planning ideas, which are reproduced in Box 6.1. I can readily relate to this valuable list, and I would add two more elements to it from my own experience, both of which are to do with timing:

- Arriving at the last minute or even late, with no time to check the available technology, thereby creating a bad start in the eyes of the audience and in particular of the meeting organizer.
- Over-running. There is nothing worse than a 15-minute presentation that takes 30 minutes (except one that takes even longer!), and the likelihood is that by the end you will have lost the attention of many members of the audience. The ability to speak for a set amount of time depends upon the ability to communicate the main points without dressing them in too much detail, and this can be related in turn to how confident you are with your material.

BOX 6.1 Common mistakes in the oral communication of planning ideas

- Misjudging the audience – giving the wrong talk to the wrong group, misunderstanding their interests or level of sophistication.
- Failing to have clear goals for the talk – that is, not being sure what one is attempting to accomplish.
- Using too much jargon – professional terms used frequently by planners may mean nothing to the average citizen.
- Telling offensive, irrelevant or just plain unnecessary jokes (as distinct from the effective use of appropriate and well-timed humour).
- Excessive verbal distractions (the ubiquitous 'um' leading the way).
- Lengthy and detailed descriptions of data, which tend to lose the audience immediately.
- Errors in technique – for example, reading the entire speech, making too little eye contact, jangling one's pocket change, fidgeting, pacing excessively, speaking in a monotone.
- Dressing too formally or too casually for the particular occasion.
- Poor use of graphic aids.

Source: Developed from Brooks, 2002, p. 191.

I can't, of course, claim that my own speaking activities have always avoided the traps listed in Box 6.1 and here, but I do think that a conscious attempt to learn from negative experiences of this nature can rapidly improve the ability of planners as speakers.

Listening is in a sense the mirror-image of speaking, because most exchanges are two-way. A planning negotiation, for example, is about the giving and the receiving of points of view which may lead to a compromise acceptable to both parties; and the ability to pick up clues from what the other person is saying about the extent to which they may be prepared to move in your direction is central to the identification of what may turn out to be points of agreement. Indeed, the strong speaker who is adept at putting across the point of view of an employing organization but is a poor listener may well turn out to be a negotiator with a relatively low success rate. So in this situation, speaking and listening skills need to be in balance. This can be particularly difficult when the customer of the service is not adept at using planning language and does not really understand the planning system. It is very easy in such circumstances to be dismissive of what is being said on the ground that it has little planning relevance, but this would be to risk dismissing the substance of what is being said in favour of its surface appearance. This is why listening was defined earlier in this chapter as being not merely about hearing, but also about trying to take the planning sense out of what is being said irrespective of how it has been expressed and then trying to relate it to the planning circumstances being addressed.

Writing skills can be very individualistic, and many planners will experience a degree of tension between the ways they would like to write and what they may see as the bureaucratic stranglehold imposed by the formal styles adopted by their employing organizations for many of their documents. There is no doubt, on the other hand, that much of this has a purpose to it, even if some organizations do take conformity with standard ways of producing written material to excess. *Mutatis mutandis*, many of the common mistakes in oral communication summarized in Box 6.1 apply also to written communication. The most important point here, in thinking about any document, is to understand its intended audience or audiences and what their needs might be. The production of planning documents should be customer-driven, rather than an exercise in self-indulgence by the individual planner. This can very easily be illustrated by thinking about three common types of planning document, all of which are still likely to be produced regularly as part of the planning process, even though we are now in the age of web-based communication:

- The leaflet that goes through everyone's door in a particular part of a town or city needs to be completely clear as to its purpose (because it cannot be assumed that anyone will necessarily know what this is), written in a simple style (because a leaflet only allows a small amount of space to communicate a message), and designed to catch the attention and interest of people who by virtue of their daily experiences of living in the area may have an intimate knowledge of it even if this has never been translated into 'planner-speak'. It should also be clear what the planning organization actually wants people to do as a result of receiving the leaflet (send in comments? attend a meeting?), and what will happen next in the process of which the leaflet forms a part. It needs to be acknowledged as well that it seems to be a characteristic of contemporary life that we all get lots of junk mail through our letter boxes, much of which gets thrown away very quickly (one hopes to be recycled, but often not). So how can you ensure that your leaflet doesn't suffer the same undignified fate? Make sure that it captures the reader's attention immediately and that its purpose is clear, so that it doesn't get confused with junk mail.
- The committee report on a planning matter designed to help a planning committee to take a decision needs to convey the essential information that the elected members on that committee will need in order to be able to exercise that function. That often means describing the issue, the planning policies that relate to it, the views of consultees where this is relevant, the options in front of the decision-makers with an analysis of the pros and cons of each, and then making a recommendation as to the appropriate course of action. Because this is a very highly structured approach, and to enable members to navigate

it as easily as possible, such a report often has numbered sections and paragraphs each concerned with one part of this process, and often also a summary and recommendations at the front to enable those who do not have the time or the inclination to read the whole report to pick up quickly what it is all about and what it is being suggested that the committee should now do. Because typically such a report will be one of very many on a large agenda, there will also be pressure to keep it as brief as possible, consistent with covering this ground. While obviously writers of reports of this nature would prefer their recommendations to be accepted, there is a strong argument for saying that the report needs to contain enough material and analysis to enable the committee to make a decision even if that is not in accord with the report's recommendation.

- The background research and policy analysis report may well be much fuller than either of the previous two documents, because it will need to demonstrate that it has assembled and reviewed the relevant evidence carefully and has covered the policy issues that arise at an appropriate depth. The readership of this report in full may be relatively small, but it is also likely to be relatively well informed about such issues, and thus the report has to be capable of carrying conviction with a knowledgeable audience. At the same time, many other people without wishing to get into the level of detail encompassed by the report as a whole may want to understand the essence of what it is saying and the evidence that has led towards its conclusions. As a result, it is common for this kind of report to include for the benefit of this wider audience an executive summary, which conveys this basic information in a very small number of pages and uses an approach nearly as spare in its written style as the 'bullet-point' format. Such an executive summary may quite possibly turn out to have a life of its own, in that it may well be detached from the report it is summarizing and be either attached to other documents or even given its own circulation, and so it needs to be drafted with the likelihood that it will be put to these sorts of uses in mind.

These three examples are but a small fraction of the range of planning documents that get produced, but they make the essential point that each document should be tailored to the needs of its particular audience. The leaflet should not be like the committee report about a policy issue, and neither of these should be like the background research and policy analysis paper, because each of these has different functions to perform.

Graphical skills are possessed at many different levels of sophistication by individual planners, ranging from the ability to draw to the standard of a piece of fine art to the ability to do little more than communicate a basic idea in drawn form quickly and simply, probably in little more than cartoon style. This range is probably appropriate as well, because the planning team will undoubtedly be stronger for having people in it who can communicate in drawn form to a very high standard, without it being at all necessary for every member of that team to possess this particular skill to the same degree. In any event, of course, many planning organizations employ specialists in the field of graphic production, whose skills will include not merely the conventional ability to draw to at least a decent standard but also the ability to use the range of technological aids now available for the production of illustrations. Very often, therefore, a planner will need to be able to do little more than to communicate effectively to a skilled colleague of this kind what is needed by way of graphic support, and will not actually produce the final piece of artwork. This is not to dismiss the need for graphic skills, however, for two very simple reasons. The first is that the public perception of what planners do, at a very simple level, is that they produce plans; and this usually means drawings of various kinds, as well as words. The second is that illustrations are essential to the process of effective communication, and planners in thinking about their output need to consider what is being communicated in the round and not (for example) to think only of the words a report will contain. The example quoted above of three different types of planning document serves to make this point as well, because all three of these are likely to be illustrated in some ways, even if in the case of the committee report this may be nothing more than a site or location plan. These documents have to work as exercises in communication, and the illustrations are integral to the achievement of this objective. The planner therefore needs to be aware of the way in which illustrations can contribute to the success of the document, and to think carefully about what can be achieved here and how to set about doing this within the parameters of the exercise such as time and printing costs. Even if the graphics skills of the individual planner in terms of the hands-on production of illustrations are rudimentary, the awareness of the contribution such material can make and of how to set about obtaining such a contribution is a very important skill in its own right.

All of these communications skills can be developed through practice. Most people as a consequence can lift up their skills in each of these four areas to a level which at least allows them to get by; and they will also be able to develop ways of avoiding the major difficulties that might arise because of their relative skills deficiencies in any particular area. As already said, most people are not equally good at all of these skills, but most well-balanced teams contain a range of performance levels which allows the team through good management to play to its strengths in these terms rather than to expose its weaknesses. This is in no sense an argument for individual team members to hide skills weaknesses behind the greater competence in these terms of some of their colleagues, however, because no matter what view is taken about the use of the team's assets in the best interests of the effective performance of its functions, the individual is still responsible for the development of his or her own skills. The team can provide a very effective framework for this process, of course, because people can learn from colleagues whose skills are at a higher level than their own in a particular area. But it can also encourage people to focus on their strengths in the interests of the team, and thereby to neglect their relative weaknesses. The best way to overcome this is to try and see the team's communication experiences in the round as a learning opportunity, so that as well as looking at their own contribution people also look at the total package and try to focus on the lessons to be drawn from the contributions of others. For example, someone who contributed the text to a report but did not make any contribution to discussions about how it should be illustrated can still try to look at the report as a whole as an exercise in communication, to see how all the elements combined and how this could have been improved.

Over and above the need to practice communication skills, and the need to create practice opportunities out of everyday workloads both of the individual and of the team, the other important dimension in improving communication skills is the need to secure feedback and to think constructively about it. Feedback of all kinds about these matters is all around us, if only we can identify it as such; and it is not just limited to being told directly what somebody thinks of our efforts. Customer reactions to an end product, for example, should force us to consider what it was about that product that may have caused those reactions to be generated. Successes and failures in the negotiation process should be analysed to try to understand the reasons for this, and in particular colleagues who appear to secure high levels of success in these terms on a consistent basis should be studied to understand how they use the communication skills they possess in order to achieve these results. A willingness to listen is an important part of this process, but so are an awareness of all the other kinds of direct and indirect sources of feedback available, an openness to inputs of this kind, and a willingness to think carefully about what is coming back in these terms. Communication skills should be treated as one of the bedrocks of planning activity which individuals are constantly striving to improve throughout their professional lives, no matter how high they may already believe some of their standards of achievement to be.

Attitudes, values and ethics

These sorts of issues are often debated most intensively when something appears to have 'gone wrong' with the planning system. In Britain over the past forty years, two different examples of this phenomenon which have given rise to considerable debate about issues of attitudes, values and ethics have been the so-called Poulson corruption scandals (Gillard and Tomkinson, 1980) and the North Cornwall case, where planning policies seemed to be systematically flouted by the council's own decision-making processes for reasons that gave rise to concerns about whether the system there was operating impartially (Department of the Environment, 1993). It needs to be said that although these cases became very prominent examples of where things had 'gone wrong' within the British planning system, in my experience they are very far from being the norm. Nevertheless, planning processes may be particularly susceptible to the possibility of corrupt practices taking place because of the huge extra value that can attach to land or buildings by virtue of the granting of planning permission, and so planning officers need to be alert to this possibility and where they have clear evidence to support suspicions to draw these to the attention of the proper authorities, so that they can be investigated. There are very few examples of writing that covers the behaviour of planners in very difficult situations such as this, where the temptation to ignore what you think might be happening in the hope that it will go away (and in the desire to avoid the difficulties for you that will almost certainly follow from taking action) must be very strong, but one example of a principled planner's experience of dealing with a situation of this nature in the form of corrupt practices in Doncaster is provided by Burley (2005). Of course, one of the primary purposes of having discussions about attitudes, values and ethics in planning is to try to ensure – in so far as problems are a consequence of the behaviour of planners (and neither of the two cases cited above was mainly about this) – that things do not 'go wrong' in the first place, and that if they do then planners have the strength of purpose and character to face up to them.

Planning as a public sector activity in a democratic society carries with it an expectation that it will operate fairly and openly, within a framework of declared and accessible policies that will themselves go through processes of consultation and consent and will then be applied with an appropriate degree of consistency. This very simple statement has a great deal to say about the attitudes, values and ethics required of the people who work within such a system, although arguably this field has been relatively neglected in the literature for most of the time (approaching sixty years, at the time of writing) that there has been a strong statutory planning system in Britain which seeks to embody the characteristics described above. This is not to say, of course, that planners operating within the system have therefore given no thought to questions of attitudes, values and ethics, although it may well be true that very often these have been implicit because they have hidden behind a very broad 'public interest' stance that regards its practitioners in these terms as being neutral exponents of an understood public good (see, for example,

Simmie, 1974). Thomas and Healey (1991) made an explicit attempt to encourage practitioners to talk about and to record their views about these sorts of matters, and recorded two themes as being dominant in these exchanges. The first was the question of the relationship between one's own personal values and one's perception of the prevailing value system in one's workplace. The second was the problem of conflicting loyalties or obligations, for example for a local government employee between loyalty to the council as employer and a sense of obligation towards a customer of the service. A number of strategies are discussed (ibid., pp. 178–82) for trying to cope with these issues:

- Discussion and collective action, both in the sense of using the strengths of the team situation and in the sense of getting issues raised through management channels.
- Exercising the degree of control that individuals do have over the direction of their work to make changes that have the effect of lessening (or, no doubt, sometimes avoiding) these problems.
- A form of 'compartmentalism' which accepts something but in effect tries to seal it off from the rest of what one is doing. Depending upon how this is done, it may well sit uneasily with much of what Chapter 5 has said about the development of customer-related skills, but it starts from the pragmatic acceptance that compromise often has to be part of life.
- Reference to a guiding principle or principles, which may for example be a particular imperative derived from strongly held beliefs or a professional code of ethics which a planner subscribes to by virtue of joining a professional organization, assuming of course that such an organization has such a code.

The importance of this was that it acknowledged the fact that practitioners recognized that they faced problems of attitudes, values and ethics as a constant part of professional life, and that they did give some thought to the question of how to deal with these issues. This has been complemented by more theoretical writing (Thomas, 1994), where a series of academic authors demonstrate that planning actions of all kinds raise a very wide range of issues about the values that are explicitly and implicitly at work, without perhaps saying very much to practitioners in those fields about how they might cope with these issues as unavoidable components of their practice lives. The first step in this process, however, must be a recognition that the idea of the value-free or the value-neutral planner is neither an appropriate concept nor an accurate assessment of how planners actually think or behave in practice. This recognition makes it incumbent upon planners to try to identify what values they are taking into their work and whether they could provide better services for their customers by seeking constructively to change some of their attitudes, values and ethics.

Beatley (1994) looks at these issues from the twin perspectives of the inherently ethical nature of land use decisions and the wide range of organizations and individuals involved in taking such decisions, each of which may well have particular ethical or value characteristics. His base is the land use planning system in the United States of America, and the fragmented nature of land use decision-making in that environment. He proposes (ibid., pp. 262–73) a broad framework of twelve principles and imperatives for ethical land use policy which is summarized in Box 6.2. This is offered as 'a theoretical agenda for the future'(ibid., p. 262), and in the context of a form of moral pluralism that recognizes that different circumstances 'will suggest the relevance and applicability of different concepts and principles' (ibid.). In other words, it is not being suggested that all twelve of these principles and imperatives will be equally relevant to every planning situation, but that this framework offers a series of ethical orientations that will help planners to think constructively about these situations. It appears to be very strongly influenced by what were then the emerging concerns of the environmental sustainability movement (World Commission on Environment and Development, 1987), which are becoming an ever more significant component of public planning policy in many parts of the world. So it is likely that much of this framework would find acceptance among the contemporary planning community. It is interesting to reflect on Beatley's framework in the context of a British planning system where the primary purpose is now seen by the government as the achievement of sustainable development (ODPM, 2005a), which could be understood as broadly what he was seeking to achieve at the time of writing. Beatley's framework also has several resonances with the principles of effective planner behaviour by public sector planners proposed in Box 5.2. At the same time, frameworks of this nature inevitably raise questions about how in practice one would work with them when in particular circumstances some of their elements appear to be in conflict with each other, or when these ideas are not being lived up to by some of the participants in the process. This makes the point that real-world issues don't necessarily present themselves in the sorts of neat boxes into which ethical frameworks can be put, and it also serves as a reminder that knowledge and understanding about such issues is likely to unfold throughout the life of a particular planning project rather than all be visible right from its outset. These things don't invalidate an ethical framework, of course; they simply caution us that applying it is unlikely to be straightforward.

In Britain in the 1990s the Nolan Committee (Committee on Standards in Public Life, 1997) recommended seven principles of public life, in effect as an ethical framework stretching across a wide range of public sector activities, including planning. These seven principles are summarized in Box 6.3. Clearly by its nature this is much more

---

Box 6.2   Key elements of ethical land use policy, according to Beatley

1. *Maximal public benefit* – 'Ethical land use seeks to promote the greatest quantity of social benefits or welfare, other things being equal.'
2. *Distributive justice* – 'Land use policy can and should be used to improve the (social and economic) conditions of (those least-advantaged in society).'
3. *Preventing harms* – 'Ethical land use policy prevents or minimises the imposition of harms (on people and the environment) ... those who cause land use harms are accountable for them.'
4. *Land use rights* – 'Ethical land use policy must protect minimum social and environmental rights due every individual irrespective of income or social position.'
5. *Environmental duties* – 'Ethical land use acknowledges obligations to protect and conserve the natural environment, both for humans and other forms of life.'
6. *Obligations to future generations* – 'All land use decisions today must incorporate consideration of their cumulative, long-term effects.'
7. *Life-style choices and community character* – 'Land use policy tolerates a diversity of life styles and assists individuals in pursuing their own fundamental life plans.'
8. *Paternalism and risk-taking* – 'Ethical land use avoids actions that are paternalistic, (but it can) constrain individual risk-taking behaviour when there are substantial social costs involved and when accurate knowledge and understanding of risk is low.'
9. *Expectations and promise-keeping* – 'Ethical land use requires that public land use authorities keep the promises they make.'
10. *The privilege of landownership and use* – 'Ethical land use views the use and development of land as a privilege, not an inviolable right.'
11. *Inter-jurisdictional land use obligations* – 'No political jurisdiction is free-standing; ethical obligations exist to other jurisdictions, particularly those which are adjacent or surrounding.'
12. *Fair and equitable political process* – 'Land use policy and decisions must be formulated through a fair and equitable political process (which requires) the opportunity for all interested and affected parties to participate (and also requires) certain minimum ethical conduct on the part of land use officials, including the avoidance of conflicts of interest.'

Source: Summary of a discussion in Beatley, 1994, pp. 262–73.

---

generalized than is the (specifically planning) framework proposed by Beatley, but nonetheless the principles set out there do identify what should be norms of public life which should certainly be applied to planning. Indeed, it could be argued that it is particularly important that the Nolan principles are applied rigorously in the planning arena, given the very large amounts of money that can be tied up in a planning permission and the temptations that might arise in various quarters as a consequence.

Box 6.3   Key principles of public life, according to the Nolan Committee

- *Selflessness* – Decisions should be taken wholly in the public interest, and not at all in the financial or other material interest of holders of public office and/or their families and friends.
- *Integrity* – Holders of public office should not put themselves under financial or other obligation to outside parties that might influence them in the performance of their duties.
- *Objectivity* – Decisions on public business should be made on their merits, and not on any other basis.
- *Accountability* – All those who make decisions in the public interest are accountable for them and must submit themselves accordingly to appropriate scrutiny.
- *Openness* – There should be as much openness as possible about public decisions, including how they were arrived at and the reasons for them.
- *Honesty* – Holders of public office must declare any private interests that might impact upon their public duties, and must take steps to resolve any conflicts of this kind that might arise in a way that protects the public interest.
- *Leadership* – Holders of public office should support and promote these principles by leadership and by example.

Source: A summary of key principles in Committee on Standards in Public Life, 1997. In essence, these principles subsequently became part of the standard code of conduct for elected members in local government, which all local authorities had to adopt in accordance with the provisions of s. 51 of the Local Government Act 2000.

The sustainable development perspective adopted by Beatley and the definition of appropriate public behaviour developed by Nolan aren't of course the only perspectives that could be used to define an ethical framework for planning and planners. To take a third possible approach, building on a growing volume of work about women and planning (see, for example, Greed, 1994), Hendler (2005) offers some broad principles that would contribute towards the construction of a feminist-informed code of planning ethics. These are reproduced in Box 6.4. There are clearly some points of connection between the contents of Boxes 6.2, 6.3 and 6.4 and also some points of departure, which suggest that the process of developing appropriate ethical frameworks for planning is still an emerging field. Whether it is possible to bring all of this material together into a single framework which integrates it all effectively without suppressing important component elements from each of the individual approaches remains to be seen, as does the question of whether supporters of each approach would accept the validity of attempts at integration. It is important whether or not this suggestion

---

Box 6.4   Principles that would contribute to a feminist-inspired code of planning ethics, according to Hendler

- To promote healthy social and physical environments.
- To act with integrity.
- To value and protect the natural environment.
- To consider consciously the whole range of domains and interests affected by a planning decision or action.
- To promote a dynamic vision of the future.
- To strive for consensus.
- To use processes sensitive to power differentials.
- To plan for equity among citizens.

Source: This summarizes the main arguments in Hendler, 2005, pp. 53–69.

---

about the possibility of integration proves fruitful that work continues in this area, because planners do need to be as clear as possible about the ethical frameworks that shape their work.

Codes of professional conduct or codes of ethics issued by professional bodies don't tend to be as prescriptive as is the framework offered by Beatley, and they tend to have a concern with the reputation of the profession as a continuing living entity as well as a concern with the individual planner. As a result, they can have both positive and negative dimensions. As Hendler puts this (ibid., p. 55):

> [P]rofessional codes may, indeed, represent the very best and the very worst moral thinking in a profession. At their best, they can provide a normative sense of what a profession is all about. At their worst, they can be window-dressing for an unsuspecting public, hiding unethical behaviour and providing an impenetrable barrier between a group of professionals and their clients, colleagues and society at large.

Gunder and Hillier (2004) follow a similar line, by suggesting that professional expectations (for which codes can be a proxy) can condition the behaviour of planners to the point where the beliefs and values that they 'think' are expected of them become more important than their own. Boxes 6.5–6.7 summarize the main principles that drive codes of professional conduct or their equivalent in the professional planning bodies in Britain, Canada and the USA. Recognizing that each of these comes from a different tradition and that they were prepared/updated at different points in time, a comparison of the three (including the

---

Box 6.5   The purposes of the RTPI's code of professional conduct

In all their professional activities, RTPI members shall:

(a) act with competence, honesty and integrity;
(b) fearlessly and impartially exercise their independent professional judgement to the best of their skill and understanding;
(c) discharge their duty to their employers, clients, colleagues and others with due care and diligence in accordance with the provisions of this code;
(d) not discriminate on the grounds of race, sex, sexual orientation, creed, religion, disability or age and shall seek to eliminate such discrimination by others and to promote equality of opportunity; and
(e) not bring the profession or the Royal Town Planning Institute into disrepute.

Source: RTPI website – www.rtpi.org.uk – consulted on 1 August 2005.

Box 6.6   Statement of Values: Canadian Institute of Planners

1. To respect and integrate the needs of future generations.
2. To overcome or compensate for jurisdictional limitations.
3. To value the natural and cultural environments.
4. To recognize and react positively to uncertainty.
5. To respect diversity.
6. To balance the needs of communities and individuals.
7. To foster public participation.
8. To articulate and communicate values.

Source: This is an abbreviated version of the *Statement of Values* of the Canadian Institute of Planners website. The full version can be found at www. cip-icu.ca/English/members/practice.htm

---

documentation that supports these statements of principle) suggests that there are some features that are broadly common to all of them:

- Promoting greater opportunity for all.
- Avoiding conflicts of interest.
- Respecting confidential information.
- Openness about financial dealings.
- Providing good-quality services that meet customers' needs.
- Promoting public engagement with planning activities.
- Maintaining confidence in the profession.
- Complying with these codes.

> ## Box 6.7 Statement of aspirational principles: American Planning Association
>
> We shall:
>
> (a) always be conscious of the rights of others;
> (b) have special concern for the long-range consequences of present actions;
> (c) pay special attention to the interrelatedness of decisions;
> (d) provide timely, adequate, clear and accurate information on planning issues to all affected persons and to governmental decision-makers;
> (e) give people the opportunity to have a meaningful impact on the development of plans and programs that may affect them, including those who lack formal organization or influence;
> (f) seek social justice by working to expand choice and opportunity for all persons, recognizing a special responsibility to plan for the needs of the disadvantaged and to promote racial and economic integration;
> (g) promote excellence of design, and endeavour to conserve and preserve the integrity and heritage of the natural and built environment;
> (h) deal fairly with all participants in the planning process.
>
> *Source*: Reprinted with permission from http://www.planning.org/ethics/conduct.html, adopted 19 March 2005, © by American Planning Association.

These are not as comprehensive as Beatley's ethical land use principles, for example, although it could be argued that they sit within them. What does appear to be clear is that ethical issues are acknowledged by both individuals and by professional organizations as an important component of professional life, of which skilled planners need to be aware and about which they need constantly to be thinking. It seems likely as a consequence that there will be considerable further developments in the years to come in the available literature about these matters, focusing not just on the behavioural standards of planners but also on the legitimate expectations of their customers (see the discussion in Prior, 2000).

Reflective skills and continuous personal and professional development

In some ways, the skills of the reflective practitioner (Schon, 1998) are at one and the same time the simplest to describe and the most difficult to develop. The reflective practitioner seeks constantly to think about and to try to learn lessons from his or her own experiences and those of colleagues so that personal and contextual understanding develop continuously. It is often said that the lessons hardest learned but best remembered are those that come from painful experience; to put this colloquially, the 'school of hard knocks' is a good school. This is only true, however, if conscious efforts are made to understand what it was about such experiences that made them so hard and to try to ensure that future experiences are not always as difficult. While the school of hard knocks may be a good school, it can also be a testing one at which to be a permanent pupil. This requires not only a process of personal reflection, but also a willingness to discuss with participants in one's own experiences as well as with non-participant colleagues what might have been done to obtain a better outcome, and how this might be achieved in broadly analogous circumstances if these were to arise in future. These working methods can also be applied to situations where things might not necessarily have been so difficult, of course; there is nothing unique in these terms about painful experiences that cannot also be applied in less painful ones. The point is that this way of working and thinking treats our own experiences and those accessible experiences that surround us as learning tools, rather than as something which has slipped away into the past.

That is not to say that the process of learning from experience is easy. As Krumholz and Forester (1990, p. 242) put it:

> How exactly do we 'learn from experience?' We do not just have experience, we have experience of *something*. 'Experience' is a joke that theory plays on history. Descending from abstract theory to the apparently firm ground of concrete history, we soon learn that experience is endless, seamless, directionless, sometimes eye-catching, sometimes tiresome and irrelevant. Without a sense of direction, we will walk backward rather than forward. Without a broad sense of purpose, our knowledge of historical experience may never seem to matter. Without a sense of pressing questions, we may review our past without ever fashioning answers to the problems facing us today.

Thus, reflective practice is at least as much about the context, the objectives and the issues that frame our experiences and those of others as it is about those experiences themselves. Sometimes, planners employed in organizations will find that the organization itself is prepared to help its staff address such questions, but more often planners will have to do this as self-starting individuals. The above quotation from Krumholz and Forester suggests that this needs to be a lifelong commitment to a way of working and thinking, rather than a series of one-off events, and that it always needs to be set in a context if we are to understand our own efforts as part of a larger picture. It is not mere aimless musing about the past; rather, it is structured reflection about contexts, processes and directions. This can, of course, be greatly assisted by the planning practice stories told by others, and also by public policy analysis work from a wide range of relevant fields where processes are similar to those of planning and where the focus is on policy analysis as individual and organizational learning (for example, Vickers, 1965; Wildavsky, 1979). Fundamentally, however, reflective practice is about making a personal commitment to lifelong learning. I return to the question of the planner as a reflective practitioner in Chapter 10, because of the importance of this concept to the arguments presented in this book.

The importance of trying to develop reflective skills of this kind lies in large measure in the fact that planning is about change, and that it is likely during the course of most people's professional lives to encompass a great deal of both intended and unintended change. The changes described in Chapter 1 of this book, for example, have occurred more or less during my professional life, and although some were undoubtedly influenced by planners others were not to any significant extent. Successful planning is therefore about both change management and the processes of adaptation to change. Although each situation is likely to contain unique elements, components of most situations can also be looked upon in the light of experience; there is very little that is strictly 'new', when taking a rigid view of what that word means. The reflective practitioner recognizes this, and recognizes also the dangers of repeating past mistakes in evolving situations through a failure to learn relevant lessons from experience. More positively, the reflective practitioner also knows that even a small percentage improvement in the way things are handled as a result of learning from relevant past experiences is an improvement worth having from the perspective of the customers of their service. Thus, developing the skills and habits of reflective practice is not just about being a good professional; it is also about being a better-performing professional, and about achieving better outcomes for our customers. Attempts to act in these ways can undoubtedly also be helped by more formal evaluations, of individual processes and actions (see, for example, Hogwood and Gunn, 1984), longitudinally of what planning processes achieve when looked at in the round (see, for example, Sies and Silver, 1996; Garvin, 2002), or in specific cases (see, for example, Sagalyn, 2001). In recent times more attention has also been paid to the identification and dissemination of good or best practice (see, for example, the work of the British Urban Regeneration Association in the field of urban regeneration: Roberts and Sykes, 2000; Burwood and Roberts, 2002), and this too can provide a valuable source for the reflective practitioner. Such individuals can also contribute to this accumulation of knowledge by writing up their own experiences in open and honest ways, and by making this material as openly accessible as possible. For most of the time, though, while sources of this nature can provide valuable inputs to the need to think creatively about planning challenges, the particularities of the individual situation and of the people active in it will be such that appropriate ways forward have to be shaped rather than taken from the shelf. Thus there is no substitute for the skills and habits of reflective practice; all of these other sources are merely useful additions to this basic activity.

Note also in this context that it is becoming increasingly common for professional bodies to require their members to commit themselves to programmes of continuous professional development (CPD) as a condition of professional membership. For example, the Royal Town Planning Institute requires members to maintain a professional development plan which identifies their personal professional development needs, and then in any two-year period to undertake a minimum of 50 hours of CPD activity in meeting those needs. For the reflective practitioner, although formally this represents an obligation, a CPD requirement of this nature should be seen as part of what they would be doing anyway in the course of the journey of personal development rather than as in any sense something that represents a burden. In a field like planning, where there is always something more to learn, CPD provides a framework within which planners and their employers can commit to continuous learning as a condition of professional life.

Being an effective member of a planning team

A great deal of planning work is teamwork, partly because of its scale, partly because of the range of skills and experiences that it requires, and partly because this can often be the only way to mobilize the resources needed to do the job in time. Even where planners are tackling jobs on an individual basis, there will almost certainly be a history, a planning context, and a series of follow-through consequences and implications; there will be, in other words, an 'invisible team', past, present and future, to which this apparently individual job is in practice a contributor. Part of the skill of being an effective team member is simply recognition of the responsibilities that go with this situation, both to the other members of the team and to the task to be performed. It is often said that the strength of a team is measured by its weakest element, and one of the responsibilities of team membership is that individuals need to strive not to be so defined.

There are many potential strengths to team-working in planning situations, some of which are:

- It allows a range of minds to be focused on a particular situation. At the outset of a task, for example, brainstorming sessions between team members can play a large part in moving quickly to an understanding both of the shape of the task and of the approach the team should adopt in tackling it. This can often be helped by 'assumptive' methods of planning, which seek to use the knowledge and experience of team members at the outset to make a series of informed assumptions about the parameters of the task. These then allow judgements to be formed about the shape and scale of the task as a whole and the relative importance of individual tasks within this broad understanding, which would otherwise have to wait until much later in the process and would inevitably make it much slower. It is, of course, necessary as the process unfolds to check on how accurate these assumptions were, and to revisit them and their consequences when and if it becomes clear that single or sets of assumptions were significantly adrift. But my experience has been that, very often, while the detail is inevitably adjusted as you go along, broad orders of magnitude can be understood quickly through this approach and can very helpfully shape much of the work when this is dependent upon the general direction rather than the finer detail.

- It allows a great deal of work to proceed in parallel rather than in sequence. The example of the use of assumptive methods given above illustrates this point very well, because when this enables a work programme to be defined within a shared raft of assumptions, tasks can then proceed without necessarily waiting for each individual assumption to be confirmed or modified.

- It allows a range of skills and personal characteristics to be brought together and focused on a job which can be appropriate to that job and which will transcend what any individual can offer. As has been said above, most people's skills are not equal across the board; most of us have strengths and weaknesses, but good management in the selection of a team can balance these attributes and liabilities so that the team as a whole is strong.

- It can be an excellent learning opportunity for individuals, because the range and the significance of the work encompassed by a team will usually be greater than that of any individual. Merely being in a team is not necessarily a learning experience in itself, however. It becomes this only if individuals set themselves to learn from the experience, but this can in turn be much helped by an attitude on the part of team managers and senior members which alongside their own needs to continue to learn recognizes a responsibility on their part to help other and more junior team members develop.

- It can be the source of a considerable amount of job satisfaction. Pride in the achievements of a team of which one is a member may seem a less likely source of job satisfaction than one's individual achievements, but because so much of planning work is involved in tackling large-scale issues or projects through team methods it is likely that someone who finds team-working difficult and does not see job satisfaction in collective achievement will simply not get the opportunity to tackle many major planning tasks.

There are also some potential pitfalls in team-working:

- It depends heavily on effective communication between team members, and on the careful and understood allocation of tasks. The anarchic, freewheeling, semi-chaotic approach of some teams may at times be creative and even be fun to be in, but it is at substantial risk of being neither efficient nor effective. Much of this depends upon the style of team management adopted (be it hierarchical or collective), and then upon its translation into everyday reality. Where these things do not function well, teams can significantly under-use the resources at their disposal and team-membership can be a frustrating experience.

- It is often easier for individuals who are not pulling their weight to hide in a team situation than it is for this to remain undiscovered when they are allocated tasks as individuals. This can be a problem not just in terms of the individual concerned but also for the team as a whole, since its dynamic is often very dependent upon each team member playing a full part. This can in turn be very disruptive of team morale, because feelings that someone is 'not pulling their weight' can lead to interpersonal difficulties within the team, the development of cliques, and other dysfunctional practices.

- Because the volume of potential human interaction increases geometrically as the size of the team expands arithmetically, there is always a possibility that human relationship difficulties between individual team members will disrupt effective team working within larger teams. In considerable measure, team management is about human relationships, and just as good teams have a good balance of skills so also do they have a series of interpersonal relationships where team members have worked out how to get along professionally whatever people may think of each other personally.

- Responsibility can become diffused in team situations, to the point at which 'the team' being responsible for certain things does not translate into identifiable individual responsibilities. This can be a particular problem if and when things start to go wrong since the location of responsibility is usually a prerequisite for correcting these findings, although what this can sometimes reflect is the inadequate allocation of tasks and responsibilities to team members in the first place.

- Teams can find the process of changing direction very difficult, at least in part because a team set up to carry out particular tasks or to perform functions in a certain way will not always be well placed to see that those tasks are no longer needed or that their ways of doing things are becoming counter-productive. The actions of teams can become self-fulfilling, and if they have developed the kind of ruling ethos which does not encourage self-criticism or doubt this can reinforce these problems. Again, much of this is about team management; the awareness of teams about the continued appropriateness of their actions is as important in its own way to the process of managing a team as are more conventional tasks such as objective definition and task allocation.

- It is possible that team members can share common assumptions (spoken or unspoken) about the situation they are addressing which are not shared by many of the other stakeholders in the process. This can create barriers which can get in the way of effective working with partners, and in the worst case it can create a damaging 'us and them' mentality. While the assumptive method of planning noted above is a valuable way of making progress quickly, one of its risks is this very point. It is important as a consequence that assumptions are stated openly and checked out where possible with other stakeholders, just to ensure that assumptions that looked very helpful from within the team don't create barriers when looked at from outside it.

This identification of some of the strengths and potential weaknesses of team-working in planning leads to some very simple ground rules for effective team operation:

- Team management is important. There needs to be an agreed process, understood by all parties, which allows whatever management arrangements are agreed time and space not only to perform the conventional management tasks but also to maintain an overview of how effectively the team is performing, paying particular attention in this process to customer feedback.
- The composition of the team needs careful attention not only in terms of the skills mix desired but also in terms of the personal characteristics of the individual team members and their ability to work with each other. The objective should be to assemble a team with all the necessary strengths, and then to play to those strengths. Many managers don't get to pick their teams in the real world for a variety of reasons, but simply have to work with the teams they are given. In these situations, the opportunities to make changes to the team when they arise are critically important, and need to be seen not just in relation to a particular post which has become vacant or been created but in relation to the needs of the team as a whole.
- The team needs to see itself as being engaged in a task for which all team members share responsibility. Important components of this include collective ownership of the objectives to be achieved, of the methods of working, and of the internal and external communication practices that the team will adopt.
- Individual team members need to be confident about their roles within the team and the relationships between these roles, the roles of other team members and the tasks of the team as a whole.

They need to accept as part of this process the responsibilities that go with team membership, both to their colleagues and to the team as a whole.

- The team needs to see itself as operating within a learning environment, where it constantly strives to improve its performance through reflecting on both its experiences and the environment in which those experiences are set and through developing the contribution of every individual team member. Awareness of the continuing relevance of the team's output and working methods is an important part of this process. In turn, this approach will provide for the individual an appropriate work opportunity through which to develop as a professional.

- The team needs to operate on the principle that it is seeking to maximize the benefits that derive from team-working methods and to avoid as far as possible the pitfalls that can arise from this method of working. Awareness both of the potential inherent in team working and of the problems that may arise is a first step in the process of translating the principle into practice.

- Team members always need to remember the wider whole of which they form a part. Most planning departments, for example, will consist of several teams that will interact with each other at various levels and in various ways, and they are in this sense mutually dependent and thus ought also to be mutually supportive. One of the problems that many organizations can face, however, is that the boundary lines that define their team or group structures can become barriers to communication across them, and this can be counter-productive for the organization as a whole. Team loyalties need to coexist with organizational loyalties, not to supplant them.

Lots of people become managers of planning teams in the first instance without any formal management training at all; in effect, they are often promoted to positions of this nature because of their effective performance as planners and not because of any management skills they have demonstrated, although their performance as planners might also have suggested some management potential. There is a huge literature about management, and it is not the intention of this book to get into this field, but a useful general introduction is provided by Fincham and Rhodes (2005). This subject is also discussed in Chapter 7.

Team membership will be a significant part of the professional lives of planners who work in public sector organizations and in many private and voluntary sector organizations as well. Even where planners are essentially working as individuals providing services directly to a known customer, it is helpful for them to think about the set of relationships of which this particular one-to-one connection forms a part as being the equivalent of a team. These experiences will give planners plenty of opportunities to reflect not only on the successes and failings of the team but also on the internal dynamics of team operation. Trying to understand what it is about some teams that makes them work more effectively than others is a complex and subtle task, because it may well be about human relationships at least as much as it is about the more obviously professional components of team-working. But it is a task that is well worth attempting as part of the continuous process of reflective practice, precisely because the team mechanism plays such an important role in so much planning activity.

Conclusions

Much of this chapter has been about the need for planners as individuals to be aware of and to work at improving elements of their own approaches to their jobs where they can make a big difference themselves – auditing and improving their own communication skills, thinking about the ethics and values which shape their approach to their work, developing the skills of the reflective practitioner, and thinking about how to improve their personal contributions in teamwork situations. My experience has been that the people who do these things regularly and well have been the people who have tended to make the most progress, both in a hierarchical sense and in terms of my own perceptions of the quality of their contributions. The people prepared to commit to developing their personal skills in this way as a result have tended to be the people who have often been asked to take on some of the most challenging opportunities, and in turn these situations have tended to provide some of the most fruitful opportunities for reflective practice. So, while planners can often feel that in the work they are doing they are not very fully in control of many of the variables that impact upon that work, this chapter has been about something that they really can influence – themselves, and their approaches to their jobs.

Self-assessment topics

1. Carry out an audit of your own communication skills. Try to evaluate honestly how effective you think your speaking, listening, writing and graphic communication skills are. Show this audit to people you can trust who are able to evaluate it independently, and discuss any points of disagreement between your self-evaluation and their perspective. Develop a personal plan which targets those areas of this audit which are the weakest, and which tries to improve them through practice to a more acceptable level. Try to identify people who are willing and able to provide relevant coaching as part of this process.

2. Take a sample of planning documents produced locally. Who are their customers intended to be? How effectively do you think these documents communicate with those customers? How might they have been improved in these terms?

3. Study carefully the key elements of the ethical and behavioural principles summarized in Boxes 6.2 to 6.7. How much of this material can you personally sign up for? What sorts of problems can you see arising from any of these principles? To what extent do you think that some of the elements in these frameworks might potentially be in conflict with some of their other elements?

4. Take any example of any teams of which you have recently been a part. It does not for these purposes need to be a planning team, or even a team tackling a planning-related job. How effectively do you think this team operated? What were the main elements that led you to this conclusion? To what extent was this about the internal dynamics of the team, and to what extent was this about the external environment in which the team was trying to operate? In relation to its internal dynamics, try to list what were its main strengths and weaknesses. How could more use have been made of the strengths, and how could the weaknesses have been overcome? How effective and how satisfying was your own role as a team member, and how might your personal contribution to the work of the team have been improved? What were the main difficulties you experienced, and how might these have been overcome?

Chapter 7

Organizational, Management and Political Context Skills

Introduction

Chapter 3 was mainly about the procedural dimensions of planning, and in particular the fact that planners need to be expert in the ways things get done because participants in the planning process need advice and guidance about this. This chapter looks broadly at this same set of issues, but from a different perspective – how to deliver planning outcomes within the structures that exist for this purpose. In other words, while Chapter 3 was about advising people how best they can relate to planning systems, this chapter is about how to make planning systems work from the inside.

The importance of this particular dimension of skills for planning practice is fairly straightforward to explain, in terms of the familiar distinction between means and ends. Most of the chapters of this book to date have been primarily about the ends or the purposes of planning, but this chapter is essentially about the means involved in delivering effective planning services. It is about the planner as an insider in complex public organizations, where there are corporate (as distinct from specifically planning), managerial and political dimensions to the process of getting things done. Ends will not be achieved without the means to do this, and planners need to be good at delivery as well as clear about what they want to achieve. So this chapter is about understanding some of the key dimensions of delivery that planners have to address when working in relatively large public organizations. These may not necessarily be local authorities, since there are several different models available for the delivery of public planning services, but they are likely to be organizations with corporate as well as planning service objectives, with managerial structures and expectations, and with processes of taking decisions which have a political dimension to them, often involving lay (that is, non-expert) people representing the intended customers of the service in some manner and operating in a way that can loosely be described as 'political'.

After a brief section which looks at decision-making in planning, this chapter proceeds by scanning the corporate dimension of organizational behaviour and its planning implications, the challenge of managing the delivery of planning services, and some of the processes of working with elected members as planning decision-makers. It concludes with some self-assessment topics designed to enable readers to explore some of the material discussed in this chapter for themselves.

Decision-making in planning

The key decisions in planning as a public service are likely to be around the nature and content of plans, the improvement initiatives that are undertaken in order to help to implement them, and decisions around permissions to develop in relation to proposals made by others in the context of the guidance provided by plans. The principles that shape such decisions in most societies are usually governed by statutes, which also specify which organizations have the power to take them on behalf of the community at large. Of itself this very simplified explanation begins to sketch in why planning decisions are not merely left to planners as experts but have a political dimension to them, even if this is often more about the framework within which the planning team works rather than about each individual decision. The powers in question are public powers, and in a democratic society we expect such powers to be exercised by people who are accountable to us in some way or another. They are also powers that are granted to organizations which are by their very nature political organizations, such as local authorities, even if this doesn't necessarily and always mean 'political' in its narrowest and most partisan sense of party politics.

There is a third reason why planning as a public activity needs to be seen as a political process. This is that, by the very nature of what it does, there are gainers and losers, sometimes on a large scale, as a result of planning decisions. An individual development proposal, for example, can have the capability of making large amounts of money for landowners and for developers, but it can also have adverse consequences for other groups in society, for example in terms of factors such as traffic, noise, visual intrusion, and hours of operation. The planning process as a consequence is about balancing these interests (whether it is doing this consciously or not), and this is an inherently political activity because it involves advantaging some people and disadvantaging others. Of course, in an ideal world all development proposals would bring all gain and no pain – the classic 'win:win' position. But in the real world development proposals on any scale are by no means always like this, and so real choices have to be made. This has given rise to the notion of 'balance' as an oft-repeated classic planners' word, but in truth the judgements that provide the basis for a balancing act in any situation stem at least as much from the values that are being applied to this situation as they do from any supposedly neutral professional appraisal, and the process of determining what these values should be must therefore at its heart be a political process.

I have commenced this section with this line of argument because it was one I really struggled to understand when I was a planning student. I know from my own dealings with planning students today that it remains problematic for many. What is the point, these doubters might suggest, in me having this extensive (and expensive) professional education in planning if the views of lay people with none of this expertise are going to take preference over mine? I hope that the above discussion has clarified at least three aspects of this:

1. Because planning powers are formally vested in organizations where formal decision-making powers rest with elected members or their equivalents.
2. Because the basis of planning decision-making is a series of stances which are about where the broader public interest is seen as lying, in terms of the future development of places and the needs of the people who live and work in them. Such judgements ought ultimately to be made by people who are accountable to the population at large in some appropriate manner.
3. Because the subject matter of planning is about who gets what and under what circumstances, and the bases on which decisions about matters of this nature are made are inherently political.

These points are much better understood today than they were in the 1960s when I was a planning student; or perhaps that would be put more accurately as: these points are better expressed in the literature today than they were then. When Alan Altshuler was debating these dimensions of his case-studies, and talking about the strategies he observed planners using to claim power for themselves rather than to acknowledge the inherently political nature of their actions (one example of which opens Chapter 2 of this book), that came as a revelation to many (Altshuler, 1965). Today, however, the inherently political nature of planning as a public activity is a starting-point for much planning theory writing (see, for example, Brooks, 2002, ch. 1). As Brooks puts it:

> Planners address the most important, and often most visible, issues confronting their communities; these issues tend to be wider problems for which definition, causes, and solutions remain elusive; and planners are subject to numerous external influences that assist in shaping their roles and responsibilities. Another way of saying all this, of course, is simply to note that planning is a highly political activity. (Ibid., p. 13)

Even if a less cerebral approach is taken, and the starting-point becomes not reflection on the planning task but the operational experiences of planners, the destination is essentially the same one. To quote Brooks again:

> Spend fifteen minutes with a planner, inquire about the project on which she or he is currently spending the most time, and you will very shortly be hearing about the politics of the situation. (Ibid.)

Thus, student doubts about the political dimension of planning need to be converted into an acceptance that it is an inevitable component of the planning endeavour in a democratic society, and that the planning task in these circumstances is one of working within the political process and in particular of giving politicians the best planning advice you can. This is not so much a matter of denying the value of professional expertise, therefore, but rather about trying to construct its proper relationships with what are inherently political processes.

Of course, the nature of the process of political involvement changes over time and from place to place. I can exemplify this in terms of the process of development control decision-making during my own career. During the late 1970s I worked for South Tyneside MBC, a then newly created local authority (it emerged from the 1974 re-organization of local government in England), where the principle applied by the controlling Labour group was that of detailed elected member control of all the workings of the authority. There may also have been an element in this of lack of trust of the officers by the elected members, not in the sense that the officers were inherently untrustworthy but in the sense that everyone was in new roles and that no tradition had built up as a consequence of officers and members working together on development control issues. The combination of these factors meant that there was very little delegation of development control decision-making to the officers. In Manchester during the 1980s and the first half of the 1990s the situation was very different (Kitchen, 1997, ch. 5). There, a long-established city council had a long tradition of development control decision-making with established and trusted procedures, and from the mid 1980s to the mid 1990s the share of planning applications delegated to the officers for determination rose gently from around 55 per cent (which itself was a much higher figure than in South Tyneside when I left in 1979) to around 65 per cent. The essence of this was that non-contentious items were delegated (ibid., p. 89). The policy of the government since 2002/03 has been that all local planning authorities should delegate a minimum of 90 per cent of planning applications for determination by their officers (DTLR, 2001, para. 6.37). The basis for this is partly that in a plan-led system a much higher proportion of decisions should be straightforward than was previously the case, but I suspect that it came mainly from a recognition that this was one of the most effective ways of speeding up the process of planning decision-making which as we have already seen was a primary government objective. The process of getting local planning authorities to go down such a road was not likely to be straightforward, however, especially when for many individual elected members this was seen as taking away their involvement in decision-making and instead handing more power to the officers. As a consequence, major efforts were made through the Local Government Association (the body that represents local authorities in England) both to argue the case for more delegation and to offer models to local planning authorities to show how this could be achieved (Local Government Association, 2004).

What these three sets of stories reveal, however, is a large-scale change over the period in question in the balance between elected member and officer involvement in development control decision-making, with the role of elected members being substantially reduced but not eliminated entirely over a period of less than thirty years. The reason it is still thought to be appropriate for elected members to be involved in up to 10 per cent of applications is that these are likely to be the complex and controversial ones where some of the judgements to be made in determining them should properly be the subject of political debate.

A similar story of how the terms of debates about the political nature of planning decision-making have changed can be found in the discussion of whether elected members of local authorities in order to serve on planning committees ought to receive specific training in planning (which is dealt with later in this chapter in the section on working with elected members as planning decision-makers). What this shows is that the debate has moved from a discussion about whether such training is desirable or necessary to a discussion of whether it should be compulsory. But what has not changed here is the recognition of the importance of the political dimension of planning decision-making. Essentially, this debate accepts that political involvement is and will remain an important component of planning activity, and then proceeds to explore the need for an element of regulation through requiring some basic training as in effect a form of entry qualification to the performance of this political role. So, this is quite explicitly recognizing the political nature of planning decision-making, and then exploring whether this should operate in ways that are completely unregulated or whether bounds should be put on this process, in this case through the creation of a training requirement.

Another element in this process is the creation of guidance about how elected members should engage in planning matters, which links to the discussion in Chapter 6 of ethics and the guidance available about professional conduct to planners (see for example, Local Government Association, 2002, 2005). Again, the significance of this is that it quite explicitly accepts that there is an important political dimension in planning decision-making, and then seeks to deal with the issues to which this will commonly give rise, such as probity and the impartiality of decision-makers. So, when we are dealing with planning as a public act, we are dealing with a process that has important political dimensions to it. This situation is inescapable; and nor should we seek to escape from it, because in several ways it is a desirable and necessary thing. The recognition of this situation, and then the development of the necessary understandings and skills to be able to operate successfully in such an environment, is one of the starting-points for this chapter.

The corporate dimension of organizational behaviour

One of the most noticeable changes that occurred during my planning practice life was that local government in England attempted to become much more corporate. That is to say, instead of it being a collection of service deliverers that each operated to a considerable extent in isolation from the other service deliverers, it sought to take a collective view of key issues and opportunities that transcended individual service delivery boundaries and that in turn provided a framework within which each of those individual services was expected to operate. A big question for service deliverers in this context was often around the extent to which they felt that their expertise had been properly drawn upon in assembling such corporate perspectives, or whether they felt that these had been imposed largely by 'the centre' without much regard to the experiences and practices of those who often felt that they had more contact with what was happening on the ground (see for example Kitchen, 1991). Such tensions, in my experience, existed throughout the rise of the corporate ethic, but they did little to deflect its course.

The intellectual argument for a more corporate approach to the affairs of a local authority has been around for a long time (see, for example, Leach *et al.*, 1994, ch. 5; Blackman, 1995, especially pp. 25–9), and has drawn much of its strength from the development of corporate thinking in relation to businesses and other organizations (see, for example, Argenti, 1968).

Taken at a very straightforward level, the fact that the various service departments of a local authority are always serving the same local population, even if by virtue of their functions many of them concentrate on particular segments of that population, would suggest that an element of working for a common good must be part of what those departments do. My experience was that this was a view many local government staff shared, but they also tended to see their priorities primarily in terms of their service delivery imperatives, which inevitably meant that at times there were tensions between these two positions. One of the reasons for this is that the requirements for successful corporate working can be quite onerous; Carmona *et al.* (2001, p. 40) put these as follows:

- Agreed authority-wide objectives, based on a strategic vision;
- A willingness to share information and resources;
- Commitment to joint working at the highest level; and
- A desire to seek collaborative, shared solutions to problems.

I have certainly worked in circumstances where between one and all of these requirements were missing from the apparent behaviour of some of the key players, and corporate working can be a real struggle in these circumstances. My experience of spending half of 1992 as acting chief executive of Manchester City Council, and therefore of being responsible for the corporate machine rather than for an individual service within it, certainly reinforced these difficulties in my mind. This perhaps helps to explain why the record of English local government in terms of successful corporate working seems to be quite patchy, and why some local authorities have appeared to be much more successful at this at various points in time than have others.

But I first came across this in practice in terms of the need to approach a task in a way radically different from the norm when South Tyneside Metropolitan Borough Council (MBC) (the authority I was working for at the time) acquired the status of 'programme authority' under the Inner Urban Areas Act 1978. What this meant for the authority was that it was being given the opportunity to obtain significant additional funds via the government's Urban Programme (usually in the form of 75 per cent grants) to enable it to tackle what today would be recognized as conventional inner city problems, but it could only obtain those funds by preparing and submitting to the government an 'inner areas programme' (Department of the Environment, 1977). Such a programme would need to include *inter alia* an analysis of the key problems, an understanding of the ways in which these were already being tackled through the application of mainstream funds and of the scope for 'bending' these to provide a stronger inner urban emphasis in their use, and a programme of further actions that could be undertaken for which specific Urban Programme funding was being sought. This was a huge challenge to the council, because these sorts of questions cut right across the formal structure of the authority; there was no part of the organization that already did things like this comprehensively and as a matter of course. At the same time, the council certainly didn't want to turn away this kind of opportunity. As a consequence, a new corporate team was established to undertake the task of preparing the first inner areas programme for South Tyneside drawn from several departments of the authority, and I found myself in the position of being the day-to-day leader of that team. Without any false modesty, I think that the reason why leadership for this process was sought from and provided by the planning service was because it came nearest to being the part of the organization 'that already did things like this com-prehensively and as a matter of course' – its perspective was the borough as a whole and the welfare of its constituent parts, rather than functional service delivery of the type provided by (for example) housing, education, and social services, important elements though all three of this latter groupings were in understanding and tackling the borough's inner city problems. The point of this, though, was that a corporate objective – that of taking this new opportunity by developing an inner areas policy posi-tion which saw service delivery in an integrated manner – became of over-riding importance, and as a result the structure of the organization had to be adapted by informal means in order to do this, with the planning serv-ice given a prominent role in this process.

Many practising planners in Britain over the past twenty to thirty years would be able to tell similar stories. Planning and planners were often playing significant parts in such processes because the spatial focus of planning made it different from the more functional focus of most other services, and perhaps more receptive to initiatives which cut across traditional structures and took area-based perspectives. Development plans also had the potential to offer a focus on place that was lacking from most of the other key policy documents prepared by local author-ities, although as we have already seen in this book this has often been a struggle for development plans in practice for a variety of conceptual and operational reasons. The new styles of plans introduced in England by the Planning and Compulsory Purchase Act 2004 are in part aimed to get back some of this potential role in providing a strategic and spa-tial focus, but developments over the intervening period have put in place some important differences as compared with previous situations. For present purposes, two of the most important (and interrelated) of these are the expectation that every local authority will have in place an over-arching community strategy, and that the process of preparing documents of this nature will not just be about the work of a local authority but will also involve extensive processes of partnership. Each of these is therefore discussed in more detail below.

The duty placed on English local authorities to prepare community strategies arises from the Local Government Act 2000. Box 7.1 summarizes essentially what these are, drawing from the government's contemporary guidance about this to local authorities (DTLR, 2000). What should be immediately obvious from this summary is just how over-arching community strategies are intended to be, because it is arguable that up until that point in time (whatever development plans in some instances might have aspired to be) no single document covered all of this ground. The nearest to this model might well have been the 'city pride prospectuses' produced by some cities in the 1990s, again to try to broaden out from pre-existing discussions of how the regeneration of these cities would be approached (see, for example, Manchester City Council *et al.*, 1994).

Box 7.1 Community strategies in England

The *task* of a community strategy is 'to enhance the quality of life of local communities and contribute to the achievement of sustainable development in the UK through action to improve the economic, social and environmental well-being of the area and its inhabitants'.

To this end, a community strategy will have to meet four *objectives*:

- Allow local communities (however defined) to articulate their aspirations, needs and priorities;
- Coordinate the actions of the council and all the other public, private, voluntary and community organizations that operate locally;
- Focus and shape the existing and future activities of these organizations so that they effectively meet community needs and aspirations;
- Contribute to the achievement of sustainable development both locally and more widely.

As a consequence, a community strategy must have four key *components*:

- A long-term vision for the area focusing on the outcomes that are to be achieved;
- An action plan identifying shorter-term priorities and activities that will contribute to the achievement of long-term outcomes;
- A shared commitment to implement the action plan and proposals for doing so;
- Arrangements for monitoring the implementation of the action plan for periodically reviewing the strategies, and for reporting progress to local communities.

And while community strategies will be different from each other to reflect local circumstances, they will all be based on four underpinning *principles*:

- Engage and involve local communities;
- Involve active participation of councillors within and outside the executive;
- Be prepared and implemented by a broad 'local strategic partnership' through which the local authority can work with other local bodies;
- Be based on a proper assessment of needs and the availability of resources.

Source: A summary of the main strands of advice in Department for Transport, Local Government and the Regions, 2000.

Box 7.2 then gives an example of a community strategy prepared within this framework, which in this instance is the community strategy for Hull prepared under the auspices of Hull Cityvision, which is the city's local strategic partnership. Again, the breadth of the approach being taken should be clear from this example. In particular, an examination of the eight strategic themes in the Hull example will show fairly quickly that the planning process could be expected to contribute in a variety of ways to all of them. Indeed, one of the challenges to plan-making in England in the light of the reforms introduced in the Planning and Compulsory Purchase Act 2004 is to find effective ways both of

---

Box 7.2   The Hull community strategy

The Hull community strategy operates at three levels. The highest level is a broad strategic vision, which is then followed through into eight key themes, which are in turn each developed in the form of an action plan.

Vision:
The 15-year vision in the Hull community strategy is that Hull should become:

'A CONFIDENT, DYNAMIC AND INCLUSIVE CITY, WHERE PEOPLE WANT TO LIVE, LEARN, WORK, VISIT AND INVEST.'

Key themes:
The strategy then identified eight key themes:

- Maintaining and improving community safety
- Improving health and social welfare
- Regenerating the city's economy
- Protecting and enhancing the environment
- Enhancing image and raising aspirations
- Creating a learning city
- Reinvigorating the housing market
- Improving transport

Actions:
There is then an action plan for each of these eight key themes, comprising four elements in each case:

- Objectives
- How will we measure success?
- What is our baseline position (that is, where are we starting from?)?
- Specific actions to be undertaken

Source: Summarized from Hull Cityvision, 2002.

---

assisting with the achievement of the outcomes sought in community strategies and also of contributing to the further development of the strategies themselves. The potential benefits of getting this relationship right might include:

- An improved understanding of community needs in the process of plan-making, given that the community strategy is expected to be grounded in those needs.
- A more holistic and integrated approach to future development.
- An approach which helps to join up community planning at the strategic and local scales.
- Recognition of the value of the local development framework (the new style of development plan being introduced in England) as a delivery mechanism.
- The scope for economies of scale through sharing resources in researching and preparing documents.

- The scope for resolving conflicting objectives through the range and extent of stakeholder involvement both processes will involve. (Entec UK Ltd, 2003).

The study that looked at these issues for the British government also looked at the things that planners might do in order to improve the likelihood of these potential benefits being achieved (ibid.), and this material is summarized in Box 7.3. Much of this is about how to handle complexity, since the situation being addressed here is very complex – a multiplicity of organizations, with multiple overlapping strategies and action plans and what may seem like a bewildering pattern of organizational participation in activities. As a consequence, work is being undertaken on the scope for the rationalization of some strategic requirements in order *inter alia* to reduce some of this complexity, in the context of having effective community strategies in place (Wells *et al.*, 2005), and it seems to me that in principle this is an inherently desirable thing to attempt. The reason for this is simply that the growth of the corporate and partnership dimensions of organizational behaviour in the process of governance, no matter how beneficial and indeed necessary this has been, has in my experience been accompanied inexorably by a growth in complexity, which in turn has contributed to the procedural problems that activities such as planning have been experiencing in doing everything that has been expected of them. This is not too difficult to understand if one reflects on the fact that the very sensible advice contained in Box 7.3 about how to tackle some of these issues will in itself be resource-expensive, because not all of it by any means is about how to do more efficiently things that would have to be done anyway.

This problem of the complexity that the corporate and the partnership dimension introduces is not just a function of having a significant number of strategies and action plans, each owned by a different organization, which need to be integrated. It also arises because some of the new organizational structures that the contemporary emphasis on working through partnerships have brought into being are themselves very complex. Box 7.4 shows one example of this, in looking at the structure of Sheffield First, which is the local strategic partnership (LSP) for Sheffield as it was up to 2005. LSPs have to be established in the 88 local authority areas which are the recipients of the government's neighbourhood regeneration funding (Social Exclusion Unit, 2001), of which Sheffield is one. In practice, however, most English local authorities have now established an LSP with their local partners because of the opportunity it offers to develop the partnership dimension of local governance; and so the problem of complexity as far as the planning service is concerned which is illustrated by this example is now a commonplace one.

Looking at the structure in Box 7.4, the overall strategic partnership on the right-hand side of the diagram is responsible for the city strategy.

Box 7.3   Advice to planners about how to link community strategies and local development frameworks effectively

NB: CS = Community strategy, which is in effect the corporate plan for the area.

LDF = Local development framework, which is the development plan for the area.

Policy content linkages

- See the LDF as giving spatial expression to those elements of the CS which relate to the use and development of land.
- Share visions where appropriate.
- See sustainable development as providing a common framework.
- Relate the strategic objectives of the CS to the requirement that the LDF should include a core strategy.
- Link the area action planning dimensions of the two documents whenever possible.
- Interpret the spatial dimensions of CS action plans.
- Use common targets and indicators wherever possible, and ensure that they are:
  S – specific
  M – measurable
  A – achievable
  R – relevant
  T – time based

Process linkages

- Programme and manage processes in linked or aligned manners.
- Contribute directly through as many channels as possible to the CS vision and strategic objectives.
- Integrate with other strategies.
- Get involved in the area planning dimensions of work on the CS and other key strategic documents.
- Integrate LDF work with wider community involvement activities.
- Use common or linked appraisal processes.
- Address cross-boundary or (in areas where there are two tiers of local government) two-tier issues.
- Share information gathering and monitoring.
- Adopt common branding to help develop community awareness and involvement.
- Link organizational and working structures where this is practicable.

Source: Information from Entec UK Ltd, 2003, pp. v–vii.

Each of the eight parallel functional partnerships in the centre of the diagram has its own strategy and action programme, with in most cases the extent of this being obvious from the title – the one that probably isn't obvious is Sheffield One, which is the urban regeneration company for

---

Box 7.4   The Sheffield First 'family' of partnerships

Sheffield First Forum	Sheffield First for Learning	Sheffield First Partnership
	Sheffield First for Work	
	Sheffield First for Investment	
Other Statutory City-wide Partnerships	Sheffield One	
	Sheffield First for Inclusion	
	Sheffield First for Safety	
Area Action Panels	Sheffield First for Health	
	Sheffield First for Environment	

Source: Sheffield First Partnership, 2003.

This structure was changed in late 2005 to align it more closely to the key strategic priorities in the new city strategy, but it wasn't made any less complex as a result.

---

the city centre. And the groupings on the left side of the diagram represent other components in the governance of the city with which regular contact/consultation is expected. So, in order to cover the ground that it needs to cover, the structure of the Sheffield First 'family' of partnerships (this is their own language, with the word 'family' no doubt being deliberately chosen because of the warm and supportive associations it conveys to most of us) is unavoidably complex – although probably no more so than equivalent structures elsewhere. This complexity is illustrated by the fact that each of these elements potentially needs to have contact on some matters with all of the others, creating possibly a very large number of interactions. My experience as chair of Sheffield First for Environment, however, has been that the number of meaningful interactions is nothing like the number of potential working connections, and it seems to be the case that the extensive nature of these potential contacts can also be a problem for external parties. The City Council's planning service, for example, sits outside this formal structure (although it is represented on Sheffield First for Environment), but potentially – and in many cases actually – it needs to liaise with all of the components of the diagram in Box 7.4 in order to understand the spatial dimensions of each of their individual strategies.

To a large extent this complexity is probably unavoidable given the way in which the task is conceptualized. It can be seen as an attempt through a formal structure to mirror the complexity of a real world which the process of partnership is attempting to represent, to serve, and to engage with. By its very nature, partnership involves working with more interests than would have been the case otherwise, because of the benefits this brings to the process of governance. The virtues of the partnership approach have been summarized succinctly by Carmona *et al.* (2001):

> The partnership approach establishes a culture of shared knowledge and understanding between partners, enabling innovative approaches to the sharing and management of information … As well as benefits at the development level, partnerships can also function as ongoing forums or panels for review, feedback and proactive involvement. (Ibid., p. 37)

These are virtues that are worth having. In my opinion, a planning service which is shaped by such interactions is likely to be a better and more effective service than one which is remote from this way of working. Put another way, this can be seen as another vehicle through which the kinds of customer-oriented planning services discussed in Chapter 5 can be developed. But one of the prices paid for this way of working is the added complexity it brings in its wake. Planners who work in systems like this need to be good at understanding that complexity, at helping others to understand it and to work with it (the types of skills discussed in Chapter 3), and at making partnership processes work effectively without slowing everything down unreasonably.

The challenge of managing the delivery of planning services

The classic tasks of the local government chief officer, which apply to its planning service just as much as they do to its many other services, are:

1. To advise the council appropriately;
2. To implement the council's decisions efficiently and expeditiously; and
3. To manage the resources the council agrees should be devoted to the service as effectively as possible.

Advising the council appropriately means a variety of different things. One element of this will be the formal decision-making structures of the authority, where advice will usually be tendered through written reports and also orally. Written reports are usually also public documents, and so they need to be seen not just as papers for the particular meeting in question but also as something that will be 'on the record' and part of the future development of the issues constituting their subject matter. In particular, in the planning world reports about development control issues can become in future key documents at a planning appeal, where in my experience they were often picked over more carefully than had been the case at the committee which made the original decision which then became the subject of the appeal. Such experiences, especially where hindsight suggests that parts of reports could have been better written, can become quite formative for planners, in the sense that they affect how report-writing is tackled on future occasions. As a result, generally I tended to find that experienced development controllers wrote competent reports, with a well-balanced description and appraisal of the proposal, identification of the key planning policy issues, presentation of the representations that had been made, and assessment of the decision options. Indeed, such reports should be written on the basis that their aim is to do these jobs well enough that the content of the report is helpful to someone who does not support its recommendations, in the sense that it still provides them with a sound basis for coming to a view.

But 'advising the council' isn't just about those formal occasions on which a written report is presented. It is also about the (often more frequent) occasions when planning advice is given orally to colleague-officers and to elected members, often as part of a much more informal meeting or discussion. Many of these are of an exploratory nature, where planning advice has the opportunity to contribute to the shaping of future possibilities but where it can also be difficult to offer clear-cut advice about issues that depend upon matters yet to be determined. So, for example, the broad planning policy position as it currently stands should be relatively easy to describe in the context of the subject matter under discussion, but what can be more difficult is the extent to which and the ways in which some of this policy guidance might be reviewed or changed and what the implications of these changes might be, as can be the case when development plan reviews are underway. Similarly, the acceptability of a development proposal depends not just upon its fit with the extant strategic policy framework but also on the quality of the development itself, and very often that is unclear at the time of such discussion. While most planners would enter discussions of this nature in a spirit of helpfulness, it is important that this does not lead them into expressing views or even giving what are perceived by others as assurances which are at risk of not standing up to future scrutiny. For example, it is unwise to forecast the outcome of a policy review process when the options being examined have not been out to public consultation, because it may well be that this process will lead to a change of view about what the preferred option might be. So planning advice in these situations often needs to be conditional, and to combine the best available view about the substantive issues with advice about the procedural aspects of the review process. In my experience, both colleague-officers and elected members were usually comfortable with this, provided that it was as clear as possible about time-scales. In other words, they accepted that it was not always possible for the planner to cover all the ground they might wish with clear-cut advice, but they wanted to know about what would be involved in clarifying the outstanding issues and over what period this could be expected to happen.

As far as the implementation of the council's decisions efficiently and expeditiously is concerned, the first point to note about this is that it is irrespective of whether or not the planning officer happens to agree with them. There is a time and a place for the planning officer to input views into the decision-making process, and essentially this is before the decision has been taken rather than after it. The council as the sovereign body is entitled to expect that its decisions will be implemented, and so too are all of its customers, and there really is no place in this process for a view which says that this process will be moderated if the planners dissent from it. For the avoidance of any doubt, this is not the 'I was only following orders' defence, because of the opportunity available to the planner to help to shape the decision in the first place which was usually denied to the users of that defence. This isn't to say that in these circumstances the planner has to agree with the decision or to represent it as their *bona fide* professional opinion (which in any event would be against the planner's code of professional conduct in the UK, as discussed in Chapter 6), but it is to say that the planner has to behave as an employee carrying out the wishes of the employer. This can be done using neutral rather than personal language ('the City Council's intention here is to ...'), and by refusing to be drawn on matters of personal opinion. Most planning decisions in my opinion are shades of grey rather than black or white, and so it is usually possible to focus on the positive elements of the chosen shade even when the individual would have made a different choice. If it is really impossible for the individual to live with a situation of this nature (and in truth I have very rarely seen this happen), then it is clearly time for that individual to move to another employer, but most planners in the public service don't seem to find it too difficult to come to terms with the fact that from time to time their employer will make decisions with which they don't agree.

Most of the action under the heading of implementation, though, will be in relation to issues where the planning officer has played an important role in helping to shape the decision in the first place, and often the necessary action will be a consequence of the advice that was given as part of that process. This ought usually to be relatively straightforward, and indeed the biggest problem I came across in this area was often not so much with the actions needing to be taken but with the need to ensure that all of the staff in the planning service were aware of this. People at the top of hierarchies can be guilty of assuming that because they are very close to the decision-making process, and because they play a role in shaping what it does, then everyone else in the organization is as well. But the truth is very often that staff are not aware of some of the things of this kind that are happening if they don't come across them in the normal course of their everyday jobs, and so the management structure of the organization needs to be effective at cascading knowledge of this nature to everyone who needs to be aware of it.

A good illustration of this kind of issue was the need in the mid 1980s to ensure that all the staff in the area teams in Manchester who took decisions on what the consultation areas for submitted planning applications should be were aware of the fact that elected members felt that these areas were often drawn too narrowly (because they said they kept getting representations from people who felt that they ought to have been consulted but hadn't been), and wanted to see them broadened. This was in practice a process that involved significant numbers of people throughout the four area teams, because it had to be a judgement made in the light of local circumstances, and almost certainly it was also a process that was being carried out by these people with a degree of inconsistency – not just because of the feedback from elected members, but also because the principles that were applied were expressed in very general terms and left plenty of room for judgement in individual cases. So the process of giving effect to this elected member view wasn't just a question of a general edict to all staff, but was about explaining what elected members wanted to do and why, trying to clarify what the principles were here so as to encourage greater consistency in their application, and trying to get staff to review their own practices positively in the light of this feedback. In other words, it was about getting staff buy-in to the process, in a situation where some adverse staff reaction might have been expected because in practice this was asking them to do more; broader consultation areas meant more work in undertaking consultations and then in taking into account the views that they produced. The reason why this approach was adopted was because in practice the key components of the implementation of this decision would not be undertaken by the senior managers; with over 2000 planning applications each year, these decisions would have to continue to be taken on a case-by-case basis by the individual caseworkers, and there was no practical alternative to this approach. So getting staff buy-in to this approach was critical to its success, and in my experience this is very often true of the process of implementing policy changes if this requires aspects of service delivery to be reviewed. It is very difficult to assess how successful this initiative was, however, because the experience seemed to be that widening consultation areas didn't stem comments to elected members to the effect that people felt they should have been consulted and hadn't been. This was therefore done as a more or less gradual process throughout much of the 1980s and early 1990s, and undoubtedly the scale of the development control consultation process in Manchester expanded considerably as a consequence (Kitchen, 1997, pp. 86, 87). Perhaps this process should be seen as one example of how the planning process tried to respond to the phenomenon discussed in Chapter 1 of this book of an ever-increasing public expectation of involvement in planning processes.

In one sense, managing as effectively as possible the resources that the council agrees should be devoted to the planning service is no different from many other kinds of management jobs. Box 7.5, for example, adapts a diagram about basic managerial functions in organizations from one of the standard management texts (Moorhead and Griffin, 1995), and it is not difficult to see how this would apply to a planning organization just as much as to other types.

There are five characteristics of the diagram in Box 7.5 that stand out for me in terms of thinking about its application to planning organizations:

1. An organization that exists to plan ought to be good at applying that same discipline to itself, in terms of working out how it wants to improve and how it intends to get there. In most local authorities now in any event there is a process of service or business planning which looks at issues like this, typically over periods of one year and of three-five years, so that development intentions in relation to the service are clearly set out and open to discussion, including in particular with the staff directly affected.

2. Leadership is a particularly important characteristic in a planning organization. It is likely that in this kind of professional organization there will be no shortage of views about what the organization might do which need to be tapped into, but which also need to be pulled together to create a shared sense of purpose, without which the organization can easily be seen to be pulling in several different directions. This is a key leadership task.

3. One of the most important pieces of feedback that planning organizations should seek is the views of their customers about the services they provide. If planning organizations aspire to be customer-oriented, it is important not only that they obtain views of this nature both from their ongoing activities and from periodic special studies but also that they act on them.

4. The most important resource that most planning organizations have at their disposal is their staff. This can all too easily degenerate into being a truism, but the skills, motivation and contacts of their staff are often the primary asset of an organization that tends not to have much disposable cash once the staff have been paid, and not to have

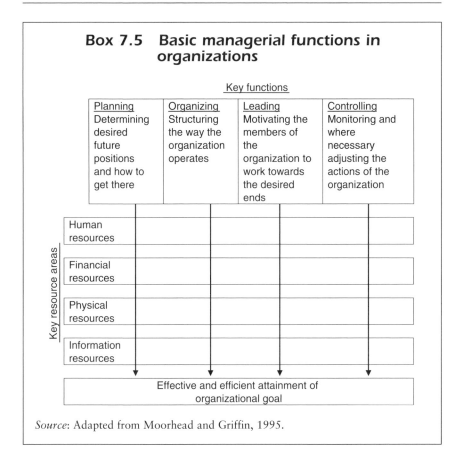

Box 7.5 Basic managerial functions in organizations

Key functions

	Planning	Organizing	Leading	Controlling
	Determining desired future positions and how to get there	Structuring the way the organization operates	Motivating the members of the organization to work towards the desired ends	Monitoring and where necessary adjusting the actions of the organization
Human resources				
Financial resources				
Physical resources				
Information resources				

Key resource areas

Effective and efficient attainment of organizational goal

Source: Adapted from Moorhead and Griffin, 1995.

much by way of physical resources either. So how this asset is used by its managers is capable of making a huge difference to the performance of the organization.

5. Second in importance to the people who staff the organization in terms of the availability of resources to a planning organization is usually its information resources. The focus on places and the people who live in or use them tends to mean that planning organizations assemble information about these matters in order to do their own job which is also seen as a valuable asset by others, and the ability and willingness to contribute in this way can often help planning organizations to gain a seat at the table in some circumstances which maybe otherwise they would not get.

In order to carry out the key functions described in Box 7.5 successfully, argue Moorhead and Griffin (ibid., pp. 32, 33) following Katz (1987), most successful managers have a strong combination of four sets of skills:

Technical Those skills necessary to accomplish specific tasks within the organization.
Interpersonal The manager's ability to communicate with, understand and motivate individuals and groups.
Conceptual The manager's ability to think in the abstract.
Diagnostic The manager's ability to understand cause-and-effect relationships, and to recognize the optimal solutions to problems.

Again, I would argue that these skills are directly relevant to the task of managing a planning organization, but the interesting question here is whether planners tend to get into such positions by displaying such skills or whether they get into them by demonstrating that they are good planners. It could be argued, of course, that the fact that they have proved themselves to be good planners will mean that they are likely to possess some of these skills anyway. For example, a successful planner is likely to have demonstrated some technical skills at least, some strong interpersonal skills (assuming that by 'successful' we mean in terms of the ability to work effectively with some of the customers of the planning services), some conceptual thinking capability (in terms of the ability to see 'the big picture' or to identify a desirable end state and to work towards it), and possibly also some diagnostic skills in the sense of finding solutions to problems. Nevertheless, my experience was that the mere fact that someone had been a successful planner was not a guarantee that they would then become a successful manager of planners; although what it did tend to mean was that they started off their managerial career with the respect of the staff working for them, and in itself that was a considerable advantage. There were two characteristics in particular that I thought marked out those who were to become successful managers. One was the ability never to lose sight of the big picture – what the organization was trying to achieve and how this particular part of it could best contribute – and to be constantly inventive about ways of moving in this direction in the given resource situation. The other characteristic of the successful planner-manager was the ability to encourage and to develop people. The importance of this was regularly reinforced for me when I saw people suddenly flourish when working for one manager when they hadn't under their previous one, and though this is undoubtedly in part about the individual it is also about the approach of the manager to developing the people he/she has got. This latter point is of particular significance because in most instances managers are appointed to extant teams rather than having the opportunity to construct their own team.

There is another important distinction in the management literature which is critical to understanding the task facing planners in key public sector positions. This is the distinction between leadership and management. Box 7.6, developed from Huczynski and Buchanan (2001, p. 704), explores this distinction.

This perhaps suggests that leadership is a more dramatic and less mundane process than management, but organizations really need both of these approaches to be working in harmony. I would certainly argue that the successful planner-manager needs to be both a leader and a manager in the terms of Box 7.6.

One particular challenge British planner-managers have faced in recent years has been the challenge of improving the performance of the planning system in response to government pressure. They have been much aided in this by the development by the organization representing chief planning officers of thinking about what constitutes excellence in the delivery of planning services (see, for example, Planning Officers Society, 2002, 2003). Much of this government pressure has focused on improving development control performance when measured by the speed of decision-making. As we have seen previously, this has arisen from the British government's near obsession with this particular element of the planning service, which has been accompanied by a regime of sticks (targets set, with the threat of government intervention if local planning authorities don't meet these targets; ODPM, 2003a) and carrots (a reward

---

Box 7.6   Leadership and management functions compared

Huczynski and Buchanan distinguish between leadership and management functions in four common types of activity in organizations:

- In creating an agenda, the task of the leader is to establish the broad vision of the future and to set the direction, whereas the job of the manager is to turn this into operational effectiveness through actions such as planning, budgeting and resource allocation.
- In developing people, the leader brings groups together, communicates visions and strategies and secures buy-in on the parts of the emergent teams, whereas the manager organizes staffing, sets up structures, and puts in place appropriate procedures.
- In the execution of key tasks, the leader motivates and inspires, energizing people to overcome difficulties, whereas the manager controls, solves problems as they arise, monitors and tasks corrective action as needed.
- In terms of the outcomes that can arise from their actions, leaders can produce positive and sometimes even dramatic change, whereas managers are more likely to produce order, consistency and predictability.

Most organizations (and planning organizations are no different) need both of these elements to be operating in complementary ways, with an appropriate balance established between them.

Source: Summarized from Huczynski and Buchanan, 2001, p. 704.

for improved performance, in the form of Planning Delivery Grant; ODPM, 2003b). In its own terms, this isn't too difficult a challenge to meet from a management perspective, since it could be achieved by putting more staff resources into development control and by being more ruthless about the operation of procedures. The difficulty, however, comes in terms of those other service delivery objectives that operate in parallel with this one and that might be affected by resource transfers of this kind (such as the need to get on with new plan-making efforts in the light of the Planning and Compulsory Purchase Act 2004), and also in terms of those service delivery objectives that could well be in conflict with this one (such as providing services that customers think are of an acceptable standard, and developing public consultation in relation to development control). Effective planning management involves achieving the best balance between these sets of objectives that is possible, taking into account the views of all the key stakeholders in the locality (that is, not just those of the government). Pragmatic planning management, however, seems in many local planning authorities to have involved doing what is necessary to achieve a reasonable Planning Delivery Grant allocation, given that this then provides resources at least for a period of time to build up the service. At the time of writing it is too early to form a judgement about the longer-term implications of this challenge, but two things can be said about it. The first is that, generally speaking, the appearance of the Planning Delivery Grant mechanism does appear to have had a positive impact on development control performance (Addison and Associates with Arup, 2004, 2005), confirming that planning managers have indeed tried to grab the carrot on offer. The second is that senior planning managers seem to be very well aware of the conflicts this challenge suggests with the imperative to improve public engagement with planning, but feel that this latter desire will need to be tempered by the necessity to obtain the extra resources on offer because they can then be used to improve the whole service and not just its development control element (Kitchen and Whitney, 2004). The longer view of all of this may turn out to depend upon how long this particular financial regime lasts, since for many local planning authorities it represents the first real opportunity to improve their planning service after years of decline or at any rate of stasis, but it does raise important questions about the extent to which a financial intervention of this kind distorts service delivery priorities or at least replaces a local view of this balance with a central one.

Working with elected members as planning decision-makers

One of the most difficult tasks facing a (usually senior) planner in the public service can be 'speaking truth to power' (Wildavsky, 1979), where 'power' is represented by the people in positions of political leadership. It can also be one of the most necessary tasks. Why might it be difficult? Benveniste (1989, pp. 9–18) begins to answer this question helpfully by separating the planning function into two broad groupings: functions where power speaks to planners and planning serves power, and functions where planners both speak to and alter power. Both of these sets of activities tend to coexist in planning organizations operating in the public service, which means that planners sometimes will have to take instructions from the sources of political leadership and sometimes will have to seek to guide those sources in coping with processes of change. Put like this, it is not too difficult to see why speaking truth to power might at times be difficult. What if the instructions given are unacceptable in some way, or are extremely difficult to implement without compromising some pre-existing political instruction? What if the process of giving advice results in that advice being of a kind that the political leadership does not wish to hear? For example, I have been in the situation where I have had to give advice to the effect that something was not achievable by the planning service, when an elected member without checking with me had said publicly that he would ensure that the planning system would do this. His reaction to my advice was that I was failing to follow political guidance; in other words, my advice rather than his untenable position was presented as the problem, and my relationship with that councillor throughout his period as a member of the council was problematic as a result. It is easy to take the normative position that the ethical planner should proceed regardless, although my experience was that the people who said things like that to me had usually never had to face situations like that themselves; setting standards for other people to fail to live up to is more common in these matters than we might hope it would be. My own experience of such situations (Kitchen, 1997, pp. 45–9) was that they could be extremely difficult for many reasons, especially when politicians were prepared to make material available to the local media in ways designed to advance their own positions.

Benveniste used the concept of 'the Prince' (following Machiavelli) as a generic term for the location of political leadership, and he offers four reasons in particular why relationships between planners and the Prince might be a struggle. These are summarized in Box 7.7. All four of the generalized reasons set out therein are reasons I can relate to in practice, as I am sure could many other planners with extensive experience of dealing with elected members.

But before all this gives the impression that the relationship between planning and the political leadership is inevitably fraught, it is important to put in place three correctives to this view:

1. My experience with this relationship was that the ability of the planning process to exercise influence through it was heavily dependent

---

Box 7.7   Why relationships between political leaderships and planners might be difficult, according to Benveniste

Benveniste uses the concept of 'the Prince' (following Machiavelli) as a generic description for a political leader. He sees four broad sets of reasons which might explain why relationships between the Prince and his planners might at times be difficult:

- The Prince will want to keep a degree of distance between himself and his planners, especially when they are floating ideas which aren't yet accepted wisdom. If these ideas run into difficulties, the Prince can distance himself from them (and indeed, if need be, hire a fresh set of planners), although if the ideas are successful he is quite likely to claim them as his own.
- The Prince will see himself as the primary adjudicator of conflicts, and that is indeed one of his sources of power. He won't want his planners to start playing roles like this, and in particular he won't want the impression to get around that it is the planners with whom deals are done rather than the Prince himself.
- The Prince is likely to see his planners as technical people performing tasks for him, rather than as administrators or managers who have to exercise political judgement ultimately on his behalf. The Prince will see himself (and his immediate advisers) as being better placed to make political and managerial judgements than the planners are, and won't want to encourage them to believe that they can expand their role in this way.
- The interests of the Prince and those of the planners won't completely coincide. The Prince's primary focus will be on the present, and on what he can achieve immediately, whereas the planners will be looking at longer-term improvements. The Prince is likely to be distrustful of the longer term, because there is not much immediate payoff and because future promises can become liabilities.

Source: Summarized from Benveniste, 1989, pp. 191, 192.

---

upon the retention of confidence. While it would be possible to argue that this is a two-way process (confidence of the planners in the political leadership, as well as vice versa), in practice this is almost entirely one way: confidence on the part of the political leadership in the planning process and in its own leadership. This is a hugely important thing in which a chief planning officer needs constantly to be investing, and which once lost is very difficult to get back. My experience was that planning advice even when its content was difficult was much more likely to be taken seriously when it was clear that the recipient of that advice was broadly confident in both the person proffering the advice and its source than when that was not the case.

2. A recognition of the difference between what can be done informally and what has to be done formally. Most of the most influential advice

I gave as city planning officer of Manchester was given in informal discussions rather than in the formal setting of committee meetings, where previously prepared papers are discussed and decisions (often themselves previously prepared) are taken. These latter occasions could be set-pieces, and nearly always took place in the public arena with the media present. Neither of these characteristics made them appropriate places to give what might be new or politically difficult advice for the first time unless that was unavoidable. Nearly always, this was best done in private, and certainly less formal, surroundings which offered time and space for these things to be debated and reflected upon. I cannot emphasize strongly enough from my own experience just how important this process of informal dialogue is, as an appropriate preparation for the public event to come.

3. A recognition of the proper territory occupied by each other's roles. The definition of the boundaries of these territories may not be very precise, but in my experience it was essential for a planner giving advice to a politician to respect what was a political decision, and not to tread on what was seen as political territory. Equally, it was impor-tant for the planner to be clear about what was properly the territory of planning advice, and to spell out its implications and its signifi-cance. Given that working relationships between senior planners and key politicians tend to be ongoing (that is to say, they last for a period of time, and are not just about one significant event), one of the most important ways in which the confidence in the planning service and its senior personnel that I have described above as being necessary can be built up is through the development of understandings of this nature. During my time as Manchester's city planning officer, for example, I worked essentially with just two politicians as chairs of the planning committee, and in each of these instances the develop-ment of this kind of implicit understanding of territory was much helped by very frequent and usually very informal discussion (Kitchen, 1997, pp. 50–2).

Any planner working in the public sector who wants to get things done has to learn to work with the grain of the political process. As stated above, this isn't always easy. It also isn't the case that the motivations and behaviour of the politicians that one has to deal with are always easy to understand, or that planners' perceptions of what should be done and how it should be done will necessarily be shared (Hillier, 2002). All of this can be particularly difficult territory for planners, especially if they take into this process fixed views about roles and behaviour which then seem not to be congruent with their experiences in the real world. Brooks (2002, pp. 16–18) records some negative reactions from American planning students to reported experiences of this nature, which appeared to make them doubt the worth of public service planning as compared with working in the private sector and thereby avoiding much of this political interaction. He concludes as follows:

> Clearly, this situation needs some attention; planners do indeed need to be prepared for that interaction and intervention. One step toward doing so is to stop thinking of the political system as a dysfunctional external disturbance – something that keeps us from being effective – and to identify and employ planning strategies that are integrated with, and make creative use of, that political system. (Ibid., p. 18)

I agree entirely with this view. Politics isn't about to go away from planning, and it is up to planners to learn how to work with it.

To date, this discussion has all been about how planners can relate to politicians and the political process. But in Britain in recent years there has been an increasingly strident debate about the scope of and necessity for moves in the other direction; whether elected members ought to receive any training in planning in order to serve on local authority planning committees. For many years the view was that this was not necessary. Essentially, elected members were seen as bringing their political and representative skills to the table, where they would receive planning advice, and so there was not seen to be a necessity for them to receive more formal training in planning in order to carry out their functions as members of planning committees. This is not the place to go into all the reasons why this view changed, but one important stepping-stone in this process was the very high-profile North Cornwall investigation (Department of the Environment, 1993). There the development control process appeared to have produced a systematic pattern of decisions that were against the principles of the development plan and in favour of particular interests in the locality as a result of inappropriate behaviour by elected members, mainly those who served on the planning committee, but also by others who were not in this position but who brought pressure to bear on planning committee members. One of the recommendations made as a consequence was that there should be more systematic training available to elected members, so that they were aware of the basis on which the planning system operates and of their own roles within it (ibid.). The consequence of all of this was the gradual development of a (very British) process whereby local planning authorities were encouraged to arrange training programmes of this nature and elected members were encouraged to attend them. The extent to which this was mandatory was very variable as between authorities, although the Nolan Committee (Committee on Standards in Public Life, 1997) had recommended that such training should be compulsory. The government issued an advisory syllabus for training programmes of this nature (Department of the Environment, Transport and the Regions,

1998b), and this provided at least a starting-point for initiatives of this kind. I had the experience during this period of preparing and delivering a planning training programme for elected members in a local planning authority, and it was a struggle both in terms of attendance and in terms of engaging some of the elected members during the sessions as compared with the demands on their time from other sources (like, for example, dealing with other council papers). Bluntly, the problem for some of the attendees appeared to be that they were there because they had been told that they had to be, rather than because they wanted to be. The government repeated the view in the Planning Green Paper (DTLR, 2001, para. 6.40) that councillors ought to undergo training before sitting on planning committees, although the Egan Committee in its review did not support compulsory training for elected members (Egan Committee, 2004, paras 4.36–4.38). So, over the years the debate has moved from a discussion of whether training in planning for councillors is necessary to a discussion of whether it should be compulsory, there being widespread agreement that it is desirable in principle that councillors should receive specific training and that the system should not just rely on their political and representative contributions.

A lot of local planning authorities that do believe in planning training for elected members have recognized how difficult it is for their own staff to carry this out successfully, and have asked independent sources to do this. An interesting reflection on the experience of providing councillor training in planning includes the following observations about officer–member relationships:

> Good relations between planning officers and the members of a planning committee are crucial to the successful delivery of the planning service. Ideally, the relationship should be based on professionalism, mutual respect and trust. The councillors must trust the officers to provide them with sound, professional, objective planning guidance and the officers must trust the councillors to take wise decisions based on the evidence before them. In the vast majority of visited councils these conditions are in place. Yet a surprising number of local authorities are found where the relationship between officers and members is very poor and officers find themselves 'under attack' when appearing at committee. In some councils, planning officers appear to be nervous and in fear of the councillors. In some cases they may have all but abandoned professionalism in favour of an 'easy life'. In others, when officers stand their ground and warn members that rejection of officer recommendations to approve an application could lead to developer appeal (possibly with costs awarded against the council), they can be challenged. Members can take legitimate caution and warning as a threat to their integrity and status as decision makers. On the other hand, the pressure for probity and caution

within the framework of national planning policies has reduced some councillors to feeling that they are forced to 'rubber-stamp' officer recommendations. (Weston and Darke, 2004, p. 430)

Weston and Darke suggest a way forward as follows:

Achieving a proper separation between the roles of officers and members and a fruitful relationship between them is difficult. It is often dependent on organizational structures, cultures and procedures. Individuals (both officers and members) can also heavily influence roles and relationships. The greatest problems seem to be where there is a lack of strong leadership on either side of the 'divide'. A key to improved relations is for councillors to accept that the planning officer is not simply an employee working for them, but a professional serving a wider constituency. The latter includes all involved in the planning process: objectors; applicants; statutory consultees; and the wider public interest in the form of national planning policy. Equally, officers have to accept the political context of planning and the role of councillors in providing democratic legitimacy for town-planning decisions. (Ibid., p. 431)

These reflections very much reinforce what has been said above about the nature of the relationship between elected members and planning officers, and confirm the view that while this can be difficult the starting-point is indeed the mutual recognition of each other's roles and contributions.

Conclusions

This chapter has been about the kinds of organizational, managerial and political context skills that planners need to develop in order to be able to operate effectively in the public service. The skills being talked about here are essential to delivery in complex situations, where corporate, managerial and political imperatives are all likely to be found, not necessarily all pulling in the same directions. Some of this, as we have seen, can be very difficult for planners. In recent years in Britain, developments in corporate and partnership working, desirable though undoubtedly they have been, have served to make the planning process more complex, with new strategies and action plans to relate to and more extensive sets of consultations that need to be carried out. Managerially, British local planning authorities have found themselves under pressure to improve their performance and at the same time to take into account a range of aspirations for the development of planning as a public activity (such as the extension of public engagement with planning, not just in terms of its scale but also in terms of its meaningfulness) which don't always sit easily with these performance imperatives. And politics is an ever-present component of planning as a public activity, and must be so by its very nature, which means that planners whether they like it or not have to learn the skills of operating effectively within political regimes.

It seems to me that there is no going back from any of this. Contemporary planning as a public activity exists within frameworks of this nature in democratic societies, and it will continue to do so. The experience of this in Britain over the last twenty years or so is almost certainly that it has made the planning job significantly harder, and the likelihood is that this will continue, given that at its heart it is fuelled by the kinds of rising expectations discussed in Chapter 1 of this book. So, if planning is fundamentally about what you do to make places better for people, as distinct from just what you say you would like to do, the public service planner has to engage successfully with the corporate, the managerial and the political dimensions of taking action. Jon Gower Davies over thirty years ago coined the phrase 'the evangelistic bureaucrat' to describe what he saw as the self-perceptions of the planners working in Newcastle at that time (Davies, 1972), and it wasn't meant as a compliment. But it seems to me that this isn't actually a bad description of what a public service planner needs to be in the contemporary world. They will inevitably be bureaucrats because they will work in large bureaucracies, and to get things done they will need to be good at making those machines work, with all that this implies. And they will need to be evangelistic because they will need to retain and promote their sense of purpose as the basis of such action, while hopefully being more prepared to listen to and to work with the customers of the planning service than were the planners Davies described.

Self-assessment topics

1. Find an example of a partnership operating in the broad planning/regeneration field. What does it aim to do, and how does it aim to do it? Who is (and who isn't) involved in that partnership? How does it relate to the public planning service in that locality, and how does the planning service relate to it?
2. Try to identify a major public policy initiative that has been undertaken in a town or city near you in recent years. How was that initiative organized, managed and funded? To what extent and in what ways did these elements determine the characteristics of the initiative? What part did the planning process play in this initiative, both formally (i.e. in terms of statutory planning processes) and informally (i.e. by other means)?

3. What is the management structure of the public planning service in any area of your choice? On what basis does this management structure seem to have been determined? What do you think its main strengths and weaknesses might be?

4. Try to carry out interviews with both a politician concerned with planning in your locality and a senior officer concerned with the management of the planning service in that area. Ask them about their perceptions of what planning is and how effectively it operates in the locality, and also about how they see the working relationship between elected members and officers on planning matters in that locality. Compare and contrast their answers, and try to find explanations for any differences you can identify.

5. Take any local example of what might be described as a 'planning controversy', and try to unpick what were the respective roles of elected members and of planning officers in that controversy. What was it about the case that actually made it controversial, and what appear to have been the key influences in the resolution of the issues?

Chapter 8

Synoptic and Integrative Skills

Introduction

None of the skills discussed in the previous chapters would be a huge amount of use by themselves unless they were pulled together and applied effectively in particular sets of circumstances. Few of them in any event exist in total isolation; for example, technical skills, customer skills, place skills and system and process skills are all likely to be applied in a discussion between a planner and a customer of a planning service about what might happen in a particular locality. The argument of this chapter is that this isn't just a question of putting all the elements together, however, but is also about the framework planners use in order to carry out this task. This framework can be described using many terms, but essentially what I mean here is that planners need to have a sense of purpose when approaching a planning task. This may come, for example, from good strategic planning policies, from understanding how the policies of the development plan might apply to a particular problem or opportunity, from an urban design exercise which tries to look at what might be desirable and achievable in physical terms, or from any combination of these things. I have chosen to call this process of establishing and maintaining a sense of purpose synoptic skills, and to distinguish it from the (still important) contribution of understanding and making sense out of a range of perspectives on a planning problem, which I have chosen to call integrative skills. I present these two together because I think that what planners ought to bring to any situation is both the integrative and the synoptic dimension.

It is unlikely, in my experience, that all planners will be equally blessed in terms of their possession to the same high levels of development of all seven of the packages of skills discussed in this book. My experience of most of the planners I have worked with is that they are better at some elements of this than they are at others, and it seems to me that this is exactly what we should expect of human beings. But I would argue that most of the really successful planners that I have known have been strong in the area of synoptic and integrative skills; whatever other skills they have had in abundance, it has usually been this area which has stood out. In addition, to link this discussion back to the discussion in the previous chapter about planning management, my experience has been that successful planner-managers usually bring these kinds of skills to bear on performing their management roles effectively. The sense of purpose is often what distinguishes the manager from the administrator; not just helping the system to work efficiently, but also driving it in particular directions. Successful planner-managers when they get the opportunity to build their teams also tend to approach that task in this way. What are the strengths and weaknesses of my team? How can I use this opportunity to tackle some of the weaknesses and to reinforce the strengths? How can I ensure that the performance of my team as a whole will be better, and that its internal chemistry will be improved? So what I am talking about in this chapter is not just the glue that sticks the other planning skills together (although it does do this), but also what is often the hallmark of the successful planner – the ability always to see the big picture and to pull everything together so as to move in the desired directions.

To this end, this chapter looks separately at each of these two components, taking synoptic skills first. It then looks at how synoptic and integrative skills get used in practice situations, before drawing some broad conclusions. The chapter finishes with some self-assessment topics, to enable readers to explore some of the material introduced here in their own particular contexts.

Synoptic skills

I want in this part of the chapter to talk about three elements of synoptic skills in particular. The first is the idea of strategic planning as a pervasive planning activity, which will involve two important definitional points: the idea that strategic planning should be seen not only in terms of planning at broad spatial scales, and the idea that the strategic and the tactical are not opposites but are intimately related and mutually reinforcing. This discussion will be completed by revisiting some reflective work I did while still an active planning practitioner trying to define some basic principles of strategic planning activity in these terms. This links back in particular to the discussion of these issues in Chapter 2 in the context of development plan-making. The second element to be discussed is the time-bound nature of planning, which I will look at in three ways: the time-span of plans; the relationship between these time-spans and the (usually much shorter) programmes of managing expenditure, which are essential for the implementation of plans; and the time taken to prepare plans. The third element to be discussed looks at some of the ways the planner's broad sense of direction gets expressed, which for convenience I will take together under the broad heading of 'vision'.

The strategic dimension of planning

As I argued in Chapter 2, my observation from my own practice experience is that all planning issues have strategic dimensions to them, be this at the level of the individual plot of land or at the level of policies for a whole city, conurbation or region. This is not thus a function of the spatial scale at which the issue presents itself, but is a product of asking a simple question; what are we trying to do here? It is important, therefore, to make a distinction between strategic planning, which is essentially about addressing this question, and planning at the broader spatial scales, which confusingly (and in my view inappropriately) is often called strategic planning. All planning has a strategic dimension; it is simply that some planning activities take place at broader spatial scales than do others, and that those at the broadest scales will probably not have the non-strategic detail attached to them that one would expect to see at the most localized scales, where very often this detail is critically important.

A second distinction important in this context is the distinction that is commonly made between the strategic and the tactical. What this tends to mean in regular use is that the former is about what you are trying to achieve and the latter is about how you are trying to steer in this direction, often with a particular emphasis on the things that need to be done to begin this process in the relatively short term. A good illustration of what thinking tactically might achieve in this context, which planners quite often use in practice situations, is the identification of 'quick wins'. What this means is that in order to demonstrate the value of the strategic approach being taken it is felt to be desirable to achieve some early successes that wouldn't otherwise have happened, so that stakeholders will be able to see the benefits of the proposed approach and so that direct participants in the process of delivery will be encouraged to continue their efforts. Sometimes, this thinking can actually distort what would otherwise be done, but nearly always it is based upon a pragmatic realization of the need to demonstrate gains relatively quickly if key parties are to be encouraged to stick with the longer term intention. Again, though, this common distinction between the strategic and the tactical isn't a wholly helpful one, if it separates the two concepts out. In many ways, the tactical is part of the strategic; a vision isn't of much use if you have no real ideas of how to get there. Equally, there are undoubtedly strategic dimensions to successful tactical thinking, because it is important never to lose sight of what the longer-term intention actually is. When this does happen (and in my experience it sometimes has, and I presume that this experience is not unique), a planning-led approach is in effect replaced by an approach which administers the system, usually around the principle of achieving its own survival in the most comfortable manner, and that is not what I am talking about here – although, regrettably, I can certainly think of some planners who aspired no higher than to comfortable survival. So, it seems to me that the common distinction between the strategic and the tactical may not be as helpful as seeing the two as a pair of mutually reinforcing activities which meld into each other without clear boundaries.

I tried to capture this view of the strategic component of the planning process as being ever present, and not as being confined to the broader spatial scales and to matters that were distant from the tactical, when asked to reflect on my experiences in these terms as city planning officer of Manchester (Kitchen, 1996). I identified eleven propositions which on the basis of that experience seemed to me to characterize strategic planning (ibid., pp. 125, 126), and these are reproduced earlier in this book as Box 2.3 (p. 29). I have chosen not to change significantly the way in which this is expressed or to put it into more academic language because its genesis was myself as a current practitioner reflecting on that practice experience. But the central point is that strategic action when thought about like this is a pervasive part of the planning process. It is thus central to the ideas about synoptic and integrative skills which are the subject matter of this chapter. This approach in particular mirrors the thinking of Friend and Jessop (1969), and more recently that of Friend and Hickling (1997), in which they argue that most of the choices of any consequence that planning has to make are in effect strategic choices. Friend and Hickling helpfully identify five kinds of 'judgements of balance' that commonly arise when managing the continuous process of strategic choice (ibid., pp. 6–8), and my own experience supports the validity of this approach. It is therefore reproduced as Box 8.1

The value of the approach summarized in Box 8.1 is that it puts in very simple and straightforward terms the key elements that constitute the strategic dimensions of planning decision-making, and in so doing demonstrates why I am arguing here that most planning acts contain a strategic component of decision-making. Even if this is not all formally set out in a written analysis but is largely intuitive, most planning decision-making processes do indeed require careful consideration of scope (how broadly or how narrowly do we conceive the issues here?), of complexity (can we cut through this to its essence, or does this case unavoidably ramify?), of conflict (because we have to be aware that planning decisions involve often sharply dissenting voices, and often also involve winners and losers), of uncertainty (because by the very nature of the fact that planning is about the future coping with uncertainty is integral to it), and of progress (how do we move this forward? What do we aim to achieve at different points in time?). There may often be nuances around the balances that planners need to strike in looking at these dimensions of strategic decision-making, but

---

Box 8.1 Making judgements about choices that are common in strategic choice processes

Friend and Hickling argue that there are five common types of issues to be addressed in the management of the strategic choice process, with the judgement in each case being one of balance – how much of this element to go for at this particular point in time? These judgements may well change over time as circumstances change, but at any time an appropriate balance will need to be maintained between the stances adopted on each issue. The issues are:

More focused ← TREATMENT OF SCOPE → More synoptic
More simplifying ← TREATMENT OF COMPLEXITY → More elaborating
More reactive ← TREATMENT OF CONFLICT → More interactive
More reducing ← TREATMENT OF UNCERTAINTY → More accommodating
More exploratory ← TREATMENT OF PROGRESS → More decisive

Source: Developed from Friend and Hickling, 1997, p. 6.

---

successful planners tend to be those who are effective at handling matters of this nature.

The time-bound nature of planning

A third element critical to this understanding of synoptic thinking in planning is around the ways in which it constructs and makes use of concepts of time. As we saw in Chapter 6 when looking at the ethical approaches that characterize planning activities, increasingly these tend to acknowledge the important role of planning in safeguarding the longer term, driven in particular in recent years by debates about sustainable communities and around the imperatives related to global warming. At the other end of the spectrum, planning also has to deal with projects (be they development proposals by the private sector or public improvement proposals) where the intended implementation timetable is fairly immediate. And very often, the plans that planners make fall between these two extremes; they are about periods that can be between, say, five and twenty years, although there may be an immediate action component (for example, the process of development control will immediately start to take account of a particular policy) and there should always be a sense in which the longer-term consequences of the actions proposed over this five to twenty-year period are understood and have been taken into account in shaping those actions. There are three particular elements of this understanding of the time dimensions of planning which need to be discussed as part of this process of trying to unpick what we mean by the application of synoptic skills in planning.

The first is the simple observation that, if it is true that many plans typically work to time-frames of between five and twenty years, there is an enormous difference between the beginning and the end of this period. To put this difference into human terms, a child born at the start of this period will be a teenager by its end, with very different needs and very different perceptions of the world. For the customers of the planning service, this time-frame matters enormously. My experience was that many of the customers struggled to think about how they would wish things to be in five years' time, let alone in twenty years, and indeed while many people were able to think in the abstract about how they would wish their areas to improve they were often unable to put any kind of time-frame to this process at all. So a very important component of the planning job is not merely to make proposals, but also to communicate effectively what the process of implementing them over time might actually mean. It is also important in trying to perform this task effectively to explain clearly why things will take the time that they will – for example, this is how long development of a particular scale will take, or this cannot start until then because of resource availability or because particular infrastructure needs to be created first – and what will happen in the interim. This latter point is often, and very understandably, of particular concern to people because they see the development process as being disruptive, and while they might be quite supportive of the end being aimed for they might be very unhappy about what they will have to live with until then. So, this sense of development taking place over time, and needing to be managed effectively so as to minimize its disruptive effects during this period, is in my experience a very important component of people's reactions to development proposals. It is important nevertheless that planners do bring to this process a sense of thinking about the longer term, because as noted above my experience was that very few others did. Indeed, it could be argued that this concern for the longer-term implications of development is one of the distinguishing elements of planners' contributions to the plan-making process, and that its value is if anything becoming of increasing importance as the need for planning to get to grips with the imperatives of sustainable development becomes more urgent.

The second element in understanding the time-bound nature of planning activities is the need to think about how plans and projects relate to the conventional programmes of managing expenditure. If the perspective of a plan is typically five to twenty years, the perspective of a public expenditure programme is in my experience typically very much shorter than this. Often, one can only be certain of expenditure programmes for one year ahead, and even then this can be only after a protracted battle over budgets. Attempts have been made in Britain in recent years to tackle this problem by making longer-term financial commitments (although there can still be an argument about what 'commitment' actually means in this context), and by creating at least indicative budgets for the longer term so that expenditure programmes can be embarked upon with at least a reasonable degree of certainty that they will be continued and not just brought to a sudden halt. Nevertheless, the process of managing implementation programmes is often much shorter-term in its horizons than is the plan from which those programmes may be drawn or which at least has inspired them. This raises major issues for planners in demonstrating the credibility of their plans to their customers; and certainly one of the reactions I have received to proposals in the past has been 'that will never happen', simply because people didn't believe that the necessary expenditure from whatever source would be available to make this happen within any time-frame to which they could relate. In this situation, incidentally, 'never' didn't actually mean 'never'; what it really meant was 'not within the foreseeable future, with my understanding of what is foreseeable being constrained by my sense in current circumstances of what is feasible'. So planning and planners have a large task to perform in explaining how events are expected to move forward beyond what they know from committed programmes and towards the achievement of the proposals in their plans. They need to be able to show that what may look like a large gap between these two elements is realistically achievable, and they need to be able to show how this might happen and over what sort of time periods the key elements can be expected to be put in place. As noted above, my experience is that this is an area where planners' credibility is often under challenge, and so if they are to generate confidence in their plans they need to address these dimensions effectively and not just to focus on the desirability of the end state.

The third element in understanding the time-bound nature of planning activities is the simple fact that they take time. To give an example, the process of producing a fresh development plan for the city of Manchester from commencement to adoption during my time as city planning officer took five and a half years (Kitchen, 1997, ch. 4). This may seem like an extraordinarily long time, and in many ways it is, but two observations in particular may help to put this in context. The first is that all ten local planning authorities in Greater Manchester received commencement orders from the Government instructing them to begin this process at the same point in time, and Manchester's was the first to go all the way through the process to adoption. In other words, five and a half years was actually the fastest pace that was achieved in Greater Manchester. Second, less than half of this time period was taken up by the process of constructing the new plan up to the point when it was placed on deposit, and more than half this period was taken up by the statutory processes involved in getting it from there to the point of adoption. This is not to belittle these processes, since clearly it is absolutely right to have in place processes of public consultation and then opportunities to challenge plan proposals in front of an independent party; but the price to be paid for these elements is the time and the resources they consume. Two comments in particular follow from this example. The first is that an awful lot of things in the world can change during the five and a half years that it takes to prepare a plan; and indeed, the longer this period the more difficult this problem is likely to be since the world has an annoying habit of refusing to stand still while it is being planned. A dramatic illustration of this is that if that period of five and a half years had been six and a half years, or if it had started one year later, the plan preparation period would have covered the destruction of much of Manchester city centre by an IRA bomb in June 1996. As it happened, the fact that there was both an up-to-date planning framework that could act as a basis for the reconstruction work in the immediate aftermath of the IRA bomb and a strong database that had been assembled to underpin that planning framework was a real advantage for Manchester city centre in these very testing circumstances (Kitchen, 2001). The second is that, as we saw in Chapter 2, ever rising public expectations about being actively involved in plan-making processes that will affect their lives have to be planned into the plan-making process, and this will have an impact upon the amount of time it takes to prepare plans. The extent of British planners' concerns about this is illustrated in Box 8.2, which draws upon a survey undertaken by the Local Government Association in the latter part of 2002 (Sykes, 2003). This tested whether planners working for local authorities felt that they could *both* meet the government's requirements around speed of plan preparation and also improve community involvement in that process. What this shows is that just over 70 per cent of authorities answered 'not very easy' or 'not at all easy' to the question that was asked, and that for every type of local authority well over 50 per cent of answers were the same. In other words, a strong majority of those that would actually have to do the tasks in question had serious reservations about whether it was possible to speed up the plan-making process and to improve community engagement with it simultaneously.

This is a hugely important issue for planning, and it is not difficult to see why this is the case. A plan that has taken so long to prepare that in some important ways it is out of date by the time it is adopted is not only of relatively little value but is also likely to carry little credibility with its key stakeholders. I have long felt that part of the solution to the very real dilemma here is that there ought to be a relationship between the effort that goes into plan preparation and the benefits that flow from having a plan. After all, it makes no sense at all in terms of the consumption of public resources (and most plans are prepared for the public sector at a cost to the public purse) for large sums to be spent on the

Box 8.2   Plan preparation time-scales

The British government, in relation to the new types of development plans being introduced via the Planning and Compulsory Purchase Act 2004, said that it expected these both to be produced within a three-year period and to engage communities more effectively in the process of plan preparation than had previously been the case. The Local Government Association wanted to gauge responses to this task from the people who would carry it out – the local authorities. The figures in the table below are based upon responses by 193 authorities, which is just under half of the number of local authorities in England.

Question:*How easy will it be to maintain and improve community involvement, and meet the target of preparing (the new style of development plan), within three years?*

Response	Type of local authority					All authorities
	Metropolitan borough	London borough	Unitary authority	County council	District council	
Very easy	0%	6%	0%	0%	3%	3%
Fairly easy	37%	19%	42%	12%	24%	26%
Not very easy	63%	69%	35%	63%	53%	53%
Not at all easy	0%	6%	23%	25%	20%	18%

So, 29 per cent of all authorities felt that this would be very or fairly easy, and 71 per cent of authorities felt that it would be not very or not at all easy.

Source: Developed from Sykes, 2003, p. 23.

production of a plan which then provides little value; at the very least, there would be a strong argument in cost–benefit terms for using the resources spent here on plan preparation in other ways were this to be the case. In the past (Kitchen, 1996), I have expressed this relationship as an equation as follows:

$$\frac{\text{Time over which plan is useful}}{\text{Time taken to prepare plan}} \geq 1$$

What this simply means is that we should get at least as much value out of the plan-making process as the effort that goes into it, and this seems to me to be a minimalist position that should be adopted. My observation at the time, however, was that few of the plans of which I was aware actually passed this test (ibid.), and I have seen little since that would change this view. The basic point being made here, though, is that we need to take a very realistic view of the timescales involved in the processes of plan-making. If it is, as a matter of social choice, the view that this needs to involve extensive and intensive processes of public engagement (as increasingly, and in my view entirely properly, it is), then both our procedures and our expectations of what we will get at the end of the process need to be adjusted as a result. It will be interesting to see whether the new-style plans introduced by the Planning and Compulsory Purchase Act, 2004 do manage to do better in these terms, or whether the kinds of perspectives summarized in Box 8.2 turn out to be accurate. Time will tell.

Visions

I am using the term 'visions' as a generic expression for the various means of setting out the longer-term future that is desired for the locality in question. Visions can take many forms. I listed six means of giving expression to them in the introduction to this chapter: broad strategic planning activities, development plans, visionary exercises, attempts to look holistically at an area, urban design exercises, or any combination of these – and that list is by no means exhaustive. What characterizes all of these, however, is that they attempt to convey in their different ways an idea of a future to be aimed for. It is vital that planning processes should be able to do this successfully, either as a basis for public debate about whether that future is actually what people want or as a vehicle for establishing a relationship between individual projects and the common goal to which they should be contributing. Indeed, if we look at the plain-language use of the term 'planning' it is about organizing in order to achieve a desired end, and so planners have to be as effective in giving expression to the 'desired end' part of this description as they are at the 'organizing' bit. Critically also, it is what the customers of planning expect the planning process to produce – plans of various kinds.

One of the critical issues in this area in my experience was the question of the credibility of the vision. I heard the phrase 'pie in the sky' on several occasions in this context, and while that might have reflected a negative view about the vision on display I think more commonly it came from real difficulty in seeing how we would get from where we are now to where this vision says we want to be, perhaps coupled with doubts about whether the resources would be available to fund this journey anyway. This sense of a lack of realism seems to me to be much more likely to occur when a vision is presented by itself, without any means also being suggested of how the route towards its achievement might be navigated. So, notwithstanding the fact that a lot of visionary work is about generating support for a view of what might be possible, and probably also about raising expectations in these terms, it is much more likely to be seen to be realistic if it is accompanied by some sort of understanding of how to get there.

A particular subset of this difficulty is around what might be described colloquially as 'artist's impressions'. Very many development proposals are accompanied by drawings or other forms of presentations which are designed to show how they would fit into the surrounding area once they had been completed, and since this is often a very important criterion in making decisions about these proposals it is clearly of much value that something like this should be attempted. Yet my experience with both elected members and the residents of localities when showing them material of this nature was that they were often inclined not to believe it, or perhaps more accurately not to trust it. In effect, the view seemed to be, this is material designed to show the proposal in the best possible light, especially when it emanated from the proposers of the development, and therefore it cannot be relied upon. I think scepticism of this nature is very understandable if one is doubtful in any event about the worth of a proposed development. Elected members (in particular) tended to say that they had seen things like this before which had turned out not to be wholly accurate representations of the reality that transpired, and thus that they were mistrustful of material of this kind. At the same time, my experience was that developers and their agents generally did not set out systematically to deceive people in these terms, not least because they were very well aware that to do so was not actually in their interests, especially if they anticipated undertaking future projects in that locality. So there is clearly a credibility gap here, which all the professionals involved in undertakings of this nature need to work at trying to close. It is important, though, that the value of activities of this nature isn't lost sight of, because the truth is that many people struggle to understand what a development idea might look like either from reading a plan or from words on a piece of paper, and they do need to be helped to understand this by accurate visual representations. Technological developments will make the process of accessing material of this nature about most sizeable developments on-line very easy in the near future, and it is important that the potential of a tool like this is not undermined by scepticism as to its reliability.

Perhaps in part because of some of the difficulties referred to above, the attention given to the visionary dimension in British planning has waxed and waned over the years. Interestingly, the government, in criticizing the performance of the British planning system and in making proposals for change in its Planning Green Paper (DTLR, 2001), criticized extant local plans as follows:

Plans are too long. Local plans have tended to address the development status of every part of their area and they often try to anticipate every development control eventuality. Rather than setting out a clear strategy for development, they have become lengthy and inflexible rule-books for development control. (Ibid., p. 12, para. 4.5)

To paraphrase, this was saying that plans had been substituting detail for strategy. It could be argued that this was exaggerating in order to make a case, and that in particular it was undervaluing the very real contributions of those plans that did have a clear strategy and were not swamped by detail. But it surely has to be acknowledged that this passage puts its finger on a real problem, which is that it is very easy for detail to push out strategy in plans, especially for areas that are under considerable development pressure. This point is reinforced in the Planning Green Paper when it puts plans in the context of the (then) recently introduced community strategies (see Chapter 7), which were characterized among other things by having 'a long-term vision for the area which focuses on the outcomes that are to be achieved' (ibid., p. 13). This line of argument is an important strand in the decision of the government to insist that local development frameworks (the new style of plans subsequently introduced via the Planning and Compulsory Purchase Act 2004) would have as a key element 'a statement of core policies setting out the local authority's vision and strategy to be applied in promoting and controlling development throughout its area' (ibid., p. 13, para. 4.8).

The refound importance that this attached to the strategic or visionary dimension of planning was then heavily reinforced in the government's guidance to local planning authorities about undertaking work on their new Local Development Frameworks:

> The core strategy should set out the key elements of the planning framework for the area. It should comprise a vision and strategic objectives for the area, along with a spatial strategy, a number of core policies and a monitoring and implementation framework. It must be kept up-to-date and, once adopted, all other development plan documents must be in conformity with it. (ODPM, 2003d, p. 15, para. 2.2.2)

There is clearly in this at least the potential for the previously identified problem (detail swamping strategy) to recur, but it is also clear that what this is attempting to do is to ensure that the statutory planning process is driven by 'a vision and strategic objectives' rather than just by policies put in place to facilitate development control.

This same sense of the importance of the visionary and the strategic being reasserted (some would say, rediscovering what planning should always have been about anyway) is also very visible in what the British government is saying about the place of urban design (ODPM, 2005a, pp. 14, 15). The process of government acceptance of an important role for urban design in planning had been going on since the mid 1990s. Mainly, I suspect, as a result of John Gummer's 'quality' initiative (Department of the Environment, 1994), the version of this guidance that was published in 1997 (Department of the Environment, 1997, paras 13–20 and annex A) was noticeably more upbeat than its predecessor. But the 2005 guidance is particularly clear on the importance (again) of getting the basic principles right and of not getting involved in matters of detail:

> Design policies should avoid unnecessary prescription or detail and should concentrate on guiding the overall scale, density, massing, height, landscape, layout and access of new development in relation to neighbouring buildings and the local area more generally. (ODPM, 2005a, p. 15, para. 38)

This pattern of reasserting the important place of urban design in planning had led some to argue that the process of urban regeneration at the more localized scales should in effect be design-led. Lord Rogers, in his introduction to the report of the Urban Task Force which he chaired, puts this as follows:

> We visited projects in all parts of England and considered the experience of Germany, the Netherlands, Spain and the United States. In the quality of our urban design and strategic planning, we are probably twenty years behind places like Amsterdam and Barcelona. What we have learned from these visits is that regeneration has to be design-led. But to be sustainable, regeneration also has to be placed within its economic and social context. (Urban Task Force, 1999, p. 7)

This process, of design-led regeneration, can take many forms, but in my opinion it is at its most effective when it combines design imagery with a strongly grounded understanding of the economic and social realities of life in the locality. A good example of this kind of process is the work undertaken in Wakefield, West Yorkshire, to create a renaissance strategy as part of the 'Renaissance Towns' initiative promoted by Yorkshire Forward (the regional development agency). Box 8.3 summarizes what this is about, and makes clear in particular what the role of urban design in this process is seen as being. The report from which Box 8.3 draws (Koetter Kim, 2005a) and its companion volumes (Koetter Kim, 2005b, 2005c) are produced to very high standards, use quite deliberately inspirational and promotional language, and are lavishly illustrated in a variety of ways that are clearly designed both to impress potential investors in the area and to galvanize local support. All of this is a very far cry from stodgy planning documents written with a fair sprinkling of jargon and with relatively few illustrations, but it has been done quite

---

Box 8.3   The Wakefield renaissance strategy

The Wakefield renaissance strategy is characterized by the following:

- It is deliberately aiming to raise the belief of readers in the potential of the locality. So it uses concepts like 'enterprise', 'optimism' and 'growth' to convey what it sees as new possibilities.
- It has a 'preparation for action' focus, so that it isn't just about broad visions but is also about things that need to be done in order to turn vision into reality.
- It is candid both about the positive assets it sees Wakefield as having (in terms of resources and amenities, which it describes as 'remarkable') and about the difficulties and obstacles to be overcome.
- So as well as broad policy stances, it identifies specific project areas and offers objectives, design principles and in some cases design studies to move the process forward to the point of implementation as quickly as possible.
- The purpose of the design studies is not necessarily to produce a worked-up design for a particular issue, but rather to illustrate how it might be tackled and to show in particular what might be possible.

More than anything else, then, what design-led urban regeneration of this kind is all about is lifting up aspirations and encouraging stakeholders to believe that it is possible to aim high successfully.

Source: Adapted from Koetter Kim, 2005a, p. 7.

---

deliberately as a means not only of presenting a vision behind which people can unite but also of raising Wakefield's game. The process of inviting in North American architects and getting them to work with a range of regional and local interests has clearly been a productive one, and has demonstrated the value that can arise when fresh eyes and ideas are combined with local knowledge. This kind of visionary work has an essential role to play in spearheading a detailed programme of change, by demonstrating what might be possible; and sometimes people have to be encouraged to believe in this in order to make it happen.

Integrative skills

One of the first things planners realize from their early practice experience, if they weren't already aware of it from their planning education, is that many different professional skills are involved in making development happen (Syms, 2002, ch. 4). For example, Paul Syms describes the key members of a team (that is to say, the group working for and advising the developer) working on a brownfield redevelopment project as being likely to be architects, engineers, landscape architects, quantity surveyors, project managers, environmental consultants, and estate agents, with solicitors, town planners, archaeologists and market research and economic consultants also likely to be involved at some stage (ibid., pp. 69–73). Clearly, then, the first thing that the planner needs to do in this kind of situation is to acknowledge and to respect this range of contributions, and to learn how to work effectively with this group of fellow-professionals rather than give the impression either that as a planner he or she can in effect do the jobs of the other professionals or that the planning contribution is somehow superior to theirs. The nature of the planning contribution, and in particular its focus on what the development initiative is trying to achieve, may well mean that the planner at various points in time will need to negotiate across this full range of professional skills, and understand and place in its proper context the significance of these other professional inputs both individually and collectively. The emphasis here, then, is on listening, understanding, and comprehending the significance of these viewpoints, in the context of what the project as a whole is seeking to achieve, especially if this causes any element of the planning framework to need to be rethought.

The planning contribution in the situation described above may be a little different from most of the others, in the sense that they are specialist contributors from a particular perspective whereas the planning contribution is likely to be about the project as a whole. This holistic approach should be one of the primary characteristics the planner brings to the table; what is the project aiming to achieve? How does it relate to the extant planning framework for the area? How can we ensure that it constitutes sustainable development, both in its initial construction and in its ongoing operations? What design requirements are likely to be necessary to enable it to 'fit in' with the surrounding area? How do the access needs of the project relate to the public and private transportation arrangements to be found in the surrounding area, and might these need to be augmented in any way? These kinds of questions should usually be addressed very early in the life of the project, with the answers to them in effect providing a framework for all the more detailed development work that is to follow. The job of the planner as a member of the development team is often to shape the strategy through finding sensible answers to these kinds of questions, and then to keep on top of its detailed development to ensure that the direction of this work doesn't distort the basic strategy that has emerged.

The range of issues that need to be considered in this kind of situation is becoming ever broader. To give just one example, it is unlikely that ten years ago very much consideration would have been given in Britain to crime prevention and the effect this might have on the design and layout of a project. Today, however, there is a clear expectation that such issues will be considered as an integral part of the design process (ODPM and the Home Office, 2004), and a likelihood that if this is not done then there will be a request for time-consuming redesign work when the project is examined by the local police architectural liaison service as part of the consideration of the planning application. As an example of a contemporary approach of this nature, Box 8.4 shows the arrangements agreed by the Bedfordshire local planning authorities and their partners for police consideration of planning applications (Bedfordshire Community Safety Working Group, 2005).

In effect, the consultation arrangements set out in Box 8.4 will catch most developments of any consequence, and the expectation is that the detailed guidance in the document (supported by and linked to policies that will be written into the new local development frameworks that the Bedfordshire local planning authorities will be putting in place) will be taken into account by development interests when assembling proposals. The process expectation in these terms is described as follows:

> [T]hose seeking planning permission and their designers are encouraged to enter into discussions with a range of interested parties before their application is submitted. This helps to resolve any potential conflicts and ensure that crime reduction measures are designed in at an early stage. (Ibid., para. 3.6.2)

And:

> When submitting a planning application it is expected that *applicants* will ... [in relation to the development types listed at point 1 of Box 8.4] ... demonstrate how crime and disorder risks have been mitigated for as part of the statement of support or design statement. (Ibid., para. 3.6.3)

The approach to handling crime prevention issues illustrated by the above example is very different from the one that would have been found a decade ago, and it shows how an issue that would have been scarcely thought about at all is being brought into the process of developing project proposals as an integral element. The person who handles negotiations on this subject may or may not be the planner, depending upon decisions on the deployment of personnel in the development team, but there can be little doubt that arrangements of the type illustrated in this example will require the planner to understand the issues being discussed and to be aware of their possible implications for the design process. In the future, when documentation such as the Bedfordshire example is more formally related to the local development framework by its adoption as part of that portfolio of documents, the planner who is a member of the development team will need to incorporate awareness of this particular issue into the process of understanding what the range of implications of the development plan's contents are for the development of a proposal.

The process of developing land can vary very considerably according to the condition and characteristics of the land itself, and as we have

Box 8.4 Emerging arrangements for police consultation on planning applications in Bedfordshire

1. The police service will be consulted on all planning applications falling into the following categories:

   - Housing developments comprising ten dwellings or more
   - Major commercial office, industrial, retail or leisure schemes
   - Development involving new neighbourhood or district community facilities
   - Proposals which include significant areas of open space/landscaping proposed as part of the development
   - Developments incorporating significant off-street parking provision
   - Proposals involving transport interchanges or other significant high-way infrastructure improvements, such as cycle lanes and new or improved footpaths
   - Applications for class A3 food and drink uses

2. In addition, the Bedfordshire local planning authorities will send weekly lists of planning applications received to the Bedfordshire police, and they will indicate within one week of receiving such lists whether they wish to be consulted on any applications on this list over and above those that fall into the above categories.

Source: Adapted from Bedfordshire Community Safety Working Group, 2005.

seen in Chapter 4 this is something planners need to know, to understand and to see both in terms of the problems it causes and the opportunities it presents. Factors such as shape, orientation, existing tree cover, drainage and many others need to be part of the critical appraisal of a site in order to understand how they should be taken into account in the development process, and this would normally be an important part of the process of preparing a development brief to which the planner has a major contribution to make. But a particular set of issues arises in this context where land has been contaminated, which may require particular specialist knowledge in order to understand how it can be properly prepared for development (Syms, 2001, 2004). This has become an issue of growing significant in Britain, as government policy has focused on encouraging the use of previously used urban land for development rather than the consumption of greenfield sites at historic rates (Syms, 2004, pp. 10–12). Unless planners have chosen to specialize in this field and have considerable experience of it (and relatively few people pass these tests), it is unlikely that they will be able to undertake this particular task themselves. But it is critically important that the planner understands enough of what is involved in the process of remediation of contamination to be aware of its implications for the future development of the site, and to be able to advise accordingly. Box 8.5

Box 8.5   Factors to be taken into account in the redevelopment of Brownfield land

Paul Syms and his colleagues, as part of a research project for the Joseph Rowntree Foundation which among other things was seeking to identify the factors that needed to be taken into account in the redevelopment of brownfield land, carried out a set of interviews with 100 people who had collectively been involved with projects on over 12, 200 brownfield sites in the previous five years. The project identified 45 separate factors in 6 broad categories, as follows:

- Site assembly factors (7)
- Regulatory and policy issues (8)
- Site remediation factors (11)
- Project viability factors (10)
- Funding issues (2)
- Additional factors, many of which were about end users or third-party interests (7)

It is easy to see why at this level of complexity development of this nature becomes a specialist task, especially when several of the 45 items on the full list are themselves specialist areas.

Source: Adapted from Syms, 2001, pp. 42–50.

---

gives an indication of the complexity of this task. It identifies forty-five separate factors which people with significant degrees of experience in undertaking the redevelopment of previously used land felt were important, to varying degrees; and it may well be the case that the passage of time since that piece of research was undertaken will have added to this list. The job of the planner in this situation will not usually be to undertake all the detailed work associated with coming to grips with such factors in a particular situation and then giving specialist advice, but it will be to understand the significance of this for the project as a whole and in particular to understand what this implies for both the principles that will determine the design and layout of future development on the site and for the processes that will need to be undertaken in order to ensure that all planning requirements are met. In particular, if either an environmental statement or an environmental impact assessment is required as part of the process of determining a planning application (ODPM, 2004g), then all this work is likely to be a significant contributor to the preparation of these documents. The planner who is part of the development team may well have an important role to play in their assembly and submission. The planner working for the local planning authority who is on the receiving end of all this material in turn has to be able to understand its significance, and to know when and where to turn for expert advice in interpreting it if not able to do this alone. So, the integrating role in this situation, even if not that of the expert doing the basic work, is a vitally important one in taking this forward as part of the planning system.

The two examples used in this section – planning for crime prevention, and the development of contaminated land – both illustrate the point that the range and the depth of issues connected with the consideration of planning matters can be both broad and deep. The planner cannot hope to be an expert in all of this, and the planner should not even try to be this because there are other people who are genuine specialists in these areas and thus who can do the job of 'expert' much better. But what the planner does have to be able to do is to communicate effectively with these experts, to understand the significance in planning terms of what they are saying, and to relate it both to the future development of the individual project in question and to the planning context for the site and its surrounding area. I have described this as an integrating role, and it is a vital one. In particular, it is essential that the significance of expert inputs is understood and put in its proper context when undertaking public consultation exercises on planning matters, because the essence of the planning contribution in such circumstances ought to be that it can make sense of complexity in such a way as to facilitate effectively the process of soliciting public views. This requires the ability to communicate the essential points without either distorting them through oversimplification or making the process too difficult for recipients to understand. Planners in the public service, in particular, will find that they are often in situations of this nature, and one of the most important skills they need to possess is this ability to knit everything together so that it tells the story as fully and as accurately as is necessary in order both to facilitate public consultation and to enable the decision-making process to proceed on the basis of sound judgement. The more complex the issues, the harder this task can become; but the more complex the issues, the more important it becomes that it is done well.

Synoptic and integrative skills together

I have presented these separately above to enable each of them to be discussed. But this is an analytical construct, because in many cases planners will be applying synoptic and integrative skills together. Indeed, I would go so far as to say that the most effective way to integrate is to do so by reference to 'the big picture ' – in other words, to use the sense of direction or purpose behind an initiative (the basis for synoptic skills) as the framework within which individual contributions are understood and pulled together. This is likely in practice to involve a series of iterations, because it may well be that individual contributions will cause elements of the big picture to be reviewed or at least to be reflected upon, and in turn it may well be that the perspective provided by the broad direction in which the initiative is trying to move will raise some questions about individual contributions that will require further work to be undertaken. Similarly, it is very difficult to make the sense of direction or purpose stick with all the other key players if they neither understand nor share it, especially when they feel that their perspectives have been ignored in shaping it. So there is a symbiotic relationship between these two elements; the basis for effective integration is the big picture of which the individual contribution is part, and the big picture in turn must be seen by all concerned to take proper account of individual contributions and not to ignore or to attempt to ride roughshod over them.

I think that in making such processes work, planning can genuinely add value, both to the project or initiative itself and to the perspectives and understandings of the individual professionals who are contributing to it. To give a simple example I have experienced many times, it is likely that if a traffic engineer is asked about the implications for the operation of the local highway system of a proposed development, that individual will come up with a response which looks at the problem from a traffic engineering perspective; after all, what else would one expect when asking a traffic engineer about that kind of issue? But that kind of response, when looked at not just as a technical solution to a traffic issue but in terms of what its impact might be on the individual project and on the wider area in which it is located, may need to be reviewed because (for example) its environmental impact upon the locality might be seen as being excessive. This process can lead to a solution that is finally adopted that is significantly different from the original response, but which represents the best balance that can be achieved between all the key interests and their objectives. At its best, this is a creative process which can test the problem-solving skills of planners and their ability to work with a range of diverse and at times conflicting interests. Planners will do best in these situations if they are seen by all parties as trying to search for the best solution for the locality that can be achieved in a manner which respects the various views expressed and which tries to find ways of accommodating them. In other words, they are applying synoptic and integrative skills together in working with a range of professional and community interests to try to find the best available solution in the prevailing circumstances, which may not be the same as the most straightforward solution. At its worst, this process can become one of simply finding the easiest compromise available between the various development interests irrespective of community views, which I would argue is a process which largely abandons synoptic perspectives and also takes a limited view of the integration of views that is necessary. While the difference between these two positions isn't necessarily a precise measure of the value that planning can add in this situation (because, for example, the political process may pick up on local resident discontent and force some rethinking), it does show what can be achieved by the determined application of synoptic and integrative skills in a mutually supportive manner.

Conclusions

This chapter has been about the various ways planning can present 'the big picture' when looking at development situations, about how it needs to pull together a broad range of contributions and interests when looking at a development situation, and about how these synoptic and integrative skills work best when they work in harmony, reinforcing each other. Many times during my practice career I was told by development interests and others that these were the skills that planners brought to the table that they valued the most, and that they were skills that were not so well developed among most of the other professions associated with the development process because their focus was elsewhere. So I would argue that one of the primary characteristics of the successful practising planner ought to be that such an individual is a 'big picture' person, and that whatever detail discussions about development get into, planners should never lose sight of the big picture and should always be trying to see individual specialist contributions in the light of it.

This is not to say that big pictures should be unchanging, because in its own way this can be as damaging as other forms of inflexibility. The characteristic of most of the types of big picture discussed earlier in this chapter, however, is that they tend to be of a relatively general nature – most visions can accommodate several different elements and lots of different ways of moving towards desired outcomes. That being so, the job of the planner is to recognize this inherent flexibility and to see it as an opportunity, but at the same time to be able to distinguish between those elements which really would present an undesirable challenge to the big picture as distinct from those elements that can comfortably be accommodated within it. Even here, it is right to think about the extent to which the challenge is actually offering something that is really worth having, in which case the big picture may need to be adjusted, or whether it should be rejected because it puts at risk desirable elements towards which the vision is striving or threatens to shatter a community consensus about desirable factors built up over a period of time and through a great deal of effort. Visions ought to be things which provide a sense of broad certainty and continuity over a period of time; there may be lots of ways of proceeding, and lots of detailed decisions to be taken along the way where there are real choices to be made, but the broad sense of direction that guides these processes remains clear. But that doesn't mean to say that anything that is inconsistent with them must automatically be rejected simply because it is inconsistent. Consistency is a virtue that is much overrated, because very often innovation comes from exploring and running with inconsistencies, and so it is here as well. The original vision may have been the best everyone could agree on at a particular point in time, but that process would inevitably have been constrained by people's knowledge and perceptions, and so it may not have conceived of something beneficial which comes forward at a later date. Furthermore, ideas move on, so something that was not considered positively at one point in time may look very different in new circumstances at a later date. So, visions, or the big picture, should be seen as essential tools to help frame contemporary action, but as well as doing this planners must constantly be monitoring whether or not new ideas or opportunities have come along which ought to cause the vision to be reviewed or adjusted.

Finally, it is important to acknowledge the value of integrative work in its most straightforward sense. One of the mantras of the New Labour government in Britain when it was first elected in 1997 was the need to 'join things up'. The sense of this was that lots of the things done through the use of public funding were not being effectively related to each other even though they undoubtedly impacted either directly on each other or indirectly on the problems that this expenditure was trying to tackle, and as a consequence the public was not getting full value out of the process of spending what were ultimately resources that it had contributed. My experience was that this analysis could also be applied on the ground in the various localities where I worked, and that one of the most valuable acts that the planning process could undertake as a consequence was to try to understand everything that was intended in a locality and to explore the relationships between these elements to see where value might be added. Planners were able to undertake this task because their perspective was not the functional approach of the individual services delivering programmes, but was the future of the places and the people living within them on which those programmes would impact. This process of looking at functional programmes to see what impact they would have on space and the people who use it wasn't always well received by programme managers, but often difficulties of this nature could be lessened by explaining what else was being undertaken in the area, what this was trying to achieve, and what the impact of the programme in question might be. Several local authorities have experimented with area management initiatives for precisely this reason (see, for example, Blackman, 1995, p. 146), but the difficulty with these has tended to be that they sit awkwardly alongside the conventional service departments with their functional approaches. Planning with its focus on locality offers another contribution to tackling this issue, and the integration that an active planning process can offer in these situations can be of considerable value.

Self-assessment topics

1. Try to identify a range of 'visions' of different kinds that apply to an area known to you. Where have these come from? How are they expressed? How would they be used in relation to the operation of the planning process? How in turn might the planning process take them into account in, for example, writing a new development plan?
2. Take the case of a major development project being undertaken in a locality. In what ways was the approach to this project influenced by the context of any of the 'visions' that relate to the wider area in which it sits? What were the other key influences on the development of this project? How important do you think the 'vision' elements were in comparison with the other elements in shaping what is happening with the project?
3. Look at any development plan document. How much of its content could be said to be 'the big picture' or 'the vision', and how much of its content is relatively more detailed? How adequate do you think the former element is, and in what ways might it be capable of being improved? How much of the detail that is presented do you think is really necessary, and why?
4. Try to identify for any geographical locality of a town or city what major public expenditure programmes are likely to impact upon it over the next five years. What do these programmes involve, and which agencies will be undertaking them? In what ways will these programmes impact upon each other and upon the area? In what ways does the planning framework for the area planning play an integrative role in this context?

Chapter 9

The Changing Planning Skills Debate

Introduction

Having looked in the previous seven chapters at the core clusters of skills needed for successful planning practice, this chapter steps back a little from this level of detail and tries to look at some of the debates that can be found about the nature and extent of planning skills from various perspectives. I would argue that what I have said in the preceding chapters about skills for planning practice is broadly consistent with much of this material, although in truth it would be hard to distil a common view about planning skills from the various perspectives presented here. One of the reasons for this, of course, is that the views presented reflect where each of these perspectives is coming from and what interests it is trying to promote. Another reason is that some of the views about the skills needed for successful planning practice change as the planning process itself changes, with at times a dash of fashion thrown into these debates as well. For example, the emphasis the Egan Committee places on 'generic skills' (which is discussed later in this chapter) would almost certainly not have been found a decade earlier, and (hopefully) neither would the management-speak in which it is presented have characterized the language of such a view about skills for planning practice. This, then, is contested territory, and what this chapter seeks to do is to display some of this thinking.

The chapter begins with a brief discussion about terminology. This is unavoidable in this field because, while some writers are careful to try to distinguish what they mean by skills from several other similar concepts, it is quite clear that much of the general usage in this field mixes up some of these concepts in a fairly indiscriminate manner. The bulk of the chapter is then taken up by a series of commentaries on perceptions of planning skills in four broad groups; historically by reference to the work of some key writers; by the changing views of an appropriate professional body (in this case the British Royal Town Planning Institute) over time; in relation to the field of urban regeneration (and particularly, in relation to neighbourhood renewal, which is regeneration at a localized scale); and in a multi-professional context as part of the process of urban management. There is no pretence here that this represents an exhaustive review of perceptions of planning skills (see Durning and Glasson, 2004a, 2004b; Sykes, 2003), but it should be enough to illustrate something both of the range of perceptions that exist and of how views have changed over time. The chapter concludes by setting the skills for planning practice presented in this book into this broader context.

Some problems of terminology

One of the greatest difficulties involved in writing about planning skills is the difficulty in much of the literature in distinguishing the concept of 'skills' from many other similar (and at times overlapping) concepts. This is relatively straightforward to illustrate, but far less easy to overcome. To take the illustration first, in carrying out research for this book I have come across fifteen concepts that appear to be used in ways that are seen by their particular users as overlapping, containing or being synonymous with the concept of skills; and there may well be more. In alphabetical order, these fifteen are as follows:

Abilities	Capabilities	Expertise	Skills
Attitudes	Capacities	Knowledge	Techniques
Attributes	Characteristics	Methods	Values
Behaviours	Competencies	Qualifications	

Box 9.1 takes each of these words and sets out selected definitions of them, all taken from the *Illustrated Oxford Dictionary*, 1998 edition. What this shows is both the existence of a considerable amount of overlap between some of these definitions and also at least something of the ways in which these concepts can be differentiated; and interested readers who want to pursue this could engage in an etymological exercise designed to identify both the differences and the similarities in the meanings of these words. One advantage of the definition of skills in Box 9.1 is that it is very broad, and this is helpful when it comes to looking at planning skills because planning too as a concept has a very broad span with some very fuzzy edges. Of course, the disadvantage of this approach is that it does lack precision; but in my view this is outweighed by the value of the broadly based approach on offer.

Essentially, then, what we are talking about in this book when we talk about planning skills is those areas of knowledge and of ways of applying that knowledge that distinguish the planner. When we talk about skills for planning practice, we are talking not only about those skills it could be said to be the objective of a planning education to cultivate but also about how those skills need to get applied in the kinds of real-world situations in which planners commonly operate. It is no part of the argument of this book that each of the seven clusters of skills introduced in this book is unique to planners, because it is manifestly the case that this is not so. The argument here is that it is this *combination* of skills,

---

Box 9.1   Some definitions of overlapping concepts

ability   Capacity or power; cleverness, talent, mental power.
attitude   settled opinion or way of thinking; behaviour reflecting this.
attribute   quality ascribed to a person or thing; characteristic quality.
behaviour   the way one conducts oneself; the treatment of others; the way a machine, chemical substance etc. acts or works.
capability   ability, power; the condition of being capable.
capacity   mental power, faculty or talent; the power of containing, receiving, experiencing or producing.
characteristic typical, distinctive feature or quality.
competency   state of being competent (which is in turn defined as adequately qualified or capable, and also as effective).
expertise   expert skill, knowledge or judgement.
knowledge   awareness or familiarity gained by experience; range of information; theoretical or practical understanding of a subject; certain understanding as opposed to opinion.
method   special form of procedure, especially in any branch of mental activity; a **methodology** is a body of methods used in a particular branch of activity.
qualification   accomplishment fitting a person for a position or purpose; a condition that must be fulfilled before a right can be acquired.
skill   expertness, practised ability, facility in an action; dexterity or tact.
technique   means or method of achieving one's purpose, especially skilfully.
values   one's principles or standards; one's judgement of what is valuable or important in life.

Source: Summarized from *Illustrated Oxford Dictionary*, 1998.

---

and the ability to bring them to bear effectively in practice situations, that distinguishes the planner. This is why the seventh of these skill clusters was that of synoptic and integrative skills, because the ability to bring together all of the others and to focus them on the task in hand is a valuable and necessary skill in its own right.

Changing views of planning skills over time – the contributions of selected writers

Since views about what constitutes planning have both changed over time and have often been surrounded by controversy (Hall, 1996), it is no surprise that consequential views about the skills needed for planning practice do not reflect a settled consensus. The purpose of this section is simply to provide a flavour of some of these views at different points in time in the context of what the writers quoted were seeking to achieve just then, rather than to present any sort of comprehensive review of this literature.

Perhaps the classic British planning textbook of the early years following the 1947 Act was Lewis Keeble's *Principles and Practice of Town and Country Planning* (Keeble, 1964), which ran to three editions between 1952 and 1964. This was an attempt to provide a comprehensive text on planning as it was then practised; and, indeed, it says something about the approach to planning at the time that comprehensiveness was seen as an achievable objective for a single volume, whereas today we would see such an undertaking in terms of the provision of an introduction with most of the detail to be found in more specialist texts. Keeble does indeed talk about the skills of the planner (ibid., pp. 20–6), but very much in terms of the debates of the time. So, much of the material is a discussion of the contemporary obsession with whether planners should be 'specialists' or 'generalists', which tended to be closely associated with debates about routes to the achievement of professional qualifications (with specialists being seen as people converting from another professional discipline, and generalists having had a comprehensive training in planning rather than converting from a different academic and/or professional background). As a result, the discussion of planning skills does not conclude with a listing of what these are seen as being, but rather looks at a range of professions and skill areas connected with planning and at how these contribute to the planning process, and at how much knowledge of these the planner needs. The areas listed (ibid., pp. 23–5) are architectural design and building construction (including landscape architecture), valuation, sociology, statistics, engineering (including traffic engineering), geology, agriculture, law, government structure, geography and economics. More generally, Keeble quoted approvingly from the Schuster Report (1950) to the effect that '[p]lanners [should] be people of wide culture, and this ought, perhaps, more specially to include a knowledge of the world and its ways, a sense of history and of human destiny' (Keeble, 1964, p. 25).

To avoid the impression that such a list might inevitably give of planning as a set of bits from a wide range of areas rather than as something which constitutes a coherent whole in its own right, Keeble then proceeded to define the special skill of planners:

> It lies, I suggest, in the ability to determine the appropriate relation of land uses spatially and quantitatively and to create a design which expresses this relation without violating other needs. This is the core of Planning skills; to reach the highest levels it needs to be accompanied by the ability to discern those aspects of a particular subject which are of particular Planning importance and to master these in some detail, together with the broad appreciation of the subject as a whole which such mastery entails. (Ibid.)

grounded in quite a wide-ranging view about the territory
by planning and the characteristics of the people who ought to
......ers, this represents nevertheless a fairly narrow view of the kernel of planning skills; it is about land use interrelationships and how they get expressed via a form of plan (described here as 'a design'). The need for planning to attempt to take a more holistic view of the urban systems it ought to be seeking to manage was at the heart of the 'systems' view developed in the late 1960s, and one of the leaders of this drive was Brian McLoughlin. His best-selling work was *Urban and Regional Planning: A Systems Approach* (McLoughlin, 1969), and this talked about the need to define and understand the central skills of the planner not in terms of a rag-bag of bits and pieces taken from elsewhere (an approach of which McLoughlin is very critical; see ibid., p. 306) but rather in terms of specialisms in the levels of planning systems (for example, regional or local) they are seeking to manage. So, McLoughlin saw planners as being people who, in relation to the planning of towns and of regions, could do the following:

(i) understand the nature and behaviour of the appropriate system;
(ii) distinguish elements and sub-systems within it and how their problems are approached by people with other skills;
(iii) co-operate in the setting of goals and objectives for the system;
(iv) devise the best methods of improving system performance;
(v) carry continuing responsibility for the performance of the whole system. (Ibid., p. 307)

This was intellectually a very attractive approach much seized on by planners at the time, perhaps because of its coherence in comparison with what had preceded it, but translating it into effective reality proved to be extremely problematic. As an approach it became associated with large-scale computer modelling, the data requirements of which were often extremely onerous. This was not merely about the sheer quantity of data, either, but also about its quality. I can easily recall as a young professional working on the provision of data for computer models for strategic planning work in South Bedfordshire, where considerable effort went into the assumptions and approximations necessary to meet the data requirements of the models being used, to the point at which it became difficult to see how the outputs could be relied upon when the inputs were considerably less than perfect. A second, and even more fundamental, difficulty was that planners did not actually have at their disposal the controls that were needed in order to deliver effective system management in these terms (however intellectually attractive the approach), but were in fact operating with more limited and partial tools. Thus the concept of the planner as an urban system manager, able to take 'continuing responsibility for the performance of the whole system', was not one that proved readily capable of being operationalized. It may have been the case that if this approach had been persisted with over a longer period of time more could have been made out of it, but the lack of powerful champions with adequate resources and the swings of fashion meant that planning thought moved in other directions.

It can be argued that since the eclipse of systems theory in planning, planning has seen two (probably interrelated) trends. The first is the rise and rise of what could almost now be termed the planning theory industry, where more and more authors worldwide have sought to offer alternative explanations of what they think planning ought to be, without always offering a route map from where planning currently is to these desired destinations (Hall, 1996, pp. 331–40). Indeed, this emphasis on the normative may offer one of the explanations for the second trend, which is the growing distance between much planning theory writing and the world of planning practice (ibid., pp. 340, 341; see also Brooks, 2002, ch. 2). This is a sweeping generalization in the sense that some planning theory does try to start from understanding practice circumstances and seeking to draw helpful lessons from them, but much of it doesn't; and this may help to explain why, as Brooks puts it, 'planning practice and planning theory constitute two distinct communities of interest, each with its own membership, forums for interaction, modes of communication and other internal dynamics' (Brooks, 2002, p. 25). Nicholson (in Thomas and Healey, 1991, pp. 53–62) reflects on this in the context of his experiences of moving from a job as a planning academic to a job in planning practice as follows:

> A more difficult issue is underlined by my experience of the transition from a research post to a local government job. I have already noted that I was able to accept, on taking up my post, the assumption that planning was a valid activity, a 'good thing', which needed little if any further analysis. However, I was acutely aware that this assumption effectively blocks out a series of questions about the role, effects and values of land use planning. As an academic these questions had been foremost in my thinking, but I found it difficult to sustain this position of objectivity while actually carrying planning out. In effect, the demands of planning as a job had come to greater prominence than my view about planning itself. (Ibid., p. 61)

What has become one of the dominant elements in planning theory writing has been the idea of planning as a communicative and a collaborative process, whereby information and views are exchanged on a more or less continuous basis and planning decisions are worked towards through a process of debate (see, for example, Healey, 1997). The rise in support for this view of planning among the planning theory community can perhaps be related to the development of the concept of

irticipation in planning discussed in Chapter 2, although the
f untangling what is cause and what effect in this relationship
.... ᴜᴄ extremely complex (but see Darke, 2000). Thomas and Healey
report evidence that planners increasingly see interactive work as a very
significant component of their practice lives, with the emphasis on the
report and the plan being of less significance than in earlier periods; in
other words, the balance between an emphasis on process as distinct
from an emphasis on product was moving in favour of the former
(Thomas and Healey, 1991, p. 195). The practical consequence of this
approach is that it puts an emphasis not just on plan-making and implementation as traditional planning skills but also on processes of seeking
support, building consensus, listening to wide-ranging views and accommodating difference; what Thomas and Healey described as 'knowing
how' as well as 'knowing what' (ibid., p. 194). As a result, Albrechts
(2002) seeks to explore planning expert opinion from both academics
and practitioners about six issues that arise from this concern:

- Including citizens in decision-making;
- Involving citizens in consultative structures;
- The implications for decision-making and power relations;
- Deliberation, collaboration and the time budget;
- Specific bottlenecks in decision processes;
- Strategies of collaboration.

Given what has been said in Chapter 1 about the constantly rising public
expectations about involvement in the planning system, and the expectations of the British government (and, indeed, many other governments)
that practitioners will 'engage' the public more effectively (that is, not
just seek views but try to ensure that they are reflected in planning outcomes), there can be little doubt about the importance of interactive
skills as a component of contemporary planning practice. What is less
clear is how activities of this nature fit into planning systems faced with
pressures that pull in other directions, such as the fragmented and
indeed oppositional nature of many of the views that are expressed, the
government emphasis on performance and delivery, the resourcing
restrictions that most planning services have had to live with in recent
years, and a political process which retains the ultimate responsibility
for decision-making. Many of the hardest challenges of contemporary
planning practice are undoubtedly around taking commitments to public
engagement (which many planners do feel personally are intrinsically
right) and turning them into operationally effective ways of proceeding
in the face of conflicting pressures.

Looking ahead to the type of planning curriculum that might produce
planners with the skills needed to operate effectively in what she sees as
the cities of the future, Leonie Sandercock in *Towards Cosmopolis*

(Sandercock, 1998), sees the task in terms of four key elements:

- Planning needs to identify the specificity of its domain in terms of socio-spatial processes which are subject to continuous change.
- Planning programmes need to be articulated with environmental and design programmes to reach a greater understanding of the problems of human settlements.
- Methods, skills and competencies need to be redefined as matters of key literacies.
- Planning must be approached as an ethical inquiry. (Ibid., pp. 222, 223)

The first of these points is seen in terms of six macrosocial processes: urbanization, regional and inter-regional economic growth and change, city-building, cultural differentiation and change, the transformation of nature (which others would talk about as a key element of sustainable development), and urban politics and empowerment. The second of these points is about breaking down barriers, which Sandercock sees as being erected and defended by professional bodies, to explore in an interdisciplinary manner built form in the environment in the context of the need to achieve sustainable development. The third point is about the need for future planners to be armed with technical, analytical, multi- or cross-cultural, ecological and design literacies. The final point is about recognizing that the real goal of planning education should not be to stuff students full of facts, techniques, methods and information, but should be about raising basic questions of values around living in the emergent human societies in sustainable ways (ibid., pp. 225–30). This challenging approach represents a view of planning skills emphasizing community, environment and cultural diversity rather than the more traditional approaches discussed in much of the rest of this chapter, but it is an important corrective to the trap of seeing planners' skills mainly in terms of making a governmental machine work.

Changing views of planning skills over time – the views of a professional body

There is considerable scope to debate the roles of professional bodies in contemporary societies, and in particular how they relate their manifest concerns for the interests of their members to their claims to be able to offer expert views about how their professional area should develop, and to their positions in relation to the public interest. There isn't the space here to debate this territory, but for readers who want to follow up some of the more conceptual literature about professions there is a considerable body of material to explore (see, for example, Durkheim, 1957; Johnson, 1972; Torstendahl and Burrage, 1990; Friedson, 2001).

The literature on how this gets applied to the specific field of planning is much smaller (but see Healey and Underwood, 1979; Reade, 1987; Thomas and Healey, 1991; Evans and Rydin, 1997; Campbell and Marshall, 2001), though perhaps the most critical elements of this are around how distinctive the set of claimed planning competencies really is (Evans and Rydin, 1997) and the balance between what can properly be seen as technical and what is really political (Reade, 1987). Of course, planning is by no means the only profession in which professional bodies are facing challenges of this nature in the early years of the twenty-first century. For present purposes, though, the critical point is that professional bodies do exist and are significant players in the field. This section therefore looks at one example of the views of a professional body in this context – the British example, which is the Royal Town Planning Institute.

As a professional body, the Royal Town Planning Institute (RTPI) is concerned among other things to promote the value of planning, to advance the interests of its members, and to seek to influence (and in so far as it relates to admission to corporate membership, to regulate) both initial and continuing education in planning. As such, it is likely to contribute statements about skills for planning practice which are of considerable significance in helping to understand the nature of those activities, but it may also in doing these things be a contributor to the creation of those very barriers in terms of the approach to planning reflected in contemporary education which Sandercock argues (in the summary we have just seen above) should be torn down. The challenge for a professional body in such a situation is clearly both to be in the van of change and at the same time to advance and protect its members' interests; and this must always be an awkward duopoly when the latter constrains the former, as it almost invariably will.

The early history of how the RTPI approached these issues is closely related to how planning itself developed as an activity in Britain (Ashworth, 1954). The development of the RTPI's views in the specific context of planning education can be seen in Cherry (1974, especially ch. 9), and for present purposes there is no need to go back into the evolution of ideas from this point over the next couple of decades. Our starting point here is a statement from 1996 (RTPI, 1996) which talks about the qualities of a planner. These elements are reproduced in Box 9.2.

A survey of academics and practitioners looking at the relative importance of the elements in this RTPI formulation was reported in the Summer 1997 edition of *AESOP News* (Oc *et al.*, 1997). This reported 60 responses from the members of the International Society of City and Regional Planners (regarded for these purposes as practitioners) and 44 responses from members of the Association of European Schools of Planning (regarded for these purposes as academics). The RTPI's list of

---

Box 9.2   The RTPI's 1996 view of the qualities of a planner

The professional planner needs to possess:

(a) *Knowledge* about:
  - The nature, purpose and method of planning (debates on the nature, purpose and methods of planning; traditions of thought in philosophy, science and social science; planning methods; and the roles and relationships of the planner);
  - Environment and development (the dimensions of the natural environment; the dimensions of the built environment; the development process; and valuing and managing the built and natural environment);
  - The political and institutional context of planning practice (the planning system in context, British law, politics and government; law, procedure and organization of British planning practice; and related areas of policy); and
  - Specialized areas in the planning field;

The key attribute of a knowledgeable planner is the ability to value relationships across these areas of knowledge.

(b) *Competence* (skills) in:
  - Problem definition
  - Research skills and data selection
  - Quantitative analysis
  - Aesthetic dimensions and design awareness
  - Strategic and synoptic dimensions and implications
  - Synthesis and application of knowledge to practice
  - Collaborative problem-solving
  - Written, oral and graphic communication
  - Information technology and

(c) Awareness of the *value dimensions* of planning work and the ethical responsibility of the planner.

Source: RTPI, 1996, para. 2.2.

---

competencies (skills) in Box 9.2 was divided into two groups – analytical and research skills, and communication and professional skills – and this distinction was carried forward into the 1997 report. The results are summarized in Box 9.3.

The outstanding point that emerges from the material in Box 9.3 is how similar the views of at least these two groups of academic and practitioners are about these sets of rank orders. In particular, while there are some minor variations, in the case of both lists both the top three and the bottom three are the same; so, problem definition/solving, synthesis and application of knowledge and strategic thinking are seen as the top analytical and research skills, and reasoning and negotiation, collaborative problem-solving and written communication are the top communication and professional skills. This might be seen as evidence

Box 9.3   The relative importance of the RTPI's 1996 view of planning skills, as expressed by academics and practitioners

Views in each case are expressed in rank order, with 1 as the highest rank.

	Academics	Practitioners
1. *Analytical and research skills*		
Problem definition/solving	1	1
Synthesis and application of knowledge	2	3
Strategic thinking	3	2
Conceptualization	4	4
Qualitative analysis	5	5
Quantitative analysis	6	7
Ability to read maps, plans	7	6
Data collection	8	8
2. *Communication and professional skills*		
Reasoning and negotiation	1	1
Collaborative problem-solving	2	2
Written communication	3	3
Management and leadership	4	4
Oral communication	5	5
Design/graphic communication	6	6
Information technology	7	9
Aesthetic awareness	8	7
Time management	9	8

Source: Developed from Oc *et al.*, 1997, p. 8.

that the much-vaunted gap between academics and practitioners may not be as great as some contend, although it could also be seen as evidence of a cosy set of shared views within elements of the same professional community.

The RTPI's view in Box 9.2 can be compared with the views of Leonie Sandercock summarized above; and it can be seen that there are considerable differences between what might be described as the mainstream view of a professional body and a radical-utopian critique. There are also some similarities, however, for example in the approach to knowledge areas, in some of the skills that are seen as necessary, and in the emphasis on values; although the Sandercock formulation would probably be seen by most readers as being considerably more broadbrush than that of the RTPI.

The perspective of employers at that time, on the other hand, seemed to be much more about immediately useable skills. The 1994–5 annual report of the Discipline Network in Town Planning reported a sample survey of planning employers which showed that the planning skills regarded as essential to planning graduates across the range of employers and given the highest ranking were the ability to read maps and plans, followed by design appreciation. The skill areas which this sample of employers felt needed greater development were communication skills, report-writing, effective meetings (including time management and group working), problem-solving and analysis (Discipline Network in Town Planning, 1995, p. 10). Looking at these survey results in more detail, the top seven transferable skills ranked as essential by all employers were

	Per cent	
Report-writing	96.1	
Written communication	96.1	
Problem-solving	84.4	
Time management	81.8	
Group working	80.5	
Problem analysis	80.5	
Negotiating skills	68.8	(Daniels, 1996, p. 8)

This view of planning skills on the part of employers (as well as reflecting the questions they were asked) is all about the practical things they expect planning graduates to be able to do, rather than the longer-term and much more philosophical view of what planning ought to be trying to achieve advanced by Sandercock. It should be noted though that this set of views by employers shows some differences from the views of practitioners summarized in Box 9.3 – where as we have seen the views of that particular sample of practitioners were not mainly about immediately usable practical skills but were more about strategy and focus and, indeed, were not very different from the views expressed by the sample of academics about these same issues. Nevertheless, the views of employers reported by the Discipline Network in Town Planning perhaps illustrates what Nicholson (in Thomas and Healey, 1991) was saying in the quote above when he moved from taking an academic perspective to a practice job, and had to focus perforce on the operation of the system as it was rather than on how it might be changed.

Just after the RTPI guidance was published, Kunzmann offered a further view on planning skills, taking as his starting point key issues in urban policy and planning in Europe over the next two decades (Kunzmann, 1997, pp. 3, 4). He considered the following five issues to be the key ones in this context:

- The conceptualization, promotion and implementation of sustainable urban development.

- The management/governance of space in increasingly fragmented and polarized urban regions.
- The conceptualization and management of urban and regional policies targeted to secure both formal and informal work in post-industrial times.
- The further development of the concept of multicultural society, and a socially acceptable management of the spatial implications of inward migration.
- The conservation of the heritage of cities and cultures.

From this perspective, Kunzmann identified seven key competencies:

- Analytical competence (defined very broadly in terms of understanding the causes and implications of spatial problems)
- Methodological competence
- Visionary competence
- Creative competence
- Social competence
- Communicative competence
- Intercultural competence (ibid.)

This formulation bears certain similarities to that of Sandercock (and, indeed, to the view of skills for planning practice developed in this book), and again represented something of a challenge to the extant view of the RTPI. Academic challenges of this nature weren't the only reasons why there was seen to be a need by the RTPI to review its stance, however. The RTPI's Planning Education Commission in its report (Planning Education Commission, 2003) identified nine sets of challenges as the context for this review:

- Societal changes – very similar to those discussed briefly in Chapter 1 of this book.
- The move to spatial planning rather than narrower definitions of land use planning.
- Devolution within Britain, and the variety this will bring.
- The growing planning significance of the work of the European Union.
- The impact of major global issues in the economic, environmental and social fields.
- The need to see planning as operating within an environment of continuous learning.
- The need to raise the profile of planning as an education and career choice among potential students.
- Adverse trends in the university world which have put the provision of planning education under pressure.
- The need for a professional body such as the RTPI to rethink its position and role in a changing world (ibid., pp. 12–17).

Box 9.4 The RTPI's new vision for planning

The core ideas are that planning is:

- *Spatial* – Dealing with the unique needs and characteristics of places.
- *Sustainable* – Looking at the short, medium and long-term issues around the achievement of sustainable development.
- *Integrative* – In terms of the knowledge, objectives and actions involved.
- *Inclusive* – Recognizing the wide range of people involved in planning.
- *Value-driven* – Concerned with identifying, understanding and mediating conflicting sets of values.
- *Action-oriented* – Driven by the twin activities of mediating space (the management of the competing uses for space) and making places that are valued and have identity.

Source: RTPI, 2001.

The central idea behind this review is the idea of planning as *critical thinking about space and place as the basis for action or intervention* (ibid., para. 4.17). This derives from the Institute's *A New Vision for Planning* (RTPI, 2001), built around six core ideas; these are summarized in Box 9.4.

The work of the Planning Education Commission starting from the philosophy espoused in *A New Vision for Planning* has been turned into a policy statement on initial planning education (RTPI, 2004), which sets out in the twenty-first century educational jargon of 'learning outcomes' what graduates from new-style planning programmes should be able to do. There are in total 24 learning outcomes identified in the Institute's 2004 policy paper, but essentially these reflect 4 basic clusters or elements, which are summarized in Box 9.5.

There is, of course, scope for argument about how radical an updating of its view about planning skills this new prescription is, and there is considerable scope for debate about how well (for example) this would perform against the views of Sandercock on how planning needs to change to be fit for purpose in the twenty-first century. Clearly also, it is too soon at the time of writing to be able to comment meaningfully about how effective a response this represents to the challenges identified by the Planning Education Commission, especially since I played a part in developing this specification and thus would not be a disinterested commentator. What surely cannot be denied, however, is that there was a need for the RTPI to face up to this agenda if it is to flourish well into the twenty-first century as the kind of professional body that it aspires to be, because the challenge to planning is to a large extent the challenge of change.

Box 9.5 The RTPI's 2004 view of the key components of planning skills

- **Critical thinking** Planning is both an art and a science, but also more than the sum of those; it is about achieving outcomes, not just operating a set of procedures; and achieving those outcomes involves processes which are qualitative as well as quantitative, and informal as well as formal.
- **Space** Planning deals with spatial relationships, and competing claims to spaces; and it deals with how sectoral and spatial relationships affect each other. In so doing, it has real effects on how economies and their infrastructures function; on how communities achieve cohesion and social inclusion; on environmental capacity and ecological impact; and on cultural identity.
- **Place** Planning focuses on the outcomes that determine the quality, form and identity of places which people experience, whether they stay there or are just passing through.
- **Action or intervention** So planning is a process of deliberation that focuses on what could and should be done, and thus a process concerned with ethics and values as well as facts. It is an active process (although it recognizes that sometimes the best course is no action), which requires management skills appropriate to securing results. And it requires sensitivity to the time dimension of decisions – how time affects decision-making, how it affects differentially the interests of the parties involved, and how decisions inevitably trade off present and future. Planners themselves need to be able to make good quality decisions, often based on imperfect information, and to help shape decision-making processes in contexts where others will make the ultimate decision.

Source: RTPI, 2004, para. 1.5.

Changing views of planning skills over time – an urban regeneration perspective

Britain has made considerable progress with what it calls urban regeneration (what is more commonly called urban revitalization or urban renewal in the USA) because as a country with a large number of old towns and cities it has had to face major problems of urban decay. Many of the tasks that fall under the heading of 'urban regeneration' are in the terms of this book planning tasks, and this section looks at how thinking about skills for planning practice has developed in this particular context.

One of the tasks the British government set itself in establishing the Neighbourhood Renewal Unit (NRU) as an arm of the Office of the Deputy Prime Minister to oversee the most localized component of its urban regeneration programmes was to look at the skills that would need to be developed among a range of stakeholders (not just professionals) to improve performance in this field. That resulted in a review titled *The Learning Curve*, published in October 2002 (Neighbourhood Renewal Unit, 2002). Before looking at this in more detail, it is important to acknowledge that the field of urban regeneration at the neighbourhood level is similar but not identical to the field of planning. The NRU express this relationship as follows:

> In order to achieve neighbourhood renewal objectives, we need a comprehensive range of skills and knowledge to improve health, reduce crime, develop housing, improve the local environment, have better schools and help more people into paid employment. (Ibid., p. 6)

So, planning is in effect one of the contributors to a comprehensive attempt to upgrade the quality of localities, both as places and in terms of the quality of life of their residents. When reflecting on the skills practitioners and professionals need to engage effectively in these processes, the NRU identifies three broad sets (Ibid., pp. 29–31); analytical skills, interpersonal skills and organizational skills. Box 9.6 summarizes the key elements in this prescription.

It is possible to argue, in the context of the discussion about terminology earlier in this chapter, that some of the elements in Box 9.6 are not in the strictest sense skills at all, but are really about attitudes or practices where the NRU wants to see change; for example, important though it undoubtedly is, is 'valuing diversity' truly a skill in the sense in which this is defined above in Box 9.1? Perhaps the most important element in the NRU's presentation, however, is the distinction it makes between analytical, interpersonal and organizational skills, and the relative emphasis it appears to be placing on the latter two elements as compared with the brief treatment of analytical skills. This may be because it takes as given the fact that different types of professionals bring different kinds of analytical skills to the table, and wants to focus on the other two areas (interpersonal and organizational skills) as being the areas where there is the greatest need and scope for adding value to those pre-existing professional packages. What may well sit behind this is the recognition of a point we have seen before; the key changes being sought are around the *process* of neighbourhood regeneration, so that it is experienced as something that is done with people rather than as something that is done to them.

Changing views of planning skills over time – multi-professional perspectives

Turf wars between built environment professions are not new. Attempts at looking at how these professions might work together to create

Box 9.6 Skills for practitioners in neighbourhood renewal, according to the Neighbourhood Renewal Unit

Key analytical skills

- The ability to apply techniques to analyse possibilities, create opportunities and evaluate alternative solutions.

Key interpersonal skills

- Effective strategic leadership, involving shaping inclusive visions, translating those visions into viable strategies, building coalitions of stakeholders, locating and deploying a wide spectrum of resources and acting as a problem-solver.
- Management of people, which requires the adaptation of traditional human resource and people management processes to the particular needs of deprived communities.
- Valuing diversity, to ensure that all sections of the community are involved.
- Working with partners, by creating opportunities for challenge and exchange across organizations and professional boundaries.
- Effective communication, including listening, negotiating and maintaining regular contact and feedback.
- Conflict resolution, consensus-building and mediation.

Key organizational skills

- Project management, to ensure the effective implementation of projects, including project appraisal and development in the phases before implementation.
- Finance and budgeting, including the ability to manage unpredictable funding streams.
- Research, monitoring and evaluation, including the central involvement of communities in evaluation processes.
- Risk assessment and management, to ensure that an appropriate stance towards the need to innovate is adopted.
- Information technology, to ensure that full advantage is taken of the benefits of IT and in particular to ensure that deprived communities aren't excluded from these benefits.
- Mainstreaming, to ensure that the major services delivered in a locality as part of an approach to service delivery that is broadly common across whole or substantial parts of urban areas are challenged to work better in deprived areas.

Source: Developed from Neighbourhood Renewal Unit, 2002, pp. 29–31.

a better end product for end users are also not new, but it is probably not too unfair to suggest that professions are often more animated when it comes to defending and promoting what they see as their territory than when they are thinking about working with others to create a better whole. There have been some attempts at this latter task in recent times, however, and this section looks at some of these from a skills perspective.

The Rogers Urban Task Force in its report (Urban Task Force, 1999) argued strongly for the role of excellent urban design in the promotion of urban regeneration. That banner has been taken up by the Commission for Architecture and the Built Environment (CABE), and several publications in recent years have added considerably to the guidance available about urban design and the planning system (see, for example, DTLR and CABE, 2000, 2001; DETR and CABE, 2001). In carrying out this work, CABE has also identified what it sees as the key problem and what it sees as the main skills lacking among the appropriate professional groups. Its diagnosis of the key problem is as follows:

> The point is simple; the levels of skills within the built environment professions have a direct effect on the quality of what they create. We only have some of the skills necessary to undertake this task and these skills are in short supply. This is not anecdotal or personal opinion, but is backed up by rigorous research. (CABE, 2003a)

The skills CABE sees as being in short supply are described in Box 9.7. This analysis bears some relationship to the views of the Neighbourhood Renewal Unit summarized above in Box 9.6, particularly in its emphasis on project management, on making partnerships work, on securing effective community involvement, and on project and financial appraisal. The big difference, of course, is the central role CABE sees for urban design. CABE has gone on to argue that it is skill shortages in this field in particular that represent a major challenge (Scott, 2004), which it supports via the results of a 2003 survey of local planning authorities in England (CABE, 2003b). Based upon a 36 per cent sample, this shows *inter alia* that 86 per cent of authorities felt they needed further design skills within their planning departments and only 13 per cent felt that they did not need such skills, which is a ratio of around 13:2 (ibid.). It has to be said that a survey of this nature with a clear design focus rather invites this kind of answer to this kind of question, but nevertheless this does suggest that local planning authorities do tend to see urban design as a particular skill which requires something over and above the general level of design expertise that a trained planner is likely to bring to them. There is also some support for this view in the survey carried out by Durning and Glasson for the Local Government Association, which, by all types of local authority except London boroughs, shows more authorities identifying design skills gaps from the menu of planning/discipline skills on offer than any of the other skills on this menu (Durning and Glasson, 2004b, table 16, p. 30).

The 'Better Together' project looked specifically at inter-professional education and comparative practice in the built environment, and it

---

Box 9.7   CABE's views about skills in short supply

CABE identifies the following five groups of skills that it says are lacking, in terms of the drive to build more sustainable communities:

- Strategic planning (particularly within local planning authorities), to inform the range of plan-making activities from statutory development plans down to site level briefs.
- Urban design, from the scale of rethinking existing urban areas or planning new developments down to design briefs for individual sites.
- Project management, especially in relation to complex mixed use schemes. CABE sees this skill shortage as having adversely affected the willingness of commercial clients to tackle complex projects.
- The management and maintenance of local development partnerships, especially in relation to the need to manage community involvement in design and development processes.
- Project appraisal and financing, including dealing with funding bodies and financial institutions.

CABE also identifies an overarching skill deficit, which it sees as the lack of leadership from decision-makers in both the private and the public sectors when it comes to making commitments to excellence.

Source: Adapted from CABE, 2003.

---

identified a set of major competencies which it saw as being necessary among built environment professionals seeking to tackle the contemporary urban agenda, based upon a previous piece of work by the Planning Network (Planning Network, 2001). The key skill groupings (described as 'major competencies') are as follows:

- Strategic thinking
- People management
- Partnership working
- Finance and risk management
- Project and programme management
- Community inclusion
- Economic development
- Implementation
- Specialist technical skills (such as spatial planning, urban design, transport, environmental protection, infrastructure, housing management and property development). (Planning Network, 2004, pp. 4–6)

Again, there is some overlap here with previous attempts at describing key skills, but perhaps the most important component of the above list is the emphasis it places on generic skills (that is to say, skills that are not the province of a single profession but that may be needed to various extents by members of all the built environment professions who seek to contribute to the achievement of the contemporary urban agenda), as distinct from the specialist or technical skills where individual professions are likely to be in the lead. This approach was also the one adopted by the Egan Committee, and this is therefore the final contribution reviewed in this section.

The work of the Egan Committee, with its emphasis on generic skills and managerialist approaches, was by no means the first step down this road as far as professional literature in planning was concerned. The Royal Town Planning Institute virtually a decade earlier had recognized that planners in practice needed a wide range of management-type skills if they were to operate successfully and, as a result, commissioned a team to look not just at what this meant but also at its implications across a range of fields including that of education. The resulting report (Higgins *et al.*, 1995) argued that planners had to see themselves not merely as professionals in possession of a range of subject-based skills but also as managers, with a focus on the effective management of processes and on delivery against agreed objectives, if they were to operate effectively in the contemporary world. This in itself was by no means an original idea, but it captured what was part of the practice experience of large numbers of Institute members which arguably was not fully embedded in the Institute's formal policy stances, particularly in relation to education. This in turn contributed to the development of thinking which led a few years later to the Institute's New Vision for Planning and to the work of the Planning Education Commission, both of which have been reviewed above.

The Egan Committee was asked by the deputy prime minister in April 2003 to review the skills and training required to deliver sustainable communities, and its report was published a year later (Egan Committee, 2004). The committee took a very broad view of its remit, which once it became public knowledge fairly quickly started to generate a negative climate for the committee's work. Its consultative processes, with their emphasis on the importance of the development of a series of generic skills that all built environment professionals should have, generated considerable (and perhaps fairly predictable) flak to the effect that this was downgrading the importance of the existing skills of existing professionals and thereby threatening those professions rather than seeing them as part of an inclusive process. This was unfortunate in the sense that it was creating antipathy to what the committee was likely to say even before it had reported, with the consequent risk that important messages might be ignored. What was also unfortunate was that the language in which the committee's material was couched, including its final report, was seen as that of the management consultant or the business guru rather than a language that was an appropriate means of communication with the key stakeholders in the drive for the achievement of sustainable communities. All of this meant that the reception this potentially very significant review was likely to receive (and, by and large, did receive) was at best lukewarm and at worst fairly dismissive. At the same time, and without trying to deny that the way the Egan Committee handled its task contributed to this outcome, the response from professionals and their representative bodies could also be seen as evidence of Sandercock's view (Sandercock, 1998) that the behaviour and attitudes of professional bodies, because of the vested interest this involves, are often a barrier to progressive change.

The Egan Committee's starting-point was an attempt to define what a sustainable community actually was, and then to itemize its key components, in order to identify the skill developments needed to move in this direction. The committee's definition was as follows:

> Sustainable communities meet the diverse needs of existing and future residents, their children and other users, contribute to a high quality of life and provide opportunity and choice. They achieve this in ways that make effective use of natural resources, enhance the environment, promote social cohesion and inclusion and strengthen economic prosperity. (Egan Committee, 2004, p. 18)

The committee then went on to present what it saw as the components of sustainable communities in the form of a 'wheel' diagram, reproduced in Box 9.8. Subsequent work by the British government has added an eighth element ('Fair for everyone') to the seven components of the Egan wheel (ODPM, 2005d), and it may well be that these elements will be further explored in subsequent work.

From this position, the Egan Committee proceeded to examine a number of process issues, where the criticisms noted above about the language in which the committee chose to express itself are particularly easy to apply, before looking at the right skills for the job (ibid., ch. 3). This they did by identifying seven types of core occupation engaged in the delivery of sustainable communities; implementers and decision-makers, built environment occupations including planners, environmental occupations, social occupations, economic occupations, community occupations, and cross-cutting occupations such as neighbourhood renewal and regeneration practitioners (ibid., p. 53). The committee followed this by defining a set of generic skills regarded as being essential, accompanied by appropriate behaviours (distinguishing between ways of thinking and ways of acting) and necessary knowledge. This set of generic skills was as follows:

- Inclusive visioning
- Project management
- Leadership
- Breakthrough thinking/brokerage

Box 9.8 The Egan Committee's view of the components of sustainable communities

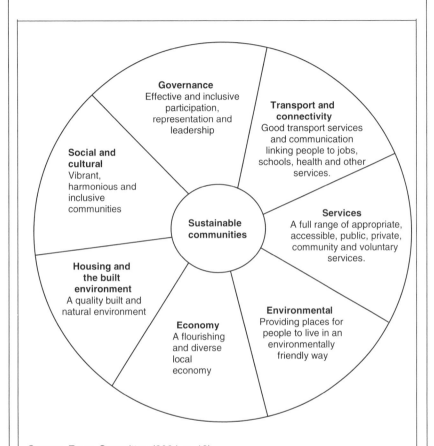

Governance
Effective and inclusive participation, representation and leadership

Transport and connectivity
Good transport services and communication linking people to jobs, schools, health and other services.

Social and cultural
Vibrant, harmonious and inclusive communities

Sustainable communities

Services
A full range of appropriate, accessible, public, private, community and voluntary services.

Housing and the built environment
A quality built and natural environment

Economy
A flourishing and diverse local economy

Environmental
Providing places for people to live in an environmentally friendly way

Source: Egan Committee (2004, p. 19).

The ODPM on its website (www.odpm.gov.uk consulted on 7 September 2005) identifies eight components of sustainable communities:

- Active, inclusive and safe
- Environmentally sensitive
- Well connected
- Well served
- Well run
- Well designed and built
- Thriving
- Fair for everyone

These map reasonably well onto the Egan definition, except that 'Fair for everyone' (which is intended in an inter-generational as well as in a contemporary sense) doesn't sit very easily and could be seen as an added eighth component of the Egan Wheel.

- Team/partnership working within and between teams, based on shared sense of purpose
- Making it happen given constraints
- Process management/change management
- Financial management and appraisal
- Stakeholder management – including ability to work with local residents and residents/community groups
- Analysis, decision-making, evaluation, learning from mistakes
- Communication – including intelligent listening to the community and promotion of development solutions
- Conflict resolution
- Customer awareness and how to secure feedback (Ibid., pp. 56, 57, 103–5)

The Egan Committee then went on to examine means to achieve skill development along these lines among stakeholders, including the creation of a National Centre for Sustainable Community Skills to lead and drive this process. The government's response to all of this could perhaps best be described as being broadly positive but in a very general way, although it did include a specific commitment to the proposed new national centre (ODPM, 2004f). In doing this, the government must have been aware of the very mixed reaction the committee's work and report had generated, and also of the challenge this would pose in terms of getting people and organizations onside whose response had been at the critical or even dismissive end of this spectrum. It remains to be seen how effectively this agenda will be taken forward, and this must in part turn on how widely accepted the message is about the significance of generic skills as against those possessed in varying degrees by existing professions.

For present purposes, it is perhaps enough to note that the Egan prescription contains quite a lot of points that overlap with those seen in previous examinations of skills for planning practice, but has a very strong process management element to it. The key question is whether these really are distinct and separate skills that should be seen as being in a box labelled 'generic skills', or whether they should be seen as part of the mainstream definition of the skills needed for planning practice, if perhaps without some of the management-speak associated with the presentation of them by the Egan Committee. The position adopted for the purposes of this book is the latter one, because in my experience planning practice is always about not just what you are doing but how, why and for whom you are doing it; but in saying this, I wholly acknowledge that skills of this nature, while necessary for effective planning practice, are by no means unique to planners. Thus, the Egan Committee may well be right to think about skills as being broadly of two kinds (profession-specific and generic) when looking across the range of professions involved in the creation of sustainable communities. It is simply that in looking at one particular grouping in this spectrum (in this case, planners), and at how that group can operate effectively in practice, it is not helpful to think of skills as being in these two distinct boxes.

Conclusion

The above review, which makes no claim to comprehensiveness, should have demonstrated two points in particular. The first is that views about skills for planning practice have undoubtedly changed significantly over the past fifty years and, given the material presented in Chapter 1, it would be both amazing and disappointing were this not the case. What that should tell us, therefore, is that further change, and perhaps on quite a substantial scale, is likely in the future; there is no credible reason to believe that the point in time at which this book is being written represents the apotheosis of the development of ideas in this field. At the same time, I believe that it is possible to be clear about the core areas of skills needed to be successful in planning practice, and that is the basis for the seven clusters of skills for planning practice identified in this book. The second point is that there is by no means a consensus either about a single package of skills for planning practice or about the ways of best describing these skills, although there are certainly many shared ideas among the literature reviewed. I would argue, however, that it is possible to look back at the four broad groupings of analysis presented in this chapter, and to see therein concepts that are very similar to (although not always expressed in the same way as) the seven clusters that constitute most of this book.

In my view, these seven packages represent the ongoing element of skills for planning practice. These are, very broadly, the skills that planners have needed for a long time, and they are likely to be the skills that planners will continue to need into the future, although of course others may be added as part of the continuous process of change. The contents of each of these packages will continue to develop, as will the balance that is appropriate between them in particular circumstances, but the packages themselves will continue to represent the key elements of what a planner needs to have in order to be able to operate successfully in practice situations. Not every planner needs all of these elements in equal amounts, but planners lacking significantly in one or more of these elements are likely to struggle. Planning teams, for sure, need to be well endowed across this spectrum. Indeed, one of the advantages of the team approach is that it can help to overcome the skill deficiencies of a particular individual, because another team member can fill the gap; and so effective team management includes the ability to make the most in this sense of the skills available within the team. The other particularly relevant advantage of team working to the present discussion is that it provides a framework for skill development, in which a problem can often become an opportunity. So, the need for another team member to step into a breach because of the skill limitations of one team member (which could be seen as a problem) is an opportunity for the latter individual to improve skills through working alongside the former individual and learning from that experience.

This particular example serves to illustrate the other key point that needs to be made, which is that the acquisition and development of skills for planning practice is seen as a lifelong process. Indeed, the skill of continuous learning is itself one component of the package described as synoptic and integrative skills. The job of initial planning education is to establish the basis for this process, both by introducing people to the range of skills they will need to develop and by helping to inculcate the skills they will need to continue learning once initial professional education is complete. But the role of initial education can never be more than this, not only because it constitutes a relatively small proportion of a professional working life but also because it takes place at a particular period of time from which point large-scale change has to be seen as inevitable. These two points are easy to illustrate. If an individual has a forty-year professional career which has included a four-year undergraduate planning course, the latter is 10 per cent of the former. It makes no sense at all, given this very simple illustration, to concentrate all our attention on the first 10 per cent of the period and to ignore completely or to undervalue very substantially the last 90 per cent. This has in very large measure nonetheless been the position in British planning to date (and, I suggest, in many other countries also, even those where the detailed figures presented above would need to change because they see planning education purely as a postgraduate activity); and the need to change this around so that we recognize the importance of and create a much more effective structure for the development of continuous learning throughout a professional lifetime is one of the biggest challenges facing the British planning profession. I return to this issue in Chapter 10. As far as the point about the nature and scale of change is concerned, the changes described in this book in Chapter 1 have taken place over little more than a forty-year period or, in other words, over a professional lifetime – indeed, over my professional lifetime. These enormous changes have had to be coped with by practitioners active over that period as best they can, and it would be completely unrealistic to assert that their primary resource for this process was their initial education in planning as distinct from their accumulated experience. And, if the pace of change is accelerating, as many authors argue (see, for example, Cooper and Layard, 2003), then the difficulties associated with coping with change are likely to be greater for someone starting a forty-year career at this point in time than they have been for someone just finishing a forty-year career. So, the development of skills for planning practice has to be seen as a continuous process rather than as a job mainly for initial planning education; and the planning practitioners who are likely to be the most successful are likely to be the ones who are most efficient and effective at the accomplishment of this particular task.

Chapter 10

Conclusions

Introduction

I think planning practice is becoming harder. The broad societal change elements discussed in Chapter 1 would tend to suggest this anyway, but two of them in particular are important in this judgement. The first is that public expectations both about involvement in the planning process and about the kinds of outcomes it will produce are rising, and I see no signs to suggest that this long-term trend is about to come to an end. The second is that the experience of planning practice has often demonstrated that our ability to know what the future might bring and to plan either to encompass it or to change it is limited. As a consequence, plans have often struggled to achieve as much as their original authors hoped, and when the process of preparing them is also often becoming longer and more complex this combination of forces has asked some awkward questions about the value of some of our plan-making activities. At the time of writing, we are seeing a resurgence in confidence in Britain about the value of having a plan-led system, accompanied by new approaches to plan-making which (hopefully) are designed to tackle these problems; although, of course, the proof of this particular pudding lies not in the rhetoric of those who are baking it but in the experiences of those who subsequently eat it. Nevertheless, it will still prove to be a real challenge to get meaningful plans produced quickly via more effective processes of public engagement than we have ever seen before, and my assertion that planning is becoming harder may be thoroughly tested by this challenge.

To say that planning practice is becoming harder, however, is not to say that the attempt to plan well is somehow any less important. I am wholly persuaded from my own experience of the value of planning, not just in terms of focusing on what we want to achieve in our places rather than leaving them to become the passive victims of circumstances but also in terms of the scope of planning processes to focus people's thoughts on these matters. I am also wholly persuaded of the value of conceiving of planning as a customer-based activity, rather as some kind of higher order and all-encompassing process at which people can only stare in wonder. I have seen during my professional lifetime a substantial shift in thinking away from the idea that planners know best by virtue of the fact that they are the planners and it is their job to know the best, and towards the idea that planning is about adding value to the ways people experience places by working with them to improve those places, and I hope that this trend continues for some time to come. What we need are styles of planning which are congruent with this way of thinking, and which couple strategic certainty (clarity about the broad direction in which we are trying to move) with as much flexibility as is practically possible within the strategic framework at the level of the individual site or project, and a more or less continuous dialogue about these matters between planning teams and their customers. This kind of approach is challenging in many ways – to our structures, our processes, our resourcing of planning, and to the skills of the individual planners who operate in such situations. But all of this says to me that it is hugely important to plan well, and this (not merely surviving within our planning systems, but making them work successfully) is probably the greatest challenge of all to the skills that planners bring into the process of planning practice. Whether this will bring a more satisfied public, or merely a public that becomes more satisfied with the ability of the planning process to provide opportunities for a growing diversity of views to be expressed, remains to be seen; but my money if I was a betting man would be on the latter option.

I want, therefore, to do two things in particular in this chapter. The first is to look again at the seven clusters of planning practice skills described in this book, but to do so in the round; that is to say, as a package available to planners to be used in the situations they face as they need them, rather than as the individual elements they have (unavoidably) been presented as in the preceding chapters. I want in particular to look at planners' individual responsibilities for keeping this package of skills not merely up to date but in a constant state of improvement, through the concept of the planner as a reflective practitioner (Schon, 1998). I then finish with some reflections on how skills for planning practice might be developed, not just in our planning schools as the major part of the job of initial professional education but also throughout professional lifetimes. Interestingly, these seem likely on average to get longer as ageing societies face up to the consequences both of providing for a growing number of elderly people on the back of smaller numbers of people of working age and of the skills they waste, by disregarding the potential contributions that people who retire after a lifetime of professional practice can still make if their skills remain sharp and focused.

Skills for planning practice revisited

I have presented each of the seven skills clusters individually in the preceding chapters, because that is an analytical device that makes it possible to look at each of them in some depth. But I have also made the point on several occasions that in the real world of planning practice it is most unlikely that planning skills will be seen as operating in separate boxes in this way. I therefore want in the following paragraphs to revisit each of the seven identified planning skills areas in this context.

In effect, successful practising planners bring their full battery of skills to the table and apply their skills in the most appropriate ways in the light of the needs of the particular situation they are facing. The particular skills combinations that individuals will be able to apply will vary, simply because individuals have different balances as between the seven clusters of skills for planning practice. So, for example, some planners will be better than others at relating to the needs of the customers of the planning service, others will be stronger in terms of their place-based skills, and yet others will be better at handling the organizational, managerial and political dimensions of the planning process. But it seems to me that all planners, if they are to succeed, need to have at least a basic level of competence in all of the seven skills clusters, so that the application of their own particular strengths is not undermined by serious weaknesses in other areas. At the same time, it has to be acknowledged that the individual who would be seen as very strong in all seven areas is likely to be a rare breed, and that is certainly confirmed by my own operational experience of working with planners over many years. So, the individual readers who might score themselves honestly on their skills in all seven areas (and this is a helpful way of identifying areas where self-improvement might be sought) should expect the pattern to be an uneven one, and should not expect to see very high scores in all seven areas. All of these issues, though, help to explain why teamwork is such an important and such a common dimension of the planning task; the skills of others in the planning team may be stronger in areas where an individual is weaker.

Most planning situations will require the application of some technical skill or knowledge to contribute to the process of finding an acceptable resolution to the issues being faced. This will vary according to the particular circumstances, and it will sometimes be necessary to recognize that the technical inputs required need to be obtained from specialist sources because they require a level of expertise or subject-based knowledge that is beyond the capacity of the individual planner. It is important that if this is the case then it should be identified quickly, and that the appropriate inputs should be sought. It is much better to acknowledge openly that this is the situation than to pretend to a competence that the individual planner does not possess. At the same time, it is also important to acknowledge that any situation of this kind is a learning opportunity for the individual planner, so that when next a situation of this nature arises the individual will be better placed to deal with it. This comment also applies to team situations, because the most successful planning teams that I have worked with don't merely try to utilize the key strengths of individual team members but also utilize the work of the team as a whole as a learning opportunity to try to improve team members in areas where their skills are less well developed. In all of this, as we saw in Chapter 2, it is important to be clear about where the boundaries of what really is technical work lie, so as not to present something as technical when in fact it turns on an economic or a socio-political judgement about key values. Equally, it is important to think of technical work not just in terms of how well in a professional sense it is being done, but also as something where it is critically important that its significance can be explained in relatively straightforward terms to other key stakeholders in the planning process. Both of these last two points illustrate the importance of seeing technical work in its broader context, and in particular of recognizing how it interfaces with other skill areas such as customer skills, planning system and process skills, and organizational, managerial and political context skills.

As the planning process has become more complex, and as nevertheless more people have sought to get involved in it because they have recognized that what planning does has the potential to impact directly upon their lives, so has the need to explain clearly and succinctly how planning processes work and how as a consequence to participate effectively in them. My experience has been that often people know in essence what they want to say; they just don't know how and when to say it to ensure that as far as possible it has maximum effect. Much of my life as city planning officer of Manchester was not spent advising about great projects or better tomorrows (although there certainly was some of that) but was about how the various stakeholders in the planning process could work within it or could make their views known to it in effective ways. Since I left the world of planning practice and moved into the university world in 1995, this pattern has continued; the majority of the requests for me to give planning advice continue to be of this kind. Planners often under-value the importance of this to others, or see it as being mundane or unex-citing compared with many other more glamorous things that they could be doing. But the truth is that if we are to have planning processes that involve large numbers of stakeholders effectively, and if we are to have planning services that are customer-oriented, then all these stakeholders and customers do need to be helped to understand how best to engage with planning. It is wholly unrealistic to expect that the citizen at large must in effect develop an entry-level qualification in planning in order to be able to engage effectively with it. Planners themselves have a major role to play both in constructing user-friendly planning processes and then in helping the customers of planning services to use them as effectively as possible, and the skills involved in doing this are an essential complement to the customer skills discussed in Chapter 5. We must demystify our planning processes if we are indeed to get the widespread public engagement with them that seems to be so broadly sought, and this should be the main goal behind the development of planning system and process skills.

If planning is indeed about making places better for people, as I argue it is, then a critical element of the planning activity must be around understanding places, how they work, what their regular users think about them, and how they might be capable of being improved in ways that their regular users would not merely accept but would positively embrace. At the time of writing, the concept of 'place-making' has become very fashionable in the planning world, as we saw in Chapter 4, and very often this is associated with the process of urban design. It seems to me that urban design does indeed have a very important role to play in thinking about how our places might be improved, but at the same time what I have described as place skills is about more than that. Ideally, I see this as being about long-term engagement with localities. It is about understanding their history, the forces that are impacting on them and causing pressures on them (positive or negative), the ways in which people use them and what they feel about them, and getting to understand what might be called the 'grain' of the place. It is also about experiencing planned change in localities and the public reactions to these changes. In many ways, these are among the most valuable lessons a planner can learn. It is (relatively) easy to draw up development ideas for a locality and then to move on to something else before those ideas have worked their way through cycles of development, never as a consequence experiencing what the impact of those ideas once implemented actually was and in particular never experiencing at first hand the public reactions to those changes. It can be much tougher to live with the consequences of your own thoughts and actions in these terms and to have to learn and adapt while still dealing both with that area and with its people. My sixteen years as a planner–senior manager in Manchester were like this, and while some of the feedback about things we had done was not as good as I would have liked the important point was that it was feedback that was easy to relate to because it was about my own experiences as well – not those of departed individuals who could easily be blamed as I washed my hands of responsibility. This kind of continuity of experience is absolutely vital to professional learning; it is another really important characteristic of the planner as a reflective practitioner, and even when a planner has moved on to other tasks, projects or localities that individual should still be seeking feedback of this kind, including going back, looking, and talking to people. Interestingly, I found some of the most valuable feedback from elected members in Manchester when we were out on site visits was often not about the individual site that was the primary purpose of the visit but about projects previously undertaken that we passed along the way. Understanding how well or how poorly our past interventions in seeking to make better places have worked out from a wide range of perspectives seems to me to be absolutely fundamental in terms of our future attempts. It is also about carrying credibility with the other stakeholders in that process; why should we expect them to have confidence in what we are saying about what we want to do if their reactions to what we have already done are wholly negative?

The growing importance of customer skills has been highlighted in Chapters 1 and 5. Essentially, planning has had to shift its sense of what it is about away from the idea that it has a superior view of how places need to be made better, and towards the idea that it needs to work on these issues with and for the people whose lives are tied up with the futures of places. In making this shift, planning has also had to acknowledge that public expectations about involvement in the process have been constantly growing, and that these are not just about expecting to be consulted but are also about expecting to have their views taken into account when planning decisions get taken. These two broad trends have probably been mutually reinforcing, and I see no evidence that they have stopped at where we are today. Thus, the skills of relating to customers, of helping them to contribute fully and effectively to the process of planning decision-making, and of identifying and where possible meeting their needs, are more important today than they have ever been; and the significance of customer skills in successful planning practice can only continue to grow. The days of planning conceived of as a neutral, value-free process which knows better than anyone else where the public interest lies have surely gone for good, if indeed it could be said that they had ever arrived other than in some planning minds. Planning today is a public activity, which means not only meeting public expectations about both effective engagement with the process and in terms of the public acceptability of the kinds of outcomes that it produces, but also working with those members of the public who wish to get involved to these ends. The skills of relating to customers are absolutely fundamental in this context, and there can as a consequence be relatively few planning activities where customer skills will not need to be brought to bear on the issues at hand.

It seems to me that what I have called personal skills, and discussed as a package in Chapter 6, are also becoming more important almost as a corollary of the kinds of changes discussed above. To operate effectively in the kind of environments I have been describing, and in particular to work with the kinds of demands that arise from the concept of planning as a public activity in the ways in which I have just described it, the individual planner needs more than anything else to be self-aware. This means not only being clear about the personal skills that the individual possesses, such as the oral presentation of ideas or the ability to listen to what people are saying about the experiences of living in a locality and to extract the planning essence from that, but also being as clear as possible about the personal and the professional values to which the individual subscribes and would be expected to uphold and to be seen to be upholding. As we saw in Chapter 6, some of this is still contested territory, and there is important work still to be done to develop our understanding about appropriate values in planning situations. But none of this takes away from the importance of the individual being as clear as they possibly can be about the values they are carrying into planning situations as individuals, and also being aware of how this affects what they do and how to behave. In my experience, the most successful planners I worked with were people who had put a lot of thought, time and effort into working these things out for themselves, who not merely expressed the outcome of these processes in fine words but also exemplified them in what they did. This has always to be a conditional process, however, because planners have to be open both to learning from their own experiences and to the general development of thought in the planning field; and so what I am saying here should not be taken as an argument for the adoption of a single set of values that are then and forever afterwards rigidly applied irrespective of changing circumstances. This balance between having clear values that frame professional practice and being constantly open to challenges that cause those values to be tested seems to me to be one of the most important characteristics of the reflective practitioner that I discuss below. It should also mean that the planner has a robust framework within which issues arising in some of the other skills areas can be addressed, such as the need to retain personal and professional integrity when 'speaking truth to power' that was discussed in Chapter 7.

As I have argued in Chapter 7, it seems to me to be inevitable that if we see planning as essentially a public activity, it is more or less bound to be tied into the operation of fairly large-scale public bureaucracies and also of public processes of decision-making with a strong political element to them. I think this is likely to be true irrespective of the precise structures of local governance within which particular planning systems happen to be placed. This inevitably means three things. First, the individual planners that serve it must relate to whatever corporate drivers currently operate; planning will not be an island, and I have explained some of these linkages in Chapter 7. The second point is that the process of managing a planning organization in this context will be a process of resource management that in its essential elements is very like many other management tasks; and the efficiency (or otherwise) of this process of management will make a big difference to the effectiveness of the planning organization. The third point is that the major planning decisions will be political decisions, and planners will need as a consequence if they are to work at this level to be effective at working with politicians. The delivery of a public planning service will involve the interaction of these three elements at least – the corporate, the managerial and the political. My experience of these elements in Manchester was that they were all interacting with each other for much of the time, and so it was difficult at times to identify where the boundary lines between them actually were. This means that planners, if they want to lead the process of public service delivery, have to become effective at operating in this kind of milieu. And to be effective, they have not merely to survive (and regrettably that appears to be the goal of some who have been worn down by what can be processes of attrition) but also to continue to keep in mind and to work towards the goal of making places better for people, in whatever forms that takes in particular areas. They probably also have to recognize that the planner will be a relatively unusual bureaucrat, in that most members of the bureaucracy will be functional specialists (education, engineering, social services, for example) whereas the planner will focus on place at various spatial scales; and this of itself can be difficult if the functional specialists don't see the value of a spatial perspective. Nonetheless, if planning is to be an effective public service then planners need to keep plugging away at getting things done in this kind of working environment, because it seems to me that these basic characteristics go with the territory that public service planning will inevitably inhabit. That is why I argued in Chapter 7 that planners in these kinds of situations probably do need to be 'evangelistic bureaucrats', notwithstanding the negative connotations of that term when it was first applied to planners.

I have argued in Chapter 8 that planners need not merely to have a range of integrative skills, because lots of different contributions can shape the making of a planning decision, but also that one of their primary contributions should be as presenters and upholders of 'the big picture' – what are we trying to do in this locality? This sense that the future of places should not merely be a passive function of the various forces that are acting upon them but the result of an active process of thinking how that can be made better for the people who make use of them is something that planners bring to the table and that other professionals tend not to because they don't think in this way. As noted in Chapter 8, there are all kinds of ways of giving expression to what 'the big picture' might actually be, and it seems to me that as long as these are appropriate for the audiences they are intended to inform or influence then it doesn't really matter all that much what methods are chosen – although, by all means, there is a lot to be said for making full use of the creative skills of the team undertaking this work and also of the communicative powers of modern technology. As was also noted in Chapter 8, this sense of planning as always having a 'big picture' dimension to it irrespective of the spatial scale at which it is operating is also one of the most important integrative tools the planner possesses. The planner, in talking to a subject specialist, is not trying to pretend to an equivalent level of knowledge, but is trying to draw out of that specialist not merely the best understanding attainable but also the implications of that understanding for the big picture – does it need to change, or by tweaking something in what the specialist has said is it possible to hang on to the big picture without detriment? My experience of planning at several different spatial scales is that there is always this kind of dimension to it. One question in particular – 'What are we trying to achieve here?' – is always an important one irrespective of the spatial scale, and it is the planner's job always to be asking that question and to be looking at various inputs into that process in the light of it. A related question, of equal value, is 'Does it matter?' Planners need to become very good at sorting out what matters from what doesn't in all the material coming at them, if they are to maintain the sense of purpose provided by the big picture. This seems to me to be a better use of the concept of 'strategic' planning than to relate it solely to planning at the broader spatial scales, which is a common usage. My experience was also that this kind of contribution, reflecting a sense of what is being sought in a locality and where that was coming from, was commonly what was seen by stakeholders as the planner's particular input to all kinds of initiatives, which was valued precisely because it was not likely to be the kind of contribution that others would make. So, synoptic and integrative skills are in many ways the hallmarks of the planning contribution, and whatever other skills planners are utilizing in particular situations these skills can be expected to be at the fore.

The above paragraphs have revisited the seven skills areas identified in this book as the core skills for planning practice, to try to reinforce the point that in practice these are used together rather than in isolation. I have also tried to make the point that each in its own different way is important because it brings something essential to the planning task, and that planners when armed with this range of skills (accepting that the make-up and balance of the skills packages of individuals will be different) can in turn tackle a very wide range of tasks. Looked at like this, it is very hard (and probably unhelpful) to argue that some skills may be more important than others, but what stands out from the above analysis is the importance of synoptic and integrative skills as being the basis of the distinctive planning contribution because they are the means of knitting the other elements together. The ability to develop a sense of the big picture, taking into account a wide range of experiences and aspirations about localities, and then the ability to keep hold of this as a vehicle for pulling together a range of contributions and steering in the desired directions, is at the heart of the planning effort. And it is also, in my experience, what others often most value in the planning contribution. Having said this, it is also important to recognize when it is time to change direction, because the big picture which is hung onto slavishly long after it was clear that it was time to move it on becomes a negative rather than a positive tool. This kind of awareness is fundamental to successful practice, and it seems to me to be another characteristic of the planner as reflective practitioner, which is the ground to be covered next.

The planner as reflective practitioner

The skills discussed in this book are not by their nature the kinds of skills that can be taught at one point in time and then be regarded as being 'finished'. There is a role for initial planning education here, which I discuss in more detail below, but by far and away the most important element in inculcating these skills is the lifelong process of learning from experience, both one's own and that of others. I have described this as lifelong because in my experience, and that of many other planners that I have discussed this with, the process of learning from experience is (or should be) never-ending. Indeed, the planner who stops learning from experience is the planner who has already started to become ineffective. To be an effective learner from practice, the planner needs to adopt the perspectives of the reflective practitioner (Schon, 1998).

Donald Schon, the driving intellectual force behind this idea, argues nonetheless that planners will find this more difficult than some other professions, mainly because of the awkward institutional context within which they work. He puts this as follows:

> The institutional context of planning practice is notoriously unstable and there are many contending views of the profession, each of which carries a different image of the planning role and a different picture of the body of useful knowledge. At the present time, for example, planners function variously as designers, plan makers, critics, advocates of special interests, regulators, managers, evaluators and intermediaries. In planning as in other professions, each role tends to be associated with characteristic values, strategies, techniques, and bodies of relevant information. But in the planning profession, images of the role have evolved significantly in relatively brief periods of time. The profession, which came into being around the turn of the century, moved in succeeding decades through different ideas in good currency about planning theory and practice, partly in response to changes in context shaped by planners themselves. The history of the evolution of planning roles can be understood as a global conversation between the planning profession and its situation. (Ibid., pp. 204, 205)

This structural uncertainty around planning, it could be argued, reinforces the need for individual planners to be clear in their own minds about the key principles guiding their work. But over and above this difficulty, another problem Schon sees is the limited frame that planners sometimes construct for their various roles. He puts this as follows:

> A professional role places skeletal demands on a practitioner's behaviour, but within these constraints, each individual develops his [*sic*]

own way of faming his role. Whether he chooses his role frame from the profession's repertoire, or fashions it for himself, his professional knowledge takes on the character of a system. The problems he sets, the strategies he employs, the facts he treats as relevant, and his interpersonal theories of action are bound up with his way of framing his role ... Further, a system of this sort tends to be self-reinforcing. Depending on the kind of role frame he has constructed and on the kind of interpersonal theory or action he has evolved, a practitioner's reflection-in-action may be more or less limited in scope and depth. (Ibid., p. 210)

So, Schon argues that sometimes planners aren't as reflective as they ought to be because of their limited conception of their role, where the contested nature of some of the territory is one element in this process of choosing a narrow frame for that role. The emphasis he places on the conceptual choices that the individual makes, as distinct from seeing this as a received wisdom from the settled ways in which the relevant worlds operate, is a major constituent in this idea of the planner as a reflective practitioner. It is about the individual's choices, and the individual's capacity to reflect on the factors in the real world which impinge on those choices. Thus, every planner can and should be a reflective practitioner, and while that individual will inevitably feel that their real-world operational situation places some constraints upon their role, it is about trying to look beyond those constraints rather than being unnecessarily bound by them. Schon sees this distinction as making a real difference to how the reflective practitioner behaves as compared with a subject expert who is not a reflective practitioner, and Box 10.1 sets these differences out in two particular contexts: how sources of satisfaction and demands for competence differ between the expert and the reflective practitioner, and the differences in the competences and satisfactions for clients that would arise from traditional and reflective contracts. The differences illustrated in Box 10.1 are striking, and while there are several positive things that can be said about the statements about the traditional expert it seems to me that the stances illustrated as the position of the reflective practitioner are the ones to which practising planners should aspire.

My own practice reflection on all of this is nothing like as elegant, but it does have the virtue of being relatively straightforward. My view was always that my practice experience was:

1. Conditioned, and
2. A wonderful opportunity for learning

It was conditioned because my view of what was happening was only one of many, and almost certainly was a biased view as well in the sense

---

Box 10.1   Differences attributable to the perspectives of the reflective practitioner, according to Donald Schon

Donald Schon sought to illustrate the differences between a traditional expert and a reflective practitioner by looking both at their sources of satisfaction and at demands for competence. For the purpose of this illustration, both types of professional are assumed to be male.

Schon sees the *expert* as someone who rests on the presumption of others that he is knowledgeable (whatever his own uncertainties), who keeps his distance from the client in order to reinforce the role of expert, and who looks for deference from the client in acknowledgement of that expertise. The *reflective practioner*, on the other hand, acknowldeges that he is not alone in having relevant knowledge, sees his own uncertainties as a potential source of learning for himself and those around him, tries to relate as closely as possible to the client, looks for respect to emerge from that connection rather than as right, and doesn't feel the need to maintain a professional facade.

Similarly, Schon sought to demonstrate the differences between these two models through what this might mean for the clients to whom they were contracted. The *traditional expert contract* emphasizes that the client is putting himself in the expert's hands, and gains comfort from the fact that all will be well if he follows the expert advice that he can now expect to receive. The *reflective contract*, on the other hand, is much more interactive, and sees both the client and the professional as working together on a joint enterprise. The process, therefore, is likely to be a developmental one for both the client and the professional.

It can be seen from these examples that in many ways the role of the reflective practitioner is not as straightforward as the role of the traditional expert. But what it does do is to recognize that the reflective professional is always in the process of learning, both for himself and in creating situations where those around him can learn as well, and is entirely open about the fact that this introduces into his use and presentation of his knowledge a conditional element which is often lacking from the way these things are typically presented by the traditional expert.

Source: Schon 1998, pp. 300, 302.

---

that I was in the position of trying to make things happen rather than being on the receiving end of that process. So a critical element in trying to be a reflective practitioner was the need to get views from as many different perspectives as possible and to reflect on those as well as on my own direct experiences – what today would be called a 360-degree analysis. And my own practice experience was a wonderful opportunity for learning precisely because it was happening to me. It was me who received letters or heard views from residents about what they didn't like in their localities, and it was me who received complaints from elected members about aspects of how the planning service had operated in a particular instance which they felt were unhelpful or inappropriate. Not all of this by any means was comfortable or comforting to receive, but all of it was the kind of feedback that I needed to have. Personal experience, no matter how painful, is the best opportunity to learn that there is. Why did those residents not like what was happening in their locality, and what might we have done about it? Was this part of a long-term trend that we ought to have been trying to modify, or was it something about which we could do very little but simply hadn't explained or communicated properly? Why did elected members not like something we had done? Was it part of our normal service that simply produced an inconvenient response, or was what happened something that we could have influenced positively by doing something differently? Such questions can be very challenging, and in particular can create a defensive mentality which tries to protect the planning service rather than to reflect on what was being said and why. But the reflective practitioner must always be open to these kinds of inputs, and never be satisfied if there is the scope to do better in the prevailing situation, or even over the longer term to challenge and to help change the situation. For the reflective planning practitioner, if the goal of planning is to make places better for people, it will always be necessary to strive to do better; we should never be fully satisfied. And as well as learning from other people's experiences in well-established ways, it is essential to learn from one's own experiences and from the broadest possible range of perspectives on those experiences.

Developing skills for planning practice

If I were to write a potted history of planning education in Britain during most of my professional lifetime, it would go something like this:

> British planning education struggled to keep pace with the constantly evolving nature of planning practice, as it tried to respond to the range of challenges that turned its traditional views of itself upside-down and to the ever-rising expectations of a public no longer willing to accept that planners know best. Its response was to keep broadening the planning curriculum, and as it tried to stuff more and more into a fixed amount of time, it did this by curtailing the kind of 'learning-by-doing' that it had largely inherited from architectural education. This typically took the form of simulated real-world projects that took considerable amounts of time at the drawing board, and it was replaced with more traditionally academic pieces of work. Nevertheless, there was a constant struggle to cope with what was seen as being the ever rising needs of professional planning education.

There was also a growing degree of disengagement with the work of planning practice, partly because more academic outputs of the kind the university world seemed increasingly to value connected less well with practice and partly because the world of planning practice was itself under pressure and struggling to find the time for this level of education. Despite all of this, planning education succeeded in producing many people who went on to become very competent practitioners, although how much of this was down to their initial professional education, to the quality of their learning from their practice experiences, and to their own personal qualities was the subject of endless debate.

This is, no doubt, a gross distortion in many ways, but maybe readers can connect with at least some aspects of this potted history. Fundamentally, it seems to me that the conundrum that was always at the heart of a process of constant struggle was how it conceptualized the relationship between initial education and professional practice. For most of this history, the view seemed to be that planning education had to produce pretty much the finished article, who simply then needed to be rounded off by immersion in practice. So it would follow, if this was indeed the ruling conceptualization, that if planning practice was getting harder (as I have argued in this book that it has been) then the process of producing largely the finished article for it would also be likely to get harder; and this certainly contributed to the continuing expansion of the planning curriculum. The expansion of the planning curriculum was also fuelled by a fear that planners with a professionally accredited qualification might not know enough about whatever was the latest thing that it was said that planners needed to understand – and there has been a lot of this (much of it, to be fair, entirely appropriate) over the last forty years or so. It was somewhat galling at times, though, to hear the fruits of this enterprise criticized by more experienced practitioners for the things they couldn't do when they first arrived in a planning post – to paraphrase a common example, he or she might be able to write an essay, but he or she doesn't know how to process a planning application.

It seems to me that an enterprise like this is doomed to failure because at its heart is a fundamentally self-defeating proposition. This is that the job of initial planning education is to produce someone who is the finished article, short of having the rough edges knocked off by practice experience. My view is that this has become increasingly untenable as a position, and would continue to be so were it to be persisted with. It seems to me that, instead, it should be replaced by the idea that initial professional education is the beginning of a lifelong journey, and that its task is to give someone a good start down this road on the basis that the continuation of learning will be a lifelong commitment. The sense of this position can easily be illustrated by some figures. The length of a professional career after the initial education phase may be (let us say) 40 years. This is 10 times the length of a British undergraduate planning programme, 20 times the length of a full-time postgraduate planning as it used to be, and 40 times the length of the new postgraduate fast-track awards introduced for the first time in the academic year 2004/05. Two observations follow from these numbers. The first is that the length of a professional practice life dwarfs the length of the initial planning education life whichever of these models is used as the basis for comparison, and thus in terms of the scope offered for learning it must be more significant. The second is that, as planning programmes get shorter – which has already happened at the postgraduate level in Britain, and in my view will undoubtedly have to happen at the undergraduate level – there is a greater need to focus on the most beneficial ways to use that time rather than to attempt the impossible task of cramming ever more material into a fixed amount of time. These two challenges, it seems to me, will inevitably cause us to reconceptualize the relationship between initial planning education and a lifetime of professional planning practice in the ways I have described, rather than to programme our planning schools to fail as our historic conceptualization will do. The Planning Education Commission has made a good start down this road, and the Royal Town Planning Institute has followed up its report with vigour, but much more remains to be done to achieve the shift I am arguing for here. Many British planning academics agree with this view, incidentally, but it still needs to be promoted to the wider profession.

Another reason why the kind of reconceptualization of the relationship between initial professional education in planning and a lifetime of practice experience that I have argued for would be desirable is that it would actually relate to the real-world experiences of the planners who go through this process. The truth is that young planners leaving planning schools to go to their first jobs are not anywhere near to being the finished article, not necessarily because of any major failings by their planning school but because there is no such thing as 'the finished article'. To use my own experience as an example, if I had stopped learning about planning at the point at which I left Newcastle University's planning school in 1968, I would have missed nearly all the developments that have shaped British planning practice since then which are discussed in Chapter 1. In particular, the dilemmas I can recall facing at that time were around two propositions which had been left unresolved by my planning education. The first was that it was clear that we were at the beginning of an age in which direct public participation in the planning process was here to stay, although I don't think in 1968 that I could have predicted the shape this would take. The problem was that nearly all the simulation projects undertaken as part of my planning degree programme were about the search for the best technical answer in a given situation within a small number of weeks, rather than about longer-lasting processes in which public views shape what happens at least as much as the views of planners, and so I had no real sense of how to handle this new phenomenon. The second dilemma was about coping with change. I was fairly sure that the world wouldn't stand still while I planned the bit of it that I was responsible for, but I had no real understanding of the dynamics of this process or of the notion that change might be at least as much an opportunity as it was a problem. My eyes (although literally it was actually my ears, because I first heard this on the radio in the form of the 1970 Reith Lectures) were opened in this latter regard by Donald Schon's wonderful book, *Beyond the Stable State* (Schon, 1971), which I still regard as the most influential book about planning I have ever read – even though it isn't specifically a planning text at all. This introduced me to the ideas that the stable state was a thing of the past, that change should be embraced because of its inevitability, and that the road ahead in this situation could be made much easier to navigate through individual and organizational learning. But for present purposes, the most important point is that I didn't read this until three years after my undergraduate planning degree programme had finished, not because of any failings on anyone's part but because the book didn't exist until then. My undergraduate planning education could actually be praised for helping me to develop the skills that enabled me to take something like this on board and to be a continuing learner, but if I reflect on the early years of my professional practice life I have to say that I learned far more then than I ever did during my formal phase of planning education. I have had this same conversation with many older planners who have all said the same thing, and so reconceptualizing the relationship between planning education and planning practice in the way that I have argued for here would simply reflect these real-world experiences.

One of the most important elements in this would be the reconnection of planning education and planning practice; although there is an argument which would say that 'reconnection' is the wrong word, because they were never really very strongly connected in the first place. If we accept the view that initial planning education is simply the first step down a lifelong road, and that the road should be viewed as a whole, then it seems to me that the future employers of the young professionals being educated in our planning schools should play a much fuller part in this process that they usually do today. That is not to argue that there are no such connections, because in my view that would not be true, but the yawning gap that I jumped over in 1995 when moving from the world of planning practice to the university world needs to be much narrower if one of the initiatives I would argue for in this context is to have any chance of success. This is the establishment of regular staff interchanges between the two. Another initiative I would argue for is the development of a true partnership in planning education, where the local planning authorities, the active planning consultancies, the regeneration agencies, and the community-based organizations in an area surrounding a planning school join together to contribute expertise and study opportunities to the work of the school on a systematic basis in return for student coursework on their issues/problems, rather than simply having an annual meeting which can achieve very little other than some mutual back-slapping. Of course, for such changes to emerge, practice-based agencies would need to rethink their own roles and to make time available to these ends, and I recognize that this would be difficult. But we need to see what the planning schools are doing, and what future employing organizations both need and will themselves be doing in terms of human resources development, as all being elements in one lifelong journey, rather than as two operations taking place in hermetically sealed compartments, as is too often the case today. The research work and outputs of planning schools are certainly capable of helping to strengthen the links between planning education and planning practice in this context (Griffiths, 2004), but there are issues to be resolved before the full potential of this is to be realized in terms of the sorts of things that planning academics choose to research and the extent to which the research that is carried out in planning schools is influenced by the funding available for research.

Another dimension to this is the need to reflect on which elements of planning education as it is currently offered are actually the most valuable in developing the skills for planning practice that I have outlined in this book. Most academics would probably (and very understandably) argue that the things they teach and to which they are usually very committed do this very well, and in my experience this would often be followed by a plea to the effect that if only students read more then all would be well. But a lot of this is inevitably subject- or topic-based, because that is how many planning curricula are constructed. And I would argue that it is not this kind of knowledge, valuable though it is in its own terms, that contributes the most to developing skills for planning practice. Nor do I think that the traditional simulation of a practice problem fully achieves this, although again this kind of approach if carefully constructed can be very useful. The two methods I have come across that offer the most in these terms are case-studies and consultancy projects.

It is important that case-studies are used in a very focused way. A case-study that involves a student writing down everything that happened in a given situation is of limited value, although the process of investigation that this involves can be a useful learning experience in its own right. A case-study starts to come to life, however, when students begin to ask why things happened as they did, and in particular get the opportunity to talk to key protagonists and to ask them about what they said and did and why they did these things. In my experience, this element is very problematic, because often practitioners and other participants will not make the time available to talk to students about such things; although it is surprising sometimes how much individuals are prepared to contribute in these terms. I think this goes back to what I have said above about the need for a true partnership between planning schools and the world of planning practice in the task of planning education, because the reason why this issue is so often problematic can be reduced to one word: priorities. Practitioners and other participants often won't make time available for such activities not because of a basic unwillingness but because their conceptualization of the priorities that govern their working lives puts this particular demand on their time low down in the pecking order. Of course, activities of this nature when undertaken in a very disorganized manner can create some quite unnecessary problems; having twenty students descending unannounced on a planning office asking to speak to a particular individual is not an efficient way to proceed, and is likely to generate an unfavourable response. But organizing something like this in as systematic a manner as possible, in partnership with practitioners, should enable practitioner time to be used in a cost-effective manner, and it will bring the lessons on offer from a case-study approach to life. The case-study should always end with some reflective questions: How might things have been done differently? Were there any issues/problems arising in this case which could have been resolved more effectively? Who benefited and who lost in terms of the outcomes of the process? And it should be noted that the practitioners who participate in processes of this nature can themselves benefit from these structured reflection opportunities, so this can be a two-way and not just a one-way process.

Consultancy projects, where students as individuals or working as small teams deal with a real-world problem for a live client, have a huge amount to offer if handled effectively. I have worked in this field ever since going to Sheffield Hallam University in November 1995, and I am absolutely convinced of the huge amount that students get out of this activity if three key tests are followed. The first is that the problem that is identified as the basis for consultancy work, and is negotiated in terms of the creation of a brief for the exercise, actually matters to the client. It should not be something made up simply because of the pressures of the situation, but should be something in which the client is happy to invest time and energy because the outcome matters. The second test is that students should manage the working relationship with the client directly throughout the life of the project, and should not have a member of staff acting as a tutor interposing themselves between the client and the student-contractor. The job of the academic member of staff is to advise and guide the consultancy team, but not to mediate with the client and therefore to rub off what might be some of the rougher edges of this experience. The third test is that the client should be fully involved in the process of assessment at the end of the work period, so that the client's satisfaction (or otherwise) both with the process and the product is directly reflected in the mark that is awarded. In the real world, successful consultancy (among other things) produces a satisfied client, and that should be the aim here as well. My experience of this is that very satisfied clients tend to award very high marks, rather more so than do academics who tend to experience palpitations once a prospective mark gets much above 70 per cent. My experience also is that dissatisfied clients tend to produce low marks, and to be fairly direct in explaining the source of this dissatisfaction. So I am convinced that the benefits of involving clients fully in the process of marking considerably outweigh the disbenefits, and contribute to the roundness of the consultancy project as a whole as a learning experience.

Both of these educational experiences are direct illustrations of the point I have argued above, which is the need for more direct involvement in the job of planning education on the part of the world of planning practice. The direct involvement of the participants in a case-study process brings that experience to life in a way nothing else can. The full involvement of the client in a consultancy project from start to finish, including in the process of marking, makes it as nearly as possible like the real world of consultancy, except that the student consultant doesn't get paid for the work other than in terms of the experience on offer. This is just one example of the benefits that such approaches can bring to the world of planning practice as well. Another is the reflective opportunities that this kind of experience should offer them. And of course if they are the kind of reflective practitioners argued for in this book then they should always be on the lookout for this kind of chance. But more than this, the direct involvement of the world of planning practice in student case-studies and in consultancy projects is about building bridges between planning education and practice, from which all kinds of benefits can flow in both directions. All of this requires a considerable amount of organizational time, and I don't want to underestimate this point; but my experience is that this kind of effort is well worth while in the creation of opportunities to develop skills for planning practice.

Concluding remarks

The nature of planning practice is constantly changing. The skills for planning practice that I have discussed in this book, however, seem to me to be both enduring (which is why I have described them as core skills in defining my seven clusters) and portable (in the sense that while I have talked about them in this book mainly in terms of British planning practice, because that is my own personal experience, they can be applied *mutatis mutandis* to planning situations and regimes across the world). I see no reason why the reflective planning practitioner cannot continue to develop the seven bundles of skills described in this book throughout an active professional lifetime. Equally, I see no reason why such a practitioner, so armed, cannot quickly become familiar with and contribute effectively to the resolution of planning issues in any part of the world, except maybe where there are language difficulties; and even here, there are ways around this. What all this comes down to, though, is the acceptance of individual responsibility on the part of the planner to be reflective, to see skills as needing constantly to be worked at and improved throughout a professional lifetime, and to get basic principles and values sorted out so that whatever the situation the focus is on what planning is really all about – making places better for people.

Bibliography

Abercrombie, P., 1945, *Greater London Plan 1944*, HMSO, London.

Adams, D., 1994, *Urban Planning and the Development Process*, UCL Press, London.

Addison and Associates and Arup, 2004, *Evaluation of Planning Delivery Grant 2003/04*, Office of the Deputy Prime Minister, London.

Addison and Associates and Arup, 2005, *Evaluation of Planning Delivery Grant 2004/05*, Office of the Deputy Prime Minister, London.

Albrechts, L., 2002, 'The *Planning Community Reflects on Enhancing Public Involvement. Views from Academics and Reflective Practitioners*', *Planning Theory and Practice*, Vol. 3, No. 3, pp. 331–47.

Allinson, J., 1996, *Appeals and Inquiries* and, *Alternative Approaches to Resolution* in Greed, C., *Implementing Town planning*, Longman, Harlow, pp. 88–109.

Allmendinger, P., Prior, A. and Raemaekers A., 2000, *Introduction to Planning Practice*, Wiley, Chichester.

Altshuler, A. A., 1965, *The City Planning Process: A Political Analysis*, Cornell University Press, Ithaca, NY.

Ambrose, P., 1994, *Urban Process and Power*, Routledge, London.

Argenti, J., 1968, *Corporate Planning: A Practical Guide*, George Allen & Unwin, London.

Arnstein, S. R., 1969, *The Ladder of Citizen Participation*, *Journal of the Institute of American Planner*, 35(4), 216–24.

Arup Economics and Planning and the Bailey Consultancy, 2002, *Resourcing of Local Planning Authorities*, Department of Transport, Local Government and the Regions, London.

Ashworth, W., 1954, *The Genesis of Modern British Town Planning*, Routledge & Kegan Paul, London.

Association of Greater Manchester Authorities, 1993, *Greater Manchester Economic Strategy and Operational Programme*, AGMA, Manchester.

Atkinson, D., 1995, *Cities of Pride: Rebuilding Community, Refocusing Government*, Cassell, London.

Bailey, N., 1995, *Partnership Agencies in British Urban Policy*, UCL Press, London.

Bailey, N., 2003, *Local Strategic Partnerships in England: The Continuing Search for Collaborative Advantage, Leadership and Strategy in Urban Governance*, Planning Theory and Practice, Vol. 4, No. 4, pp. 443–57.

Bartelmus, P., 1994, *Environment, Growth and Development: The Concepts and Strategies of Sustainability*, Routledge, London.

Beatley, T., 1994, *Ethical Land Use: Principles of Policy and Planning*, Johns Hopkins University Press, Baltimore, MD.

Bedfordshire Community Safety Working Group, 2005, *The Draft Bedfordshire Community Safety Design Guide*, Llewellyn Davies, London.

Bennett, L., 1997, *Neighbourhood Politics: Chicago and Sheffield*, Garland, New York.

Benveniste, G., 1989, *Mastering the Politics of Planning*, Jossey-Bass, San Francisco.

Blackhall, J. C., 1998, *Planning Law and Practice*, Cavendish, London.

Blackman, T., 1995, *Urban Policy in Practice*, Routledge, London.

Blowers, A., 1993, *Planning for a Sustainable Environment*, Earthscan, London.

Booher, D. and Innes, J., 2005, *Living in the House of Our Predecessors : the Demand for New Institutions for Public Participation*, Planning Theory and Practice, Vol. 6, No. 3, pp. 431–5.

Booth, C., 1996, *Gender and Public Consultation: Case Studies of Leicester, Sheffield and Birmingham, Planning Practice and Research*, Vol. 11, No. 1, pp. 9–18.

Booth, P., 1996, *Controlling Development: Certainty and Discretion in Europe, the USA and Hong Kong*, UCL Press, London.

Bracken, I., 1981, *Urban Planning Methods: Research and Policy Analysis*, Methuen, London.

Briggs, A., 1982, *Victorian Cities*, Pelican Books, London.

Bromley, R. D. F. and Thomas, L. J., 1993, *Retail Change: Contemporary Issues*, UCL Press, London.

Brooks, M. P., 2002, *Planning Theory for Practitioners*, American Planning Association, Chicago.

Bruton, M. J. and Nicholson, D., 1987, *Local Planning in Practice*, Hutchinson, London.

Bryan, H., 1996, *Planning Applications and Appeals*, Butterworth-Heinemann, Oxford.

Burley, K., 2005, *Probity and Professional Conduct in Planning : A Personal Perspective*, Planning Theory and Practice, Vol. 6, No. 4, pp. 526–35.

Burns, W., 1967, *Newcastle: A Study in Replanning at Newcastle-Upon-Tyne*, Leonard Hill, London.

Burrows, R., Ellison, N. and Woods, B., 2005, *Neighbourhoods on the Net: The Nature and Impact of Internet-based Neighbourhood Information Systems*, Policy Press, Bristol.

Burwood, S. and Roberts, P., 2002, *Learning from Experience: The BURA Guide to Achieving Effective and Lasting Regeneration*, British Urban Regeneration Association, London.

CABE, 2003a, *Building Sustainable Communities: Developing the Skills We Need*, Commission for Architecture and the Built Environment, London.

CABE, 2003b, *Survey Results: Review of Local Authority Planning Departments*, Commission for Architecture and the Built Environment, London.

CAG Consultants and Oxford Brookes University, 2004, *The Planning Response to Climate Change: Advice on Better Practice*, Office of the Deputy Prime Minister, London.

Campbell, H., 2003, *Is There More to Place Than Design?*, Planning Theory and Practice, Vol. 4, No. 2, pp. 205, 206.

Campbell, H. and Marshall, R., 2002, *Values and Professional Identities in Planning Practice* in Allmendinger, P. and Tewdwr-Jones, M. (eds), *Planning Futures: New Directions for Planning Theory*, Routledge, London.

Campbell, S. and Fainstein, S., 1996, *Readings in Planning Theory*, Blackwell, Cambridge, MA.

Carmona, M., Carmona, S. and Gallent, N., 2001, *Working Together: A Guide for Planners and Housing Providers*, Thomas Telford, Tonbridge.

Castells, M., 1989, *The Informational City*, Blackwell, Oxford.

Chapin, F. S., 1970, *Urban Land Use Planning*, University of Illinois Press, Urbana.

Cherry, G., 1974, *The Evolution of British Town Planning*, Leonard Hill, Heath & Reach.

Cherry, G., 1988, *Cities and Plans*, Edward Arnold, London.

Cherry, G., 1996, *Town Planning in Britain Since 1900*, Blackwell, Oxford.

Claydon, J., 1996, *Negotiations in Planning* in Greed, C., *Implementing town Planning*, Longman, Harlow, pp. 110–120.

Coleman, A., 1990, *Utopia on Trial*, Hilary Shipman, London.

Committee on Standards in Public Life (the Nolan Committee), 1997, *Third Report: Local Government*, HMSO, London.

Cooper, R. N. and Layard, R., 2003, *What the Future Holds*, MIT Press, Cambridge, MA.

Coppock, J. T. and Sewell, W. R. D., 1977, *Public Participation in Planning*, Wiley, Chichester.

Countryside Agency, English Heritage, English Nature, Environment Agency, 2005, *Environmental Quality in Spatial Planning*, no publisher or place of publication named.

Daniels, I., 1996, *Discipline Network in Town Planning: Report of Survey*, Discipline Network in Town Planning, London.

Darke, R., 2000, *Public Participation, Equal Opportunities, Planning Policies and Decisions* in Allmendinger, P., Prior, A. and Raemakers, J. (eds), *Introduction to Planning Practice*, Wiley, Chichester, pp. 385–412.

Davidoff, P., 1965, *Advocacy and Pluralism in Planning*, Journal of the American Institute of Planners, Vol. 31, No. 4, pp. 331–8.

Davies, J. G., 1972, *The Evangelistic Bureaucrat*, Tavistock, London.

Deas, I., Peck, J., Tickell, A., Ward, K. and Bradford, M., 1999, *Rescripting Urban Regeneration, the Mancunian Way* in Imrie, R. and Thomas, H., *British Urban Policy*, Sage, London, pp. 206–30.

Department of the Environment, 1977, *Policy for the Inner Cities*, Cmnd. 6845, HMSO, London.

Department of the Environment, 1992a, *Development Plans: A Good Practice Guide*, HMSO, London.

Department of the Environment, 1992b, *Planning Policy Guidance: General Policy and Principles* (PPG 1), HMSO, London.

Department of the Environment, 1993, *Enquiry into the Planning System in North Cornwall District by Audrey Lees*, HMSO, London.

Department of the Environment, 1994a, *Quality in Town and Country: A Discussion Document*, Department of the Environment, London.

Department of the Environment, 1994b, *Planning Out Crime*, Circular 5/94, HMSO, London.

Department of the Environment, 1997, *Planning Policy Guidance 1: General Policy and Principles*, Department of the Environment, London.

Department of the Environment, Transport and the Regions, 1998a, *Modernising Planning: A Policy Statement by the Minister for the Regions, Regeneration and Planning*, DETR, London.

Department of the Environment, Transport and the Regions, 1998b, *Training in Planning for Councillors*, DETR, London.

Department of the Environment, Transport and the Regions, 2000, *Our Towns and Cities: The Future: Delivering an Urban Renaissance*, CM 4911, HMSO, London.

DETR, 2001, *PPG13: Transport*, Department of the Environment, Transport and the Regions, London.

DETR and CABE, 2001, *The Value of Urban Design*, Thomas Telford, Tonbridge.

Discipline Network in Town Planning, 1996, *Annual Report 1994–95*, University of Westminster Press, London.

DTLR, 2001, *Planning: Delivering a Fundamental Change*, Department for Transport, Local Government and the Regions, London.

DTLR and CABE, 2000, *By Design: Urban Design in the Planning System: Towards Better Practice*, HMSO, London.

DTLR and CABE, 2001, *By Design: Better Places to Live: A Companion Guide to PPG3*, Thomas Telford, Tonbridge.

Duncan, S. and Goodwin, M., 1988, *The Local State and Uneven Development*, Polity Press, Cambridge.

Durkheim, E., 1957, *Professional Ethics and Civic Morals*, Routledge & Kegan Paul, London.

Durning, B. and Glasson, J., 2004a, *Skills Base in the Planning System: A Literature Review*, LGA Research Report 9/04, Local Government Association, London.

Durning, B. and Glasson, J., 2004b, *Skills Base in the Planning System: Survey Results*, LGA Research Report 21/04, Local Government Association, London.

Egan Committee, 2004, *Skills for Sustainable Communities*, Office of the Deputy Prime Minister, London.

Entec UK Ltd, 2003, 'The *Relationships between Community Strategies and Local Development Frameworks*', Office of the Deputy Prime Minister, London.

Evans, B. and Rydin, Y., 1997, *Planning, Professionalism and Sustainability*, in Blowers, A. and Evans, B. (eds), *Town Planning into the 21st Century*, Routledge, London, pp. 55–69.

Fernandez Arufe, J. E. and Diamond, D., 1998, *Spatial Aspects of Innovation Policies: Theory and Application*, Progress in Planning, Vol. 49, Part 3.4, Pergamon/Elsevier Science, Exeter.

Field, B. and MacGregor, B., 1992, *Forecasting Techniques for Urban and Regional Planning*, UCL Press, London.

Fincham, R. and Rhodes, P., 2005, *Principles of Organizational Behaviour*. Oxford University Press.

Fowler, E. P., 1992, *Building Cities that Work*, McGill-Queen's University Press, Montreal.

Freidson, E., 2001, *Professionalism: The Third Logic*, Polity Press, Cambridge.

Friend, J. K. and Jessop, W. N., 1969, *Local Government and Strategic Choice*, Tavistock, London.

Friend, J. K. and Hickling, A., 1997, *Planning Under Pressure*, Butterworth-Heinemann, Oxford.

Fyfe, N. R., 1998, *Images of the Street*, Routledge, London.

Garner, J. F., 1995, *Planning Law in Western Europe*, North-Holland, Amsterdam.

Garvin, A., 2002, *The American City: What Works, What Doesn't*, McGraw-Hill, New York.

Geddes, P., 1968 (first published in 1915), *Cities in Evolution*, Ernest Benn, London.

Gillard, M. and Tomkinson, N., 1980, *Nothing to Declare*, John Calder, London.

Gilpin, A., 1995, *Environmental Impact Assessment: Cutting Edge for the Twenty-First Century*, Cambridge University Press, Cambridge.

Glasson, J., Therivel, R. and Chadwick, A., 1994, *Introduction to Environmental Impact Assessment*, UCL Press, London.

Goodman, R., 1972, *After the Planners*, Pelican Books, Harmondsworth.

Graham, S. and Marvin, M., 1996, *Telecommunications and the City*, Routledge, London.

Grant, L., 1995, *Arena!* Cornerhouse Publications, Manchester.

Grant, L., 1996, *Built to Music: The Making of the Bridgewater Hall*. Manchester City Council, Manchester.

Greed, C., 1994, *Women and Planning*, Routledge, London.

Greed, C., 1996, *Implementing Town Planning*, Longman, Harlow.

Griffiths, R., 2004, *Knowledge Production and the Research-Teaching Nexus : the Case of the Built Environment Disciplines*, Studies in Higher Education, Vol. 29, No. 6, pp. 709–26.

Gunder, M. and Hillier, J., 2004, *Conforming to the Expectations of the Profession: A Lacanian Perspective on Planning Practice, Norms and Values*, Planning Theory and Practice, Vol. 5, No. 2, pp. 217–35.

Guy, C., 1994, *The Retail Development Process: Location, Property and Planning*, Routledge, London.

Hall, D., Hebbert, M. and Lusser, H., 1993, *The Planning Background*, in Blowers, A. (ed.), *Planning for a Sustainable Environment*, Earthscan, London.

Hall, P., 1996, *Cities of Tomorrow* (updated edn), Blackwell, Oxford.

Hall, P., Thomas, R., Gracey, H. and Drewett, R., 1973, *The Containment of Urban England* (2 vols), George Allen & Unwin, London.

Halman, G., 2004, *Dire Delays that Jeopardise the Reformed Systems*, Planning, 29th October 2004, p. 11.

Hambleton, R., 1995, *Cross-National Urban Policy Transfer – Insights from the USA* in Hambleton, R. and Thomas, H., *Urban Policy Evaluation:Challenge and Change*, Paul Chapman, London, pp. 224–38.

Hambleton, R. and Thomas, H., 1995, *Urban Policy Evaluation: Challenge and Change*, Paul Chapman, London.

Hampton, W. A., 1977, *Research into Public Participation on Structure Planning* in Coppock, J.T., and Sewell, W.R.D., *Public Participation in planning*, Wiley, Chichester, pp. 27–42.

Harris, N. and Hooper, A., 2004, *Rediscovering the 'Spatial' in Public Policy and Planning: An Examination of the Spatial Content of Sectoral Policy Documents*, Planning Theory and Practice, Vol. 5, No. 2, pp. 147–69.

Hastings, A. and McArthur, A., 1995, *A Comparative Assessment of Government Approaches to partnership with the Local Community* in Hambleton, R. and Thomas, H., *Urban Policy Evaluation:Challenge and Change*, Paul Chapman, London, pp. 175–93.

Haughton, G. and Hunter, C., 1994, *Sustainable Cities*, Jessica Kingsley Publishers and the Regional Studies Association, London.

Hayter, R., 1997, *The Dynamics of Industrial Location*, Wiley, Chichester.

Healey, P., 1992, *A Planner's Day: Knowledge and Action in Communicative Perspective*, Journal of the American Planning Association, Vol. 58, No. 1, pp. 9–20.

Healey, P., 1997, *Collaborative Planning: Shaping Places in Fragmented Societies*, Macmillan, Basingstoke.

Healey, P. and Underwood, J., 1979, *Professional Ideals and Planning Practice*, Progress in Planning, Vol. 9, Part 2, Pergamon, Oxford.

Heap, D., 1991, *An Outline of Planning Law*, Sweet and Maxwell, London.

Hendler, S., 2005, *Towards a Feminist Code of Planning Ethics*, Planning Theory and Practice, Vol. 6, No. 1, pp. 53–69.

Herbert, D. T. and Smith, D. M., 1989, *Social Problems and the City*, Oxford University Press.

Higgins, M., Prior, A., Boyack, S., Howard, T. and Krywko, J., 1995, *Planners as Managers: Shifting the Gaze*, Royal Town Planning Institute, London.

Hill, D., 1994, *Citizens and Cities: Urban Policy in the 1990's*, Harvester Wheatsheaf, Hemel Hempstead.

Hillier, J., 2002, *Shadows of Power: An Allegory of Prudence in Land-Use Planning*, Routledge, London.

Hogwood, B. W. and Gunn, L. A., 1984, *Policy Analysis for the Real World*, Oxford University Press.

Hospers, G-J., 2003, *Jane Jacobs: Visionary of the Vital City*, Planning Theory and Practice, Vol. 4, No. 2, pp. 207–12.

Huczynski, A. and Buchanan, P., 2001, *Organizational Behaviour: An Introductory Text*, Financial Times Prentice Hall, Harlow.

Hull Cityvision, 2002, *Hull Community Strategy*, Hull Cityvision, Hull.

Imrie, R., 1996, *Disability and the City: International Perspectives*, Paul Chapman, London.

Imrie, R. and Hall, P., 2001, *Inclusive Designs: Designing and Developing Accessible Environments*, Spon, London.

Imrie, R. and Thomas, H., 1999, *British Urban Policy: An Evaluation of the Urban Development Corporations*, Sage, London.

Innes, J. E. and Booher, D. E., 2004, *Reframing Public Participation: Strategies for the 21st Century*, Planning Theory and Practice, Vol. 5, No. 4, pp. 419–36.

Jacobs, J., 1964, *The Death and Life of Great American Cities: The Failure of Town Planning*, Penguin, Harmondsworth.

Jenks, M., Burton, E. and Williams, K. (eds), 1996, *The Compact City: A Sustainable Urban Form?*, Spon, London.

Johnson, T. J., 1972, *Professions and Power*, Macmillan, London.

Judge, D., Stoker, G. and Wolman, H., 1995, *Theories of Urban Politics*, Sage, London.

Katz, R. L., 1987, 'The Skills of an Effective Administrator', *Harvard Business Review*, September–October, pp. 90–102.

Kaufman, J. L. and Jacobs, H.M., 1996, *A Public Planning Perspective on Strategic Planning* in Campbell, S. and Fainstein, S., *Readings in Planning Theory*, Blackwell, Cambridge, MA, pp. 323–43.

Keeble, L., 1964, *Principles and Practice of Town and Country Planning*, Estates Gazette, London.

Keene, D., 1993, 'Plans, Policies, Presumptions: How the Law is Approaching the Plan-Led System', *Proceedings of the Town and Country Planning Summer School 1993*, Royal Town Planning Institute, London, pp. 25–8.

Kitchen, T., 1972, 'The Generation and Coarse Evaluation of Alternatives in Regional Planning: A Case Study of the Work of the Roskill Commission', *Journal of the Royal Town Planning Institute*, Vol. 58, No. 1, pp. 8–12.

Kitchen, T., 1990, 'A Client-Based View of the Planning Service', *Planning Outlook*, Vol. 33, No. 1, pp. 65–76. Also in Thomas and Healey, 1991 (see below).

Kitchen, T., 1991, *A Client-Based View of the Planning Service*, in Thomas, H, and Healey, P., *Dilemmas of Planning Practice*, Avebury, Aldershot, pp. 115–42.

Kitchen, T., 1996, *A Future for Strategic Planning Policy – a Manchester Perspective* in Tewdwr-Jones, M., *British Planning Policy in Transition*, UCL Press, London, pp. 124–36.

Kitchen, T., 1997, *People, Politics, Policies and Plans*, Paul Chapman, London.

Kitchen, T., 1999, 'The Structure and Organisation of the Planning Service in English Local Government', *Planning Practice and Research*, Vol. 14, No. 3, pp. 313–27.

Kitchen, T., 2001, 'Planning in Response to Terrorism: The Case of Manchester, England', Journal of Architectural and Planning Research', Vol. 18, No. 4, pp. 325–40.

Kitchen, T., 2002, 'The Balance between Certainty, Speed, Public Involvement and the Achievement of Sustainable Development in the Planning System: The Impact of the Planning Green Paper', in Kitchen, T. (ed.), *Certainty, Quality, Consistency and the Planning Green Paper: Can Planning Deliver the Goods?*, Yorkshire Conference Series Partners, Sheffield, pp. 21–34.

Kitchen, T., 2002, 'Crime Prevention and the British Planning System: New Responsibilities and Older Challenges', *Planning Theory and Practice*, Vol. 3, No. 2, pp. 155–72.

Kitchen, T., 2004, 'Modernising the British Planning System', in Syms, P., *Previously Developed Land: Industrial Activities and Contamination*, Blackwell, Oxford, pp. 105–23.

Kitchen, T., 2005, 'New Urbanism and CPTED in the British Planning System: Some Critical Reflections', *Journal of Architectural and Planning Research*, Vol. 22, No. 4, pp. 342–57.

Kitchen, T. and Whitney, D., 2001, 'The Utility of Development Plans in Urban Regeneration: Three City Challenge Case Studies', *Town Planning Review*, Vol. 72, No. 1, pp. 1–24.

Kitchen, T. and Whitney, D., 2004, 'Achieving More Effective Public Engagement with the English Planning System', *Planning Practice and Research*, Vol. 19, No. 4, pp. 393–412.

Koetter, K., 2005a, *Wakefield: A Strategic Framework for the District*, Wakefield City Council.

Koetter, K., 2005b, *Wakefield: Developing the Vision*, Wakefield City Council.

Koetter, K., 2005c, *Five Towns: Strategic Development Framework*, Wakefield City Council.

Krumholz, N. and Forester, J., 1990, *Making Equity Planning Work*, Temple University Press, Philadelphia, PA.

Kunzmann, K. R., 1997, 'The Future of Planning Education in Europe', *Aesop News*, Summer 1997, pp. 3–6.

Land Use Consultants and Business Efficiency, 2002, *Information Communications Technology in Planning*, Department for Transport, Local Government and the Regions, London.

Larkham, P. J., 1996, *Conservation and the City*, Routledge, London.

Laurini, R., 2001, *Information Systems for Urban Planning: A Hypermedia Collaborative Approach*, Taylor & Francis, London.

Layard, A., Davoudi, S. and Batty, S. (eds), 2001, *Planning for a Sustainable Future*, Spon, London.

Leach, S., Stewart, J. and Walsh, K., 1994, *The Changing Organisation and Management of Local Government*, Macmillan, Basingstoke.

LeGates, R. T. and Stout, F., 2003, *The City Reader*, 3rd edn, Routledge, London.

Lichfield, N., 1996, *Community Impact Evaluation*, UCL Press, London.

Local Government Association, 2002, *Probity in Planning*, Local Government Association, London.

Local Government Association, 2004, *Delivering Delegation*, Office of the Deputy Prime Minister, London.

Local Government Association, 2005, *Member Engagement in Planning Matters*, Local Government Association, London.

Low, N., 1991, *Planning, Politics and the State: Political Foundations of Planning Thought*, Unwin Hyman, London.

Manchester City Council, 1995a, *The Manchester Plan: The Unitary Development Plan for the City of Manchester*, Manchester City Council Planning Department.

Manchester City Council, 1995b, *Manchester: 50 Years of Change*, HMSO, London.

Manchester City Council, Salford City Council, Trafford Metropolitan Borough Council, Trafford Park Development Corporation, Central Manchester Development Corporation, 1994, *City Pride: A Focus for the Future*, Manchester City Council.

Mandelker, D., 1972, *A Rationale for the Zoning Process*, in Stewart, M., *The City: Problems of Planning*, Penguin, Harmondsworth, pp. 267–75.

Marcuse, P. and van Kempen, R., 2000, *Globalizing Cities: A New Spatial Order?*, Blackwell, Oxford.

McCarthy, P., Prism Research and Harrison, T., 1995, *Attitudes to Town and Country Planning*, HMSO, London.

McCarthy, R., 2004, Presentation to the Local Government Association and National Planning Forum Annual Conference, 3 March 2004, Office of the Deputy Prime Minister, London.

McLoughlin, J. B., 1969, *Urban and Regional Planning: A Systems Approach*, Faber & Faber, London.

McNulty, T., 2003, *Putting Planning First: Culture Change for the Planning Profession*, Office of the Deputy Prime Minister, London.

Meyerson, M. and Banfield, E. C., 1955, *Politics, Planning and the Public Interest*, Free Press, New York.

Ministry of Housing and Local Government, 1970, *Development Plans: A Manual on Form and Content*, HMSO, London.

Moorhead, G. and Griffin, R. W., 1995, *Organisational Behaviour*, 4th edn, Houghton Mifflin, Boston, MA.

Morgan, P. and Nott, S., 1995, *Development Control: Law, Policy and Practice*, Butterworths, London.

Mumford, C., 1966, *The City in History*, Pelican Books, London.

National Economic Development Office, 1970, *Urban Models in Shopping Studies*, NEDO, London.

Neighbourhood Renewal Unit, 2002, *The Learning Curve: Developing Skills and Knowledge for Neighbourhood Renewal*, Office of the Deputy Prime Minister, London.

Newman, O., 1973, *Defensible Space*, Macmillan, New York.

Newman, P. and Thornley, A., 1996, *Urban Planning in Europe*, Routledge, London.

Nicholas, R., 1945, *City of Manchester Plan, 1945*, Jarrold, Norwich.

Nicholson, D., 1991, *Planners' Skills and Planning Practice* in Thomas, H. and Healey, P., *Dilemmas of Planning Practice*, Avebury, Aldershot, pp.53–62.

Oc, T., Carmona, M. and Tiesdell, S., 1997, *Needs of the Profession into the Next Millennium: Views of Educators and Practitioners*, Aesop News, Summer 1997, pp. 7–10.

ODPM, 2002, *Sustainable Communities: Delivering Through Planning*, Office of the Deputy Prime Minister, London.

ODPM, 2003a, *Guidance on Best Value Performance Indicators for 2003/04*, Office of the Deputy Prime Minister, London.

ODPM, 2003b, *Planning Delivery Grant 2004/05*, letter to all regional planning bodies and local planning authorities in England dated 9 April 2003.

ODPM, 2003c, *Planning and Access for Disabled People: A Good Practice Guide*, HMSO, London.

ODPM, 2004a, *Planning Policy Statement 12: Local Development Frameworks*, HMSO, London.

ODPM, 2004b, *Consultation Paper on Planning Policy Statement 1: Creating Sustainable Communities*, Office of the Deputy Prime Minister, London.

ODPM, 2004c, *Community Involvement in Planning: The Government's Objectives*, HMSO, London.

ODPM, 2004d, *E-Planning Programme Blueprint*, Office of the Deputy Prime Minister, London.

ODPM, 2004e, *Creating Local Development Frameworks: A Companion Guide to PPS12*, HMSO, London.

ODPM, 2004f, *Government Response to the Egan Review: Skills for Sustainable Communities*, Office of the Deputy Prime Minister, London.

ODPM, 2004g, *Planning Policy Statement 23: Planning and Pollution Control*, Office of the Deputy Prime Minister, London.

ODPM, 2005a, *Planning Policy Statement 1: Delivering Sustainable Development*, HMSO, London.

ODPM, 2005b, *Sustainability Appraisal of Regional Spatial Strategies and Local Development Frameworks: Interim Advice Note on Frequently Asked Questions*, HMSO, London.

ODPM, 2005c, *Planning Policy Statement 6: Planning for Town Centres*, HMSO, London.

ODPM, 2005d, *Sustainable Communities: People, Places and Prosperity*, Cm 6425, HMSO, London.

ODPM and the Home Office, 2004, *Safer Places: The Planning System and Crime Prevention*, HMSO, London.

Parfect, M. and Power, G., 1997, *Planning for Urban Quality: Urban Design in Towns and Cities*, Routledge, London.

Peck, J. and Tickell, A., 1994, *Too Many Partners... The Future For Regeneration Partnerships*, Local Economy, Vol. 9, No. 3, pp. 251–65.

Planning Advisory Group, 1965, *The Future of Development Plans*, HMSO, London.

Planning Education Commission, 2003, *RTPI Education Commission: Final Report*, Royal Town Planning Institute, London.

Planning Officers Society, 2002, *A Guide to Best Value and Planning: Second Edition: Summary*, Planning Officers Society, London.

Planning Officers Society, 2003, *Moving Towards Excellence in Planning: First Edition*, Planning Officers Society, London.

Planning Network, 2001, *Defining the Educational and Training Needs for the New Urban Agenda*, University of Westminster, London.

Planning Network, 2004, *Higher Education, Professionalism and Skills in the Built Environment: The Impact of the New Urban Agenda on Teaching and Learning*, University of Westminster, London.

Policy Action Team 16, 2000, *National Strategy for Neighbourhood Renewal: Report of Policy Action Team 16: Learning Lessons*, Cabinet Office, London.

Porteous, J. D., 1996, *Environmental Aesthetics: Ideas, Politics and Planning*, Routledge, London.

Poyner, B., 1983, *Design Against Crime: Beyond Defensible Space*, Butterworths, London.

Prior, A., 2000, *Ethics and Town Planning* in Allmendinger, P., Prior, A. and Raemakers, J., *Introduction to Planning Practice*, Wiley, Chichester, pp. 413–22.

Punter, J., 1990, *Design Control in Bristol, 1940–1990: The Impact of Planning on the Design of Office Development in the City Centre*, Redcliffe, Bristol.

Punter, J. and Carmona, M., 1997, *The Design Dimension of Planning: Theory, Content and Best Practice for Design Policies*, Spon, London.

Ratcliffe, J. and Stubbs, M., 1996, *Urban Planning and Real Estate Development*, UCL Press, London.

Reade, E., 1987, *British Town and Country Planning*, Open University Press, Milton Keynes.

Reeves, D., 2005, *Planning for Diversity: Policy and Planning in a World of Difference*, Routledge, London.

Roberts, P. and Sykes, H. (eds), 2000, *Urban Regeneration: A Handbook*, Sage, London.

Rogers, R. and Power, A., 2000, *Cities for a Small Country*, Faber & Faber, London.

Ross, S., 1991, 'Planning and the Public Interest', *Proceedings of the Town and Country Planning Summer School 1991*, Royal Town Planning Institute, London, pp. 55–7.

Royal Commission on Environmental Pollution, 1995, *Transport and the Environment*, Oxford University Press.

Royal Town Planning Institute and Planning Aid for London, 2005, *Planning Aid: Engaging Communities in Planning*, RTPI, London.

Royal Town Planning Institute, 1996, *The Education of Planners: Policy Statement and General Guidance for Academic Institutions Offering Initial Professional Education in Planning*, London.

Royal Town Planning Institute, 2001, *A New Vision for Planning*, London.

Royal Town Planning Institute, 2004, *Policy Statement on Initial Planning Education*, London.

Rydin, Y., 2003, *Urban and Environmental Planning in the UK*, Palgrave Macmillan, Basingstoke.

Sagalyn, L. B., 2001, *Times Square Roulette: Remaking the City Icon*, MIT Press, Cambridge, MA.

Sandercock, L., 1998, *Towards Cosmopolis*, Wiley, Chichester.

Sandercock, L., 2003, *Out of the Closet: The Importance of Stories and Storytelling in Planning Practice*, Planning Theory and Practice, Vol. 4, No. 1, pp. 11–28.

Satterthwaite, D., 1999, *The Earthscan Reader in Sustainable Cities*, Earthscan, London.

Savitch, H. V., 1988, *Post-Industrial Cities: Politics and Planning in New York, Paris and London*, Princeton University Press.

Schneider, R. H. and Kitchen, T., 2002, *Planning For Crime Prevention: A Transatlantic Perspective*, Routledge, London.

Schon, D. A., 1971, *Beyond the Stable State*, Temple Smith, London.

Schon, D. A., 1998, *The Reflective Practitioner: How Professionals Think in Action*, Ashgate, Aldershot.

Schoon, N., 2001, *The Chosen City*, Spon, London.

Scott, L., 2004, *Fine Design Needs Skills, Not Luck*, Regeneration and Renewal, 16 April 2004, p. 8.

Seneviratne, M., 1994, *Ombudsmen in the Public Sector*, Open University Press, Buckingham.

Sewell, J., 1993, *The Shape of the City: Toronto Struggles with Modern Planning*, University of Toronto Press, Toronto.

Shaw, D. and Sykes, O., 2005, *Addressing Connectivity in Spatial Planning: The Case of the English Regions*, Planning Theory and Practice, Vol. 6, No. 1, pp. 11–33.

Sheffield First Partnership, 2003, *Sheffield City Strategy 2002–05*, Sheffield.

Shelter Community Action Team, Undated, *Public Inquiries: Action Guide*, SCAT, London.

Sies, M. C. and Silver, C., 1996, *Planning the Twentieth Century American City*, Johns Hopkins University Press, Baltimore, MD.

Simmie, J., 1974, *Citizens in Conflict*, Hutchinson Educational, London.

Simmie, J., 1997, *Innovation, Networks and Learning Regions?*, Regional Studies Association and Jessica Kingsley Publishers, London.

Skeffington, A., 1969, *People and Planning* (The Report of the Committee on Public Participation in Planning), HMSO, London.

Social Exclusion Unit, 2001, *A New Commitment to Neighbourhood Renewal: National Strategy Action Plan*, Cabinet Office, London.

Stein, J. M., 1995, *Classic Readings in Urban Planning*, McGraw-Hill, New York.

Stewart, M., 1972, *The City: Problems of Planning*, Penguin, Harmondsworth.

Sykes, R., 2003, *Planning Reform: A Survey of Local Authorities*, Research Briefing 1.03, Local Government Association, London.

Syms, P., 2001, *Releasing Brownfields*, Joseph Rowntree Foundation, York.

Syms, P., 2002, *Land, Development and Design*, Blackwell, Oxford.

Syms, P., 2004, *Previously Developed Land: Industrial Activities and Contamination*, Blackwell, Oxford.

Taylor, N., 1994, *Environmental Issues and the Public Interest*, in Thomas, H., *Values and Planning*, Avebury, Aldershot, pp. 87–115.

Taylor, R. B., 2002, 'Crime Prevention through Environmental Design (CPTED): Yes, No, Maybe, Unknowable and All of the Above', in Bechtel, R. B. (ed.), *Handbook of Environmental Psychology*, Wiley, New York, pp. 413–26.

Technology Foresight Panel on Retail and Distribution, 1995, *Progress Through Partnership*, HMSO, London.

Teitz, M., 1996, 'How Stands American Planning?', *Town and Country Planning*, Vol. 65, No. 64, p. 193.

Tetlow, R., 1996, *York Gate: Context* and *York Gate: Process* is Greed, C., *Implementing Town Planning*, Longman, Harlow, pp. 139–63.

Tewdwr-Jones, M., 1996, *British Planning Policy in Transition*, UCL Press, London.

Tewdwr-Jones, M., 2002, *The Planning Polity*, Routledge, London.

Thomas, H., 1994, *Values and Planning*, Avebury, Aldershot.

Thomas, H. and Healey, P. (eds), 1991, *Dilemmas of Planning Practice: Ethics, Legitimacy and the Validation of Knowledge*, Avebury, Aldershot.

Thomas, K., 1997, *Development Control: Principles and Practice*, UCL Press, London.

Thornley, A., 1991, *Urban Planning Under Thatcherism*, Routledge, London.

Timmins, N., 1996, *The Five Giants: A Biography of the Welfare State*, Fontana, London.

Torstendahl, R. and Burrage, M. (eds), 1990, *The Formation of Professions: Knowledge, State and Strategy*, Sage, London.

Urban Task Force, 1999, *Towards an Urban Renaissance*, Spon, London.

URBED, 1994, *Vital and Viable Town Centres: Meeting the Challenge*, HMSO, London.

Vickers, G., 1965, *The Art of Judgment: A Study of Policy-Making*, Chapman & Hall, London.

Wagner, F. W., Joder, T. E. and Mumphrey, A. J., 1995, *Urban Revitalization: Policies and Programs*, Sage Publications, Thousand Oaks, CA.

Wakeford, R., 1990, *American Development Control*, HMSO, London.

Warburton, D. (ed.), 1998, *Community and Sustainable Development*, Earthscan, London.

Wathern, P. (ed.), 1992, *Environmental Impact Assessment: Theory and Practice*, Routledge, London.

Wen-Shyan, L., Williams, W. P. and Bark, A. W., 1995, 'An Evaluation of the Implementation of Environmental Assessment by UK Local Authorities', *Project Appraisal*, Vol. 10, No. 2, pp. 91–102.

Wells P., Dowson L. and Percy-Smith, J., 2005, *Process Evaluation of Plan Rationalisation: Formative Evaluation of Community Strategies – Consultation Findings and Evaluation Framework*, Office of the Deputy Prime Minister, London.

Weston, J. and Darke, R., 2004, 'Reflections on 10 Years of Councillor Training', *Planning Practice and Research*, Vol. 19, No. 4, pp. 427–33.

Wildavsky, A., 1979, *Speaking Truth to Power: The Art and Craft of Policy Analysis*, Little, Brown, Boston.

Williams, R. H., 1984, *Planning in Europe: Urban and Regional Planning in the EEC*, Allen & Unwin, London.

Willams, R. H., 1996, *European Union Spatial Policy and Planning*, Paul Chapman, London.

Woltjer, J., 2005, 'The Multidimensional Nature of Public Participation in Planning: Comment on Innes and Booher', *Planning Theory and Practice*, Vol. 6, No. 2, pp. 273–76.

Wood, C., 1992, *EIA in Plan-Making* in Wathern, P. (ed.), *Environmental Impact Assessment:Theory and Practice*, Routledge, London, pp. 98–114.

World Commission on Environment and Development (the 'Brundtland Commission'), 1987, *Our Common Future*, Oxford University Press.

Index